A HOPEFUL JOURNEY

with helpful angels and
roiling black spots

Memoirs of an Only Child

BEATRICE SHARP PITCAIRN

Edit Date: August 2, 2020
Author: Beatrice Sharp Pitcairn
Editor: Tessa Rose
Designer: Michelle Chapin
Angels on Front Cover: Carey Smith

Printed in the United States of America

First Printing, 2020

ISBN 978-1-7351004-0-1

Printed by Kindle Direct Publishing
Amazon.com Services LLC
410 Terry Ave N
Seattle, WA 98109

TABLE OF CONTENTS:

I am assuming repetition and exaggeration "make the heart grow fonder." And in deference to Gertrude Stein:

A ROSE stands tall, suffusing the air with its enchanting fragrance, then wilts, bends over and dies.....

IS A ROSE brightens the spirit, is a symbol of love on the one hand, and untouchable thorns on the other hand......

IS A ROSE in a fulsome bouquet displays nobility, evokes contemplation, stirs passion.............

Roses correspond to: "The delights of the truth of wisdom"

- Emanuel Swedenborg

INTRODUCTION:

When I started writing this memoir about ten years ago, I didn't think I could conjure up enough memories for what I wanted to convey. But I started carrying around 3x5 index cards and a pen, and thinking about my childhood. Memories bubbled up to the surface, and I caught them before they could slink away.

I had a friend who lived an exotic life. She spent the Depression in a chateau in France, traveled to places like South Africa, and summered in Cape Cod. My childhood seemed boring in comparison. But I then realized that everyone has a story—an interior story of their own reflection on their surroundings, whether glamorous or humble.

I wrote this book for my grandchildren and others of the younger generations who did not have the opportunity to live through the parts of history that I and my parents and grandparents did. I hoped to give them a sense of what it was like to live in England early in the 20th century, on a self-sustaining farm in Ohio, and through the Great Depression and World War II. This is book is part memoir, and part history.

I am grateful for the inspiring education I was privileged to receive at the Academy of the New Church Girls' School and College, which gave me the skills I needed to write a book.

Editor's Note:

I want to thank some people who helped us make this book more accurate and complete: Ian Ashley, Sid Green, and the people at the Colchester New Church website got us local details; Emmy Lou Echols added some wonderful tidbits; Janna King and Carla Odhner did some editing; Siri Hurst gave us information about the Theodore Pitcairn home and family; Greg Jackson and Marvin Clymer got information from the Swedenborg Library and Archives; Bill Kay provided details about Drexelbrook; Reed Asplundh found answers to obscure questions about Bryn Athyn and the Academy; and Alan Taylor gave us permission to use his drawings of Wivenhoe.

We made a great effort to get all the facts and attributions correct in this book. Please contact us if you find any errors, misattributions, or typos. We changed one name to protect a family's privacy.

—Tessa Rose

DEDICATION:

This book is dedicated to my three wonderful children: Stirling, Andrew, and Gwendolyn. They brought great joy to me and my husband, Robert Pitcairn, who died in 1985. They are now 52, 51, and 49. They gave us five granddaughters—Alyssa, Emily, Rachel, Chloe, and Morgan; and two grandsons—Christopher and Timothy.

—BEA PITCAIRN

The Ashley Family:

Herbert Anthony Ashley (1866-1912), mariner

Beatrice Susannah Roper Ashley (1867-1911), homemaker

Herbert William (1889-1973), postman
Married: Jessie Maud Ball. One daughter
Married: Jane Allen, Nellie Taylor.

Beatrice Eleanor (1891-1971), nanny

Annie Susannah (1892-1927), domestic

Nora Lillian (1895-1955), dietician

Charles John (1898-1986), plumber
Married: Emily Coles. Children: Ursula, Anthony, Michael

Dorothy Eva (1899-1973), nurse
Married: Albert Sharp. Child: Beatrice

Phyllis May (1901-1906), child

Alice (1902-1902), infant

Elsie Elmonah (1904-1992), nurse
Married: Leroy Barnes. Child: Dwain

Felix Anthony (1908-1985)
Married: Kathleen Bailey. Children: Peter, Pauline
Married: Beryl Aubrey.
five more children

THE SHARP FAMILY:

Samuel Edward Sharp (1873-1935), farmer

Magdelena Eva Tamme Sharp (1873-1924), homemaker

Ida Rosalie (1897-1983), homemaker
Married: Charles Washburn. Stepchildren: John, Doris

William Henry (1898-1957), farmer
Married: Mary Alberta Pierson. Child: Sharon

Albert Lewis (1901-1994), mechanic
Married: Dorothy Ashley. Child: Beatrice

Marie Cecelia (1903-1993), homemaker
Married: Leslie Foster. Children: Maxine, Joanne.

Raymond Edward (1905-1984), railroad worker
Married: Essie Bradford. Children: Ethelyn, Everett, Edward, Erma

Marcella Elizabeth (1908-1992), homemaker
Married: Lester Matheny. Children: Vera, Elbert, Elizabeth, Laura

Anna Louise (1911-1990), homemaker
Married: Earl Matheny. Children: Norma, William.
Joyce, Keith, Eileen, and Eloise Matheny (not sure which Matheny)

Laura Etta (1914-2005), homemaker
Married: Harry Jodrey. Children: Shirley, Alberta, Carolyn, Robert, one more

Lawrence Edwin (1914-1914), baby

Robert Harold (1917-1945), Staff Sergeant U.S. Army

PART ONE: ORIGINS

"Alma Street, Wivenhoe" by Alan Taylor, 1969 (used with permission)

CHAPTER ONE:
DOROTHY ASHLEY

Dorothy Ashley at 14

EIGHT ORPHANS

In March of 1914, the dark clouds of World War I were gathering over the little town of Wivenhoe on the east coast of England. Dorothy Ashley, the girl who would be my mother, was packing her finished clothes into a sturdy black trunk with brass corners, lock, and clasps. At the age of fourteen, she was preparing to cross the Atlantic Ocean to the great country of America. She still had a skirt to hem, and a blouse that needed buttons.

Dorothy was one of the eight surviving orphans of Herbert and Beatrice Ashley. Her mother had died of cancer at the age of 43, and her father of tuberculosis at the age of 45. Thirteen-year-old Dorothy had been left with her five older siblings—Herbert, Beatrice, Annie, Nora, and Charles—and two younger ones, Elsie and Felix. Though her parents had worked hard to pay for insurance, for one reason or another, after they were gone, the insurance company had given the children nothing.

The plight of the Ashley orphans came to the attention of John Pitcairn in America. They were fellow members of a small, close-knit Christian group called "The New Church," and John Pitcairn was one of the founders of a New Church community near Philadelphia, Pennsylvania. He decided to bring four of the Ashley sisters to the community to work for his large extended family of in-laws. Miss Rowena Acton, who traveled from the community to visit family in England, would accompany the four sisters to America. Annie and the three boys would remain in England.

As Dorothy was packing finished clothing into her trunk, her sister Bea was already working as a nanny for Mr. Pitcairn's grandchildren. Dorothy was apprehensive about leaving her familiar surroundings, but comforted by the thought that Bea was waiting for her in America.

The day before her departure, Dorothy took a walk through Wivenhoe, down narrow streets that meandered to the quay of the River Colne. There were several churches, and a theater among the eighteenth-century buildings that lined the riverfront. She wondered if she were seeing those familiar sights for the last time.

She was. Dorothy would never return to England.

HERBERT AND BEATRICE ASHLEY
THE SUN NEVER SETS ON THE BRITISH EMPIRE

"Wivenhoe Quay" by Alan Taylor, 1969 (used with permission)

Dorothy's parents were both children of mariners. There is some question about the ancestry of Herbert's father, William Turner Ashley. Cupid doesn't always follow the rules, and it was whispered that William was born "on the wrong side of the blanket" and left on the doorstep of a seafaring family. According to family lore, a Hessian soldier had an affair with the daughter of a local gentleman whose name I won't mention.

Beatrice grew up in Rowhedge, across the river, the second child of Walter and Susannah Roper. By the time Beatrice was fourteen, they had seven children. But that year, two younger daughters died, and Susannah gave birth to twins who also died. She had no more children after that. Beatrice finished growing up with her three brothers and younger sister, Mable. Her eldest brother, Walter, also died young at 28. Children frequently died of diseases in those times, and many occupations were hazardous.

Herbert Ashley looked to the sea for his living like his own father and most of the inhabitants of Wivenhoe, which had always been a fishing and boat-building town. Oyster fishing was an im-

William Turner Ashley

Susannah Wilkins Roper

Beatrice Roper Ashley

Herbert Anthony Ashley

portant industry there, and Wivenhoe's oysters were well known for their succulence. Wivenhoe thrived as a port for the larger town of Colchester, farther up the river, and the railroad brought the town to its peak of prosperity in the 19th century. Homes and streets got gas lighting—boat races and regattas became regular events. Shipbuilders made seagoing yachts for the gentry, including the playwright W. S. Gilbert, who produced *HMS Pinafore* and *The Pirates of Penzance* and made "Gilbert and Sullivan" a household name. Crewmen on these cruising yachts could spend time ashore in pleasant and exotic places, often around the Mediterranean Sea.[1]

Herbert and Beatrice were approximately 22 and 21 when they married in 1888, and their first home was in Wivenhoe.[2] They had a son, Herbert William, and a daughter, Beatrice Eleanor.[3] Then came Annie Susannah, Nora Lillian, and Charles John. When Dorothy Eva was born in December of 1899, they were living in Colchester. Phyllis came about a year later, and then Alice, who died the day she was born.

Herbert's mother did not approve of how many children her son's wife was having. Whenever she noticed that Beatrice was pregnant again, she would stick her nose in the air and walk past her without speaking. Herbert's father had died when Herbert was 21, but his mother, Julia Bennett Ashley, lived to be 90.

Herbert and Beatrice bought a house for their growing family on Ernest Road in Wivenhoe, up the hill from their first home. It was a small, red brick workingman's house in a row of identical houses. A gate opened through a wall in front, leading into a tiny front garden. The name "Elmoneth" was etched into the transom over the front door, which opened into a small parlor that they reserved for guests and holidays. Entering guests would see a narrow staircase separating the parlor from a dining room with a large oval table.

The family didn't use the front door, but took the side walkway to the door of the scullery behind the kitchen, where food was stored. The home was heated by a coal-burning stove, and they had running water to the kitchen. At night they used chamber pots, which had to be emptied into the privy in the backyard. The Ashley girls had

---

1 Nicholas Butler, *The Story of Wivenhoe*. Wivenhoe: Quentin Press, 1989

2 Records from www.freebmd.org.uk

3 Beatrice's sister Mabel lived with her when Beatrice Eleanor was born. Later she married and moved back to Rowhedge with her husband, Frederick Collison.

Beatrice with Bert, Bea, Annie, Nora, Charlie, Dorothy and Phyllis
at Elmoneth in Wivenhoe

Mable Roper Collison

Beatrice and Herbert with
Bert and Bea

nervous temperaments, which made for a lively and quarrelsome household.

Herbert was a seaman at a time when Britain held sway over a third of the world's countries. He sailed on yachts all over the world, sending postcards to his children from India, Ceylon, and other exotic places. He shared a round of rum with his shipmates when they were safely in their home port and their work was done. Though he did achieve some higher rank above the lowly crewmen, in his daughter Dorothy's eyes, he was a Captain. He was also an avid Swedenborgian.

SWEDENBORGIANISM

Simple, noisy, and mystical, this was a religion well suited to men who risked their lives in the pitiless North Sea.

—Nicholas Butler, *The Story of Wivenhoe*[4]

Emanuel Swedenborg was a Christian theologian, scientist, and philosopher born in Sweden in 1688. In later life, he had waking trances during which he visited Heaven and Hell, and spoke with both angels and devils. The inner meanings of Bible stories were also revealed to him.

After Swedenborg's death in 1772, his voluminous writings inspired a few men to establish a New Church movement in England. The first General Conference of the New Church was held in London in 1789, and societies formed in England throughout the 19th century. Across the ocean in the United States, the first General Convention was held in 1817. By 1848, a group in Wivenhoe was having regular services with a visiting minister, Reverend David Goyder, who became the group's pastor. A Wivenhoe boat-builder financed the building of a Swedenborgian Chapel on Alma Street. By 1900, however, enthusiasm had waned, and that chapel had become home to the Salvation Army Band.[5]

With no chapel in Wivenhoe, and her husband away most of the time at sea, Beatrice pushed her baby carriage four miles alongside the river to attend services with the society in Colchester. The

---

4 Butler, *Wivenhoe*, p 96

5 Butler, *Wivenhoe*

Herbert A. Ashley on board ship

Colchester Church Assembly, August 7, 1905. Photo by William Gill.
Taken behind the King's Head Pub at the top of Lexden Road, Colchester.
The King's Head is now a private home, and the thatch building is gone.

older children trotted along behind her.[6]

When Herbert was at home, he invited fellow Swedenborgians to their house in the evening to discuss the Writings. In 1905, the Colchester society hosted a church Assembly. By that time, they had become affiliated with a new organization called the General Church

_____

6 The Colchester society was formed in 1882, meeting in the Shaftsbury Hotel in Culver Street. By 1902, the society had moved to Priory Street. In 1924, they built the church on Malden Road where they are today. "Colchester New Church, Our History." *newchurch.org.uk* © 2019 New Church UK

of the New Jerusalem. Herbert and Beatrice became members of the General Church that year.[7]

Even when she wasn't walking four miles to church, Beatrice must have been on her feet all day. When she had time to sit down and sew, her treadle sewing machine kept her feet moving. She made all the clothes her growing family needed, and earned a little extra money by sewing uniforms for the British Army.

Two more children were born: Elsie Elmonah in 1904, and Felix Anthony in 1908. But between these births, five-year-old Phyllis became ill and died. Dorothy was seven at the time, and she thought her sister died of either diphtheria or scarlet fever.

Later in her life, Dorothy would blame her own illnesses on her bad diet in England. Breakfast was bacon drippings on bread. When there wasn't enough food for everyone in the house, Dorothy was sent over to Aunt Mabel's for tea. "Dinner" was the main meal, in the middle of the day. "Tea" was an evening meal, like supper. Aunt Mabel made her tea scones from bacon fat and flour, and one day as Dorothy was eating a scone, a maggot crawled out of it. She refused to eat the scone, and did not go to Aunt Mabel's for tea again.

Life in Wivenhoe

> They learnt about hygiene, the importance of ventilation in bedrooms and of brushing one's teeth.
> —Nicholas Butler, *The Story of Wivenhoe*[8]

Education was compulsory in England up to age 13 at that time. Small children used slates to learn reading, writing, and arithmetic, and learned painting with watercolors. At age seven, boys and girls were separated. They began the day at 9:00 a.m. with the Lord's Prayer and a hymn accompanied by piano. [9]

Girls learned grammar, composition, spelling, and arithme-

---

7 General Church database and *New Church Life* card files

8 Butler, *Wivenhoe*, 184

9 Butler, *Wivenhoe*

tic. They memorized and recited poetry, and Dorothy could still recite Rudyard Kipling's poetry in her later years. They also learned needlework, dancing, drawing, and painting.[10] At midday, students walked home to have their dinner, and returned for an afternoon session. After school they played with tops and wooden hoops, and spun with a whip. Dorothy loved to play "shuttlecock," which is similar to badminton.

Dorothy especially remembered building a Maypole for the Maypole ceremony on the first day of May. The girls wove colored ribbons around the pole, and danced to welcome spring. Nicholas Butler tells of the girls going door to door through the town, wearing flowers and singing:

> Please remember the May Lady,
> My Father has gone to sea,
> My mother has gone to fetch him,
> Please remember me.

One of the girls would then say, "Coo, coo, coo, coo," to invite the householder to give them a penny.[11]

Wivenhoe Park (now the campus of the University of Essex) had been a gentleman's estate for centuries. In Dorothy's time, it was occupied by Charles Edmund Gooch, an "old Etonian gentleman of leisure." The Gooches helped people in need, and gave parties in their refurbished 18th century mansion. They kept things up with the help of a "butler, footman, cook, kitchen-maid, scullery-maid, head housemaid, second housemaid, between maid, nurse, under nurse, lady's-maid, tutor, governess, coachman, under coachman, one or two grooms, and a boy who cleaned the boiler and helped in the garden...."[12]

"Empire Day" was a holiday instituted to imbue the younger generation with love and pride for the British Empire. Schoolgirls performed a small play celebrating Great Britain and her colonies.

---

10 Butler, *Wivenhoe*, 184
11 Butler, *Wivenhoe*, 168-169
12 Butler, *Wivenhoe*, 136-137

Schoolboys marched past the Union Jack, saluted the flag, and sang patriotic songs. The children would be exhorted by Mr. Gooch and other local notables to prove themselves worthy members of the empire, after which they got a half day off from school.[13]

With such extreme disparity between the lives of the upper and lower classes, it's not surprising that the socialist philosophy was creeping into Wivenhoe in the late 19th century. The Reverend John Sinclair Carolin, rector of the Church of England, called himself a Christian Socialist. One Sunday he put forth from the pulpit, "The day is long past when we used to say, 'God bless the squire, and his relations, and keep us all in our proper stations.'" Reportedly, when he heard this, the conservative Mr. Gooch got up and left the church, "never to return."[14]

A new parish council focused its efforts on making the town a cleaner and healthier place to live. Prior to this, ubiquitous filth and rampant disease had simply been accepted and endured as part of town life, but now sanitary improvements such as paved roads and sewers were becoming possible. A water tower was built, providing many homes with fresh running water. Children no longer had to fetch water in buckets from the brook before school.[15]

Wivenhoe had a "town crier" who went around town with a hand bell, ringing it before announcing important news and events. Around the turn of the century, telephone service began with one operator serving seven subscribers. But the last town crier in Wivenhoe held his post until 1934. [16]

DEATH OF PARENTS

Dorothy's sister Bea described her mother as a kindly person who often helped other people. Even when she herself was dying of cancer, Beatrice was caring for her own widowed mother, who had

---

13 Butler, *Wivenhoe*

14 Mrs. P.L.J. Le Poer Power, as quoted in Butler, 141

15 Butler, *Wivenhoe*

16 Butler, *Wivenhoe*

Elsie, Felix, and Annie Ashley

Beatrice Eleanore (Aunt Bea)

Nora Lillian (Aunt Nora)

come to live in her home. Mabel thought cancer was contagious, and wouldn't come near her dying sister.

When Beatrice died in June of 1911, her two eldest daughters, Bea and Annie, were working as domestics for families in Hornsey, north of London. Herbert was sick with tuberculosis, and may have been in a sanatorium, where he spent some time before he died. He passed away early in 1912, less than a year after his wife.

Beatrice Eleanor left England for America at age 22, about a year and a half after her father's death. Dorothy and Nora followed

Charles John Ashley

Herbert William Ashley

Elsie Elmonah (Aunt Elsie)

the next year, and Elsie about a year after that. Elsie was eleven years old. Felix, now seven, had gone to live with other relatives.

Annie was considered "unstable." She had been working in domestic service for an upper-middle-class family. She lived in their home, sewed her own uniform, and was paid the equivalent of 50¢ a week. Something "terrible" was said to have happened to her while she was there, and she had a mental breakdown.

Dorothy was never told what the "terrible thing" was. In those days, it was vital to "keep up appearances." To "let it all hang out" was unacceptable. Neighbors, ever ready to disapprove, peeked out from behind translucent curtains to see what was going on. Annie stayed in England and died at age 35 in Colchester.

Charles would serve in World War I, and continue to live in the Ernest Road house. The family was not aware that Herbert Sr. had written a will in 1910, stipulating that the house be sold and the proceeds divided among his surviving children. Charles stayed in the house and wrote a will of his own. When Charles died in 1986, his father's will was found hidden away in the house.

Herbert William, the eldest brother, had fancied himself an actor, and performed at the local theater. He went into the Royal Navy in 1908, and married Jessie Maud Ball in 1917. Eventually he would go to London and become a postman.

Dorothy and Nora boarded the ocean liner *RMS Baltic* in Liverpool to traverse the rough seas of the Atlantic Ocean. The voyage would last about ten days, and Dorothy was sick in her bunk for most of the trip. She never wanted to travel by ship again. They came ashore in New York on April 5, 1914, and traveled by train to the little borough of Bryn Athyn, Pennsylvania.

❦

ALNWICK GROVE AND BRYN ATHYN

Bryn Athyn Cathedral
Photo by Stephen Conroy, 2019

Several decades before Dorothy's arrival on American soil,

Swedenborgians from the Advent Society in Philadelphia were traveling by train to a station called Alnwick Grove to enjoy a beautiful park. In summer, the city was unbearably hot. At Alnwick Grove Park, they could picnic in the shade of tall trees, go boating or fishing in the scenic Pennypack Creek, or dance in the pavilion.[17] The Advent Society began using this lovely spot for church events.

John Pitcairn, an immigrant from Scotland, had made a fortune in oil in western Pennsylvania and founded the Pittsburgh Plate Glass Company. He married late in life, at age 42, after courting his beloved Gertrude Starkey for four or five years. Robert Glenn and John Pitcairn were two of the founders of the Academy Movement, a group of New Church men who believed that church members should raise and educate their children in a distinctively New Church culture. The Academy of the New Church was established in Philadelphia in 1876 to provide this distinctive education.

Glenn had purchased land near Alnwick Grove for a summer retreat, and he encouraged Pitcairn to buy land there also, with the aim of establishing a New Church community away from the temptations and problems of the city.[18] Pitcairn bought two farms in the vicinity, and began building a retrospective French-style mansion for his own growing family. A few years after that, the Advent Society decided to move the Academy schools out there. The decision caused some controversy, and resulted in the Academy separating from the General Convention and forming The General Church of the New Jerusalem. They chose a name for their community that they believed meant "Hills of Unity" in Welsh. In 1899, Alnwick Grove train station was renamed "Bryn Athyn."[19]

Cairnwood estate, designed by Carrère and Hastings in the

17 "Alnwick Grove Park," May 1, 2008. Posted by: Ed and Kirsten Gyllenhaal in *New Church History Fun Fact*. NewChurchHistory.org

18 "Farmers Sell Land to John Pitcairn for New Church Community and School (1891)" December 7, 2006. Posted by: Ed Gyllenhaal in *New Church History Fun Fact*. NewChurchHistory.org

19 "The Naming of Bryn Athyn (1899)" February 23, 2010 | Posted by: Ed and Kirsten Gyllenhaal in *New Church History Fun Fact*. NewChurchHistory.org

Beaux Arts style, was completed in 1895.[20] John and Gertrude moved into their beautiful new home with their children—Raymond, Theodore, and Vera. Harold was born a year later, and was only two years old when his mother died of a ruptured appendix.[21] Vera also died from a ruptured appendix at age 22.

Despite this tragedy, the Academy and the General Church community continued to grow, and by 1914, when Dorothy and Nora arrived, there was a college building, dormitories with a dining hall, an elementary school building, and a combined library and museum.[22] Just weeks after their arrival, the cornerstone was laid for the Bryn Athyn Cathedral.[23]

John's son, Raymond Pitcairn, had been entrusted with building a house of worship for the New Church, and plans were underway for a majestic cathedral in the Gothic and early Romanesque styles. Raymond was a "devoted student of medieval art and architecture," and wanted to build a church with "craftsmanship worthy of the great medieval churches of Europe."[24]

To achieve this, he didn't use fixed architectural plans. He brought skilled craftsmen, some of them trained in Europe, to Bryn Athyn to work on site. These craftsmen collaborated with designers in a dynamic creative process. Models were built in different sizes and scales to evaluate and improve ideas. A small village of sheds and studios appeared in Bryn Athyn: for stone work, metal work, wood

---

20 cairnwood.org/the-estate/history/ Cairnwood, 2018

21 Gertrude Pitcairn's father was Dr. George Starkey, a homeopathic doctor who taught at Hahnemann, which was a homeopathic hospital at the time. Her appendicitis was treated homeopathically and her appendix was not removed.

22 "New Academy School Buildings (1901-1911)" September 30, 2009 | Posted by: Ed and Kirsten Gyllenhaal in *New Church History Fun Fact*. Academy of the New Church

The Academy of the New Church, 1876-1926: An Anniversary Record, by Members of the Academy Schools. Bryn Athyn, 1926. NewChurchHistory. org

23 Glenn, E. Bruce. *Bryn Athyn Cathedral: The Building of a Church*. Charlotte, NC. Bryn Athyn Church, 2011. Page 6

24 Bryn Athyn Cathedral, Front Jacket

work, and stained glass.[25]

Teams of draft horses pulled vast logs up the quarry road to the hilltop. Stained glass and stone carving were done with authentic medieval methods, and straight lines were deliberately avoided.

❧

Get down on your hands and knees and straighten it properly!

Dorothy and Nora had landed in a dedicated, optimistic, and growing New Church community. John Pitcairn died a couple of years after their arrival, and Raymond lived at Cairnwood with his wife, Mildred Glenn Pitcairn, and their nine children.

Dorothy and Elsie attended the Academy's Girls Seminary in Bryn Athyn. Although the census places her at Cairnwood, Dorothy lived with families in the community that she worked for. She did housework and cared for children, and sometimes missed school when a child she was caring for was sick. She attended the Seminary until 1920, and received a gold pin, which was the custom in the early years. Elsie's class of 1923 was the first class of girls to receive diplomas. Dorothy became friends with other girls who worked at Cairnwood. Celestine Schwindt, Eunice Bond, and others. The girls would gather in the upstairs sitting room and servants' quarters to visit with each other on Sunday afternoons. They saved the money they earned. Nora went to Temple College to become a dietitian.

Dorothy worked for Raymond Cranch's first wife, the Simons family, and others. At one of the homes where she worked, the man of the house told her to straighten the foyer rug, which she did, using her foot. "Get down on your hands and knees and straighten it properly!" he barked.

Upset by this rebuke, she left the house in tears and went to Cairnwood to tell her sister. Bea was annoyed. "Well, you can't stay here!" she said emphatically. Dorothy went back and apologized. Later she said she was grateful to those families and learned a lot

---

25 Bryn Athyn Cathedral, Front Jacket

from them.

As Dorothy entered her twenties, so did the country.

THE ROARING TWENTIES

The Volstead Act became law in 1919 after a protracted campaign against alcohol, ushering in the period of Prohibition. Throughout the 1920s, the manufacture and sale of alcoholic beverages was illegal, though people were allowed to make it for personal use or religious sacraments. People still wanted to drink, so they had to find a "bootlegger" to supply their liquor. Bootleggers were plentiful, some making large sums of money smuggling liquor from Canada by car or boat. Average people who couldn't buy whiskey would make "bathtub" gin. It wasn't made in the bathtub, but the large containers used to make it had to be filled from the bathtub faucet. Sometimes desperate people drank rubbing alcohol, which is highly poisonous and can cause blindness. "Medicinal" potions containing alcohol became a thriving business.[26]

With alcohol forbidden, people seemed to drink more than ever in protest. Women starting smoking cigarettes to be risqué, chic, and up-to-date. Women's skirts were shorter than ever before, and flounced or pleated. Their knees showed as they enthusiastically danced the Charleston, their legs bouncing up and down. They wore bands that matched their dresses in their bobbed hair, and they were called "Flappers."

With hemlines so high, women rolled their stockings up just above the knee and held them on with a round elastic garter. In the thirties, most women switched to girdles and garter belts. But Dorothy never gave up the Flapper method, and eventually she had permanently indented circles above her knee caps.

Women swooned over Rudolph Valentino, the original Latin Lover, in silent movies called "flickers." Valentino died unexpectedly in 1926 at the age of 31. Al Jolson starred in *The Jazz Singer*, credited

---

26 For a comprehensive treatment of the Prohibition era, see *Last Call: The Rise and Fall of Prohibition* by Daniel Okrent. New York: Scribner, 2010

as the first feature-length "talkie" in 1927.[27]

Clara Bow, dubbed the "It Girl" after playing a saucy shop girl in the movie "*It*," was a big star in the silent movies, and young women aspired to her up-to-date ways. She transitioned to "talkies" with great success, as the careers of many other silent screen idols ended. They lost their gloss when their voices and accents were not what movie-goers expected. The talkies used actors trained to speak in a semi-English accent. William Powell and Myrna Loy were sophisticates in the movies, which were all in black and white. Charlie Chaplin provided the comedy.

F. Scott Fitzgerald wrote fiction that chronicled the age. In one famous incident, he and his wife Zelda had too much to drink one night and jumped into a water fountain near a swanky New York Hotel. Another writer, Ernest Hemingway, introduced a sparse writing style in his fiction. He created a mood with fewer words. Both writers had lived in Paris and were marinated in its mystique. They had enjoyed the explosion of happiness and sophistication on the French Riviera.

NURSE TRAINING

Dorothy Ashley

Elsie Ashley

27 Jennifer Rosenberg, "The Jazz Singer: The First Feature-Length Talkie." www.thoughtco.com/the-jazz-singer-1779241

Dorothy and Elsie saved their money until they were both able to enroll in the Presbyterian Hospital Nurses' Training program, which did not require a high school diploma.

Nurses wore white uniforms and nurse's caps. Each hospital had its own style of cap. Presbyterian Hospital's cap was a half-moon shaped piece of cotton. The nurses had to starch this, crease about seven tiny pleats in each side, and fasten the pleats with white ball-topped pins. Each nurse was given a round gold pin with the Presbyterian emblem on it, which she affixed to her uniform on the left side of her chest.

One of the perils of their hospital training was that sleeping on night duty could result in expulsion. One night Dorothy caught herself dozing off to sleep. No one saw her, but the incident was so upsetting that she never forgot it. The risk of being expelled weighed heavily on her. She would have nowhere else to go.

One of Dorothy's nursing friends had flaming red hair and a brash manner. Dorothy got a shock one day when her bold friend came into her room and pulled off her wig, revealing short, mousy brown hair. Her features were suddenly plain and nondescript, and she smiled meekly, as if she had transmogrified into an ordinary person.

Part of their nurses' training took place in a psychiatric hospital. Dorothy found it unsettling to care for alcoholics, derelicts, and the mentally ill. Alcoholics experiencing delirium tremens were particularly frightening. They would see scary human faces, weird animals, or monsters emerging from the walls. They became agitated, sometimes screaming with fright and trying to get up, and she would have to tie them down.

When working in public health, Dorothy walked through unsavory parts of Philadelphia with only her nurse's uniform to protect her. She believed there was a house of ill repute on one street where workmen stared at her as she walked by. She heard a disturbing story in which a plumber, called to fix a clogged drain in a nunnery, found a fetus inside the pipe.

Dorothy and Elsie graduated from the program in 1927, and got an apartment together near 52nd Street in Philadelphia, close to the hospital. They were proud to be Registered Nurses, and enjoyed their work of helping people. Dorothy loved America and all the opportunities it offered, and was proud to be an American. I believe that Dorothy and Elsie went to the Swedenborgian Convention Church on 22nd and Chestnut Street at that time.

Shortly after her graduation, at the age of 27, Dorothy had all her teeth removed and got dentures. She blamed her bad teeth on her diet in England, and she told me this often. But her teeth always looked straight and perfect, as dentures do.

All the Ashley sisters as well as their mother suffered from migraine headaches, which Dorothy called "neuralgia" or "sick headaches." She would be in bed for a day or two, unable to keep down food or liquid. She would have to call another nurse to take her place, and reciprocate when the other nurse was sick. The nurses helped each other out.

Chapter Two:
Albert Sharp

Far away there in the sunshine
are my highest aspirations.
I may not reach them,
but I can look up and see their beauty,
believe in them,
and try to follow where they lead.

—Louisa May Alcott

Albert Lewis Sharp

Albert Sharp, who would be my father, was born on February 21, 1901. He liked to say that he was one day older than George Washington, whose birthday was February 22. Albert was born into a new century that promised more wonderful discoveries and inventions building on the internal combustion engine, usable electricity, and other inventions of the late 19th century. Dreams that were previously unimaginable were becoming possible in this explosion of inventive thought. Dreamers imagined cars for everyone. The plow and mule would be put aside; a tractor would do the work. The light of imagination filled many a dreamer with hopes of discovering new secrets of nature and the cosmos and making a better life for mankind. Albert was one of those dreamers.

THE SHARP FAMILY

The Sharp Family. Back row: Henry, Ida, Albert, Marie, Raymond. Middle: Anna Lou, Marcella, Laura. Front: Edward, Robert, Magdelena.

The forebears of Albert's father, Samuel Edward Sharp, had trekked across the country and cleared land for farming in Brown County, southern Ohio, near the Ohio River. The Sharps were an upstanding Methodist family, quiet and soft-spoken. My cousin Elbert said years later, "There's not a scoundrel in the bunch."

> The early settlers of Brown County were plain men and women of good sense, without the refinements which luxury brings, and with great contempt for all shams and mere pretense.[28]

---

28 *The History of Brown County, Ohio.* Chicago. Beers, 1883, pages 263-4

Albert's mother was Magdelena Tamme. Her parents came over from Austria, had ten children, and were respected members of St. Mary's Catholic Church. They believed that Magdelena's marriage outside the faith was a sin, and her whole family shunned her for the rest of her life. As a result, Albert carried a life-long antipathy for the Catholic Church.

Edward and Magdalena had eleven children: Ida, Henry, Albert, Marie, Raymond, Marcella, Anna Lou, Laura, Lawrence, and Robert. Lawrence was Laura's twin, and died at birth. Albert thought that being third was the worst position in the family. He was always tagging along behind his older brother and sister. They would go off with their schemes and leave him behind, crying.

LIFE ON THE FARM

The family started out in a rudimentary farmhouse in Brown County. But as more children were born, they moved to a better, 100-acre farm in Adams County near West Union. On the farm, life depended on the good graces of nature: the proper amount of rain for seeds to germinate, the proper amount of sun to bring the plants to full flower. In spring they harnessed mules to the plow, and mules and man worked together to turn over the soil so the seeds could go in.

When a pig was slaughtered, they took the innards out, coated the carcass with salt, and hung it by its hind legs from the rafters of the smokehouse to feed the family through the winter. They raised sweet corn to eat, and field corn and wild oats for livestock. They made bread from milled flour.

The girls planted vegetables and canned them in Mason jars for winter storage. They stored the canned vegetables in a cellar under the smokehouse. The girls did the washing and other housework. They made their dresses from the printed cloth of the seed sacks. They made feather beds (we would call them quilts) from goose or duck feathers. They ironed clothes by heating an iron on a wood-burning stove.

Kerosene lamps provided light. A gutter pipe on the roof edge collected rainwater to fill the cistern under the floorboards. A hand pump brought the water through a pipe to the kitchen sink. In the backyard was a wooden privy. Inside was a board with a round hole in it over a pit. The pages of old Sears Roebuck catalogs served as toilet paper.

In the fall, they hung tobacco in the barn on stretchers to season. In winter, the men repaired equipment to be ready for spring planting.

> The production of tobacco was found to be the greatest and most profitable industry on the limestone lands of the Ohio River counties—the most profitable crop in Southern Ohio. ... The Germans, by their skill and industry, had made these steep hillsides the best producing land in Ohio.[29]

Tobacco was the main source of income for the Sharp family. The tobacco was not of fine quality; it was used to wrap cigars. They also raised cows, chickens, and pigs, and grew vegetables. They were completely self-sustained. They had to be.

The child is the father of the man.

—William Wordsworth

---

29 *The History of Brown County, Ohio.* Chicago. Beers, 1883. Page 306

Albert's family had three bedrooms in their one-story farmhouse: two for the girls and one for the parents. The boys slept in the attic under the rafters. Heat came from a wood-burning stove below them in the kitchen. They would hear sounds of the wild outside and an occasional squirrel scampering across the roof overhead.

At night, on his bed under the rafters, Albert dreamed of the future. Farming was a hard and precarious existence, and he longed to see the wide world beyond West Union, Ohio. Envisioning his future was like looking through a window pane, seeing a foggy vista of uncertain shape, undefined, evaporating and reappearing.

A Spotty Education

One-room schoolhouse in Ohio

Albert and the other Sharp children went to a one-room schoolhouse, with one teacher and 25 or 30 children from first grade to eighth. They used McGuffey's *Eclectic Readers*, which taught proper behavior and virtues as well as reading, grammar, and public speaking, including many selections from the Bible as well as respected British and American writers.

But for those who lived off the land, schooling was secondary to survival. In the fall, all hands were needed to harvest crops, so

Albert often missed parts of school. He sometimes missed school during spring planting time also. As a consequence, his education was spotty. All his life he revered educated people.

West Union was about four miles away, or 45 minutes by horse and cart. On Saturdays, the farmers congregated there to sell their produce, buy staples like flour and sugar, talk, and have a little whiskey. In the evening, the locals played lively music on the accordion, fiddle, and harmonica. People would sing and dance and be in a good mood after a week of hard work. At the end of the evening, they went home and tallied up their money. In later years, Albert felt nostalgic about farm life and Saturday nights with the "Ole Time Music." But he never missed the hard work.

A New Century

In this new century, young people could reach for new possibilities and aspirations—some modest, some grandiose. Henry Ford was selling millions of Model T cars, and paying his workers enough that they could afford to buy what they produced. People rushed to buy the new radio receivers and telephones. Gradually the whole country was becoming electrified. This was a time when "tinkerers" could come up with new devices in their garages and basements. Men aspired to find their fortunes, to be an Edison or a Ford, to help the march of prosperity into the future, or maybe just get a patent on a device helpful to the homeowner or housewife.

Albert was one of these men. The first time he saw a mechanical "horseless carriage" sputter into town, he wanted to know how it worked. It looked like a carriage, but was powered by an engine. They were rare in southern Ohio in the early 20th century—objects of amazement and wonder to the people who stopped to admire them. Albert wanted to learn how to fix cars and work as a mechanic. On the farms, neighbors helped each other fix machinery and tools. Albert and his brothers were considered good at this.

When the United States declared war in 1917, Albert was too young to serve. By 1920, the slaughter of World War I was over. The United States had come into the war late, but lost 116,516 soldiers.

The influenza epidemic, called the Spanish flu, had just petered out, but had taken 675,000 Americans. Everyone expected a great future, and better living for themselves than their parents had. About a year after the Great War ended, however, there was a sharp recession. Unemployment rose and prices fell as the economy adjusted from war to peace. But the recovery was robust.

❧

ALBERT'S ROARING TWENTIES

The 1920s were full of hope and optimism. The stock market rose to astronomical heights. Not just the elites, but everyone could get into the stock market. You could buy on margin, which meant you didn't have to put much cash down. You could read the stock market page in the newspaper and watch it go up and up. You would be worth more and more, making money without lifting a finger. Times were good, and people were happy.

Very few of us are born as a completed puzzle. We spend our lives trying to fabricate the missing pieces or making do with what we have. I picture Albert lying on the hillside in the dark of a summer evening, looking up at a myriad of stars, wondering what the world was like and what his future would hold. He was a callow young man, unformed by much interaction with other people, a trusting farm boy. He had no reason to be otherwise.

He saved up his money, and when he had enough, he signed up to study automobile mechanics in South Bend, Indiana. It must've been a thrill for him to ride the train to South Bend. He loved trains for the rest of his life, and would stop whenever he could to watch one go by. In those days, they huffed and puffed steam from the engine upward to the sky, and rumbled as they grazed the tracks on long journeys to far-off places. But it was automobiles that he wanted to learn about.

After graduating from the automotive school in South Bend, Albert headed down to Tampa, Florida. He had always wanted to see the ocean and live in a warm climate. And he wasn't the only one. Sunny Florida was booming, with real estate prices rising higher and higher. Albert got a job in a filling station, fixing cars and pumping

Albert in South Bend, Indiana

gas. He did well and saved money. But in 1926, a depression hit Florida. Banks and credit began to fail, and real estate prices fell. Two major hurricanes, two years apart, wreaked havoc across the state, killing thousands of people and destroying infrastructure. Tourism evaporated, and people began to leave Florida in droves.

Albert witnessed this great exodus from Florida, and became part of it. Many people stopped at his gas station, heading north as fast as they could. One man pleaded with him to accept what he said were fine cuff-links as payment for a full tank of gas. Albert kept those cuff-links in the top drawer of his bureau for the rest of his life.

He never wore those or any other cuff-links. They were a reminder of the precariousness of existence.

❧

PHILADELPHIA

When a young flower is wilting and the stalk is bent over, give it a little water and it will summon up its inner strength to stand up straight again.

—Beatrice Pitcairn

Albert left Florida and went north to Philadelphia. He lived in a boarding house and worked at whatever jobs he could get. He had some money saved, and a man named Henry Ferris suggested a partnership in a filling station and auto repair shop. Ferris put in most of the money, and the partners set up shop in Ardmore, a Philadelphia suburb. The business thrived for several years as more and more cars came onto the roads.

The highs of the stock market and of alcohol were both intoxicating. Through the twenties, spirits were on an uphill run. But the stock market highs were based on nothing but thin air and high hopes. Every intoxicating excess has its morning hangover.

In October 1929, the stock market took a precipitous downward turn. People watched the ticker tape fall. Traders on Wall Street panicked. They sold and sold, hoping to salvage something. Ordinary people ran to their banks to withdraw their money. The banks didn't have enough cash to cover the withdrawals, and one by one the banks had to close. People's hopes, like deflated balloons, floated down to a sad repose on the ground. The wheel of history had just run over them and they were unprepared. Millionaires became paupers overnight, and some financiers jumped to their deaths from the high windows of the New York Stock Exchange.

Albert and Henry's filling and service station went bankrupt. They were left with a raft of debts, and Albert owed a large amount of money to Henry Ferris. As a shell bruised on the outside forms a new layer inside, Albert formed a layer of caution that lasted all his life.

AL AND DOT

Albert and Dorothy on their wedding day

The McIntyres were an Irish family living in a row house near Albert's boarding house. Shy Albert must have been attracted to this outgoing, boisterous family. Dorothy was often there, too, being friendly with Edna McIntyre who had gone through the nursing program with her. So that's how Mother and Daddy met, and an attraction was sparked. They never told me about their first meeting or any dates they went on. It wasn't the kind of thing they talked to me about. Their friends called them "Dot" and "Al."

THE GREAT DEPRESSION

As the United States slid into the Great Depression, President Herbert Hoover said "prosperity is just around the corner." Before the stock market crashed, Hoover had campaigned on the claim that the Republican Party was putting a chicken in every pot and a car in every garage. That claim was now thrown back in his face as homeless working-class people bundled up together around fires and constructed shelters of tin, cardboard, and tar paper. Their settlements were called "Hoovervilles" as a rebuke against the president, who was defeated by a landslide in the election of 1932.

Dour Herbert Hoover was described as constitutionally gloomy, while his opponent, Franklin Delano Roosevelt, was ebullient and optimistic. Just what the times required. People were joyful when the Democrat Roosevelt was elected.

For thirteen tumultuous years, crime had increased exponentially due to bootlegging and the growth of organized crime. John Linthicum, a "wet" Representative from Maryland, said that when Prohibition was repealed, "The Depression will fade away like the mists before the noonday sun," and that "the immorality of the country, racketeering, and bootlegging will be a thing of the past."[30] The Volstead Act was repealed, and states would be allowed to choose if they would be wet or dry. Everyone would be singing *Happy Days Are Here Again.*

Well, not quite. Roosevelt promised a new beginning and began instituting some socialist ideas from Europe. The W.P.A. (Works Progress Administration) was formed to put people to work. The government hired workers to build roads and buildings, and artists to decorate the buildings. But the economy did not improve. Amity Shlaes, in *The Forgotten Man*, tells how the Depression in 1937 was worse than in 1932. Soup kitchens were manned by churches and service groups like the Salvation Army. People stood in long lines waiting for a bowl of soup and a piece of bread. Long lines of men

---

30 Okrent, Daniel. *Last Call: The Rise and Fall of Prohibition.* New York: Scribner, 2010. Pages 349-350

stood around in heavy, threadbare coats, fedora hats or workmen's caps, hands in pockets, hoping to get a job—any job. Men stood on street corners selling apples. They went up to people and asked, "Brother, can you spare a dime?"

Albert had a lot of debts to repay, to Henry Ferris and other suppliers of their bankrupt business. But he was fortunate enough to get a full-time job at the Autocar Company's truck factory in Ardmore. Autocar began when Louis Semple Clark put a gasoline engine on a tricycle in 1897. That vehicle (Autocar No. 1) is now in the Smithsonian Museum. Autocar No. 2 is a four-wheeled vehicle now residing in the Henry Ford Museum. Shortly after that, the company moved from Pittsburgh to Ardmore. Autocar put America's first truck on the market, and after 1911, the company focused on making trucks.[31]

This was the scene when Albert and Dorothy married in February, 1932, at the depth of the Great Depression. She had a job in nursing, and he had a job with the Autocar Company. Together they could afford a small apartment and a second-hand car. They had to put their things in Dorothy's name so Albert's creditors couldn't go after them.

---

31 www.autocartruck.com/history

PART TWO:
WE THREE DREAMERS

CHAPTER THREE:
THE EARLY YEARS

Bea at Cairnwood

No matter what type of childhood you have, there's a feeling that you're sensing more than what you're seeing in front of you. That's one of the things I remember from being young. A lot of information comes to us, not in the form of words or pictures, it's a feeling in the air.[32]

We think we understand the rules when we become adults but what we really experience is a narrowing of the imagination.[33]

—David Lynch, artist and filmmaker

Daddy wasn't sure that he and Mother should have children with the country in such a precarious financial situation. But Mother

32 *David Lynch: Interviews.* Edited by Richard A. Barney. University Press of Mississippi, 2009. p 153

33 "David Lynch, Interview March 8, 1992" by Kristine McKenna (taken from) Colección Imagen: *David Lynch, 1992.* www.thecityofabsurdity.com/intpaint.html © Mike Hartmann

wanted a baby desperately. She'd had a miscarriage, and she prayed to the Lord to send her a baby daughter. She did become pregnant again, and I was born on September 6, 1934. After I was born, they moved to another apartment so that Daddy could walk to his job at the Autocar Company.

The year that I came into the world, a long and terrible drought had begun in America's breadbasket. Soil was depleted, and rain was not falling. In parts of the South, Oklahoma, and Texas, people called it the Dust Bowl as the wind picked up the parched soil and blew it around. Farmers could not raise a crop, and those who had jalopies trekked to California to find work. People called these desperate travelers "Okies."

Daddy's eldest sister Ida came out from Ohio to help when I was born. Ida had been caring for her younger siblings who were still at home when their mother Magdelena died of a brain tumor at age 50 in 1924. Their father, Edward, died a year after I was born, at age 62, while attending a square dance.

❦

EARLY MEMORIES

Aunt Ida Sharp holding newborn Bea

My first memory is of lying on my stomach. I opened my eyes briefly and looked at the white padding inside my bassinet. I was aware

37

of pleasant, gushing voices. I felt secure, and went back to sleep.

In my next memory, I recall that Mother had just made herself a nice new church dress—navy blue with white polka dots. (Mother always made all her own clothes.) We had gone to Bryn Athyn for church, and to visit with Aunt Bea. When we got home, Mother sat on the toilet seat with me on her lap to change my diaper, and I peed on her new dress. She was flummoxed.

"You ruined my new dress," she said. She was shocked that I could do such a thing. "You're naughty. You deserve a spanking!" That was my first protest against the world.

In another very early memory, my parents were hosting a doctrinal class of about ten to twelve people in our apartment to study Swedenborg's Writings. They would take turns hosting, and a minister would lead the class. In my crib next to the bedroom window, I heard the Boom! Boom! Boom! of drums and the tooting of bugles. I looked out to see costumed people walking down Spring Avenue. The people in the living room were saying the prayer, and I knew I should be quiet, but I called out anyway: "Mommy, Mommy, there's a parade!"

PETER RABBIT

Daddy the farmer

I learned about the precariousness of life when Daddy read *The Tale of Peter Rabbit* to me. Peter snuck under the fence into Mr.

McGregor's garden. He was hungry and wanted to pick out a nice carrot to eat. Mr. McGregor got mad and chased Peter, threatening him with a hoe. This upset me.

"Why was Mr. McGregor so mean, Daddy? Peter only wanted to get something to eat?"

Daddy, the farm boy, tilted his head back and laughed. With a quizzical smile and a twinkle in his pale blue eyes, he said, "If you have a garden, it's to grow food for people to eat. You don't want rabbits to come in and eat it all."

I thought it was very unfair. On the farm, there is nothing sentimental about it; either the animals would eat the vegetables, or the family would. I had learned about the cruel world, where some have to sacrifice so others can live.

We went on a trip to Ohio when I was a toddler. On the way home, we stayed overnight in an old, inexpensive hotel in Pittsburgh. There was no Pennsylvania Turnpike yet. There were no motels. My parents found the cheapest hotel they could, and bathrooms were shared with other patrons. We were on the road after leaving the hotel when I asked for my Betsy Wetsy doll. Oops! To everyone's dismay, the doll had been left in the hotel room. I was consumed with grief, and cried. When we got home, Mother telephoned the hotel. They searched and found the doll, and sent her to us. By the time the doll arrived home, I had forgotten her, and we had to be introduced again.

BLACK SPOTS

Mother read me stories from the Bible before I went to sleep. She sat me on her lap in the rocking chair in the living room or she sat beside my bed. I liked the stories of baby Moses in the bulrushes, and Joseph's coat of many colors. We would kneel and say the Lord's Prayer together. Then she would tuck me into bed and tell me more stories. She told me about fairies that danced in gossamer dresses and had adventures. Those stories were my favorites. She also read *Aesop's Fables*, and *Stories That Never Grow Old*. That book got very worn on the edges. She told me Swedenborg's stories about little girls growing up in heaven. Whenever they were naughty or didn't tell the truth, BLACK SPOTS appeared on their pretty dresses. She implied that if I did something wrong, these BLACK SPOTS would appear on the clothes of my doppelgänger in the spiritual world.

◌

When I was a small child in the crib, I used to look up at the ceiling and see many shaped configurations there. Thin cracks and slight watermarks turned into a rabbit or a barking dog in my mind. I mostly dreamed of the fairies that Mother told me about. I stayed in the crib for a long time because of the space constraints of our tiny bedroom. After a while, Daddy took the sides off so I could get in and out.

◌

Daddy and I would walk down Spring Avenue to the vacant lot on the corner of Sutton Road. He would hold my hand as we crossed the street. In May, delicate wildflowers bloomed lilac and yellow in the open areas. There were bright dandelions, butter-cups, and violets. Fields of clover could be hiding a four-leaf clover that would bring good luck. Nature swooped around filling the bare spots with weeds.

We picked black-eyed Susans and took them home to put in a milk bottle. Daddy remembered black-eyed Susans from the farm. I would watch baby squirrels leaping around, fine-tuning their nervous systems so they could scurry across the road without being smashed by an oncoming car.

Daddy would bring me sour balls when he came home from work. They were different flavors: cherry, orange, lemon, and lime. I liked sucking on them. Daddy liked surprising me with things. One time he brought home two little dog-shaped magnets, one black and one white, about two inches long. He loved discovering how things worked, and he loved explaining how things worked to me. He put one dog on top of the bed tray table and held the other dog underneath. As he moved the dog under the table, the one on top moved around. That's how I learned about magnetism.

☙

THE MILKMAN'S HORSE

When I was about three, I spent a lot of time looking out of the living room window, which faced Spring Avenue. I wanted to see the goings-on in the wide world outside our apartment. On alternate mornings, I would see the milkman coming down the street in his horse-drawn wagon. The horse was brown, and wore blinders so he wouldn't be distracted. I watched as the horse clop-clopped down the street. He knew which houses to stop at—the houses where people drank the Suplee brand of milk, and ate their eggs. The milkman carried the bottles to the front door, left them there, and took the empty ones away to be sterilized and refilled.

The milk was not homogenized. We had to shake it up to mix in the cream that floated to the top. We always got "A" milk, which was considered superior because it had more butterfat. "B" milk looked bluish with its lower fat content, and was considered inferior.

One morning, a truck came instead of the horse. I cried. I kept looking each day after that, hoping the horse would come back. He did, once or twice. But then Mother said, "The horse won't be coming anymore. It will be the truck instead."

I was very upset—I wanted the horse to come.

"What will happen to the horse?" I asked.

Mother didn't know. "He will probably be put out to pasture," she said.

Every morning I looked out, hoping to see the horse again, but he never came back. I learned about loss.

I remember many times in the winter I would stand in front of the window eating a Delicious apple and watching the snowflakes fall. I tried to follow a snowflake as it drifted past into oblivion on the street, or placed itself gently on a blade of grass on the Driscolls' lawn across from us. The snowflakes piled up until the blades of grass could not be seen. Pretty soon it would look crusty. Then when the sun came out, it got shiny and slippery. That was when Mother would pull me up the Grandview Road hill on my little sled. She pulled me up by the rope and I sledded down. We had to do that before the cars came out and ruined it.

A few years later, another child hit me in the eye with a snowball, so it wasn't all fun.

Other times I would look out at the houses around us, each one different, and for the occasional passerby. I would watch the orange school bus as it stopped on the corner across the street to pick up the Junior High students. I would go on that bus one day. I watched the few students as they waited for the bus in the cold of winter, the girls switching from one foot to the other because their feet were cold. They were so grown up, and laughing and giggling. I couldn't wait to grow up and be one of those students.

We all went down to Philadelphia to see the Mummers Parade on New Year's Day. It was a tradition for members of groups in south Philadelphia to work through winter and summer preparing elaborate costumes and practicing their string bands. Each group had a theme. The brightly colored costumes had plumes and bangles. When I was small, Daddy would hold me up on his shoulders so I could look over the heads of the taller people in front of me.

SHIRLEY TEMPLE

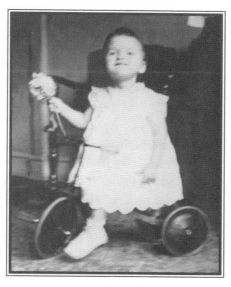

Bea with no hair

The year I was born, Shirley Temple was launched to stardom in the movie *Bright Eyes*. Shirley Temple lifted people's spirits during the Depression and transformed the concept of childhood.

Her influence was great! Readers of the movie magazine *Silver Screen* said that only Shirley's good example could induce their daughters to eat their spinach and drink their milk.[34] The studio publicists promoted Shirley Temple look-alike contests. Children would have photos taken and displayed in theaters, where movie-goers would cast votes. Winners would get an autographed photo of Shirley and free tickets to a movie.[35] These contests became an international phenomenon, and "Shirley Temple became a global standard of what a little girl should be."[36]

---

34 Kasson, John F. The Little Girl who Fought the Great Depression: Shirley Temple and 1930s America. New York: Norton, 2014, Page 126

35 Kasson, 123-124

36 Kasson, 125

Parents wanted their little girls to have blonde hair and curls like Shirley. But as my hair grew in, it became clear that it would be poker straight and brown. Someone had told Daddy that if you shaved all the hair off, it might grow back curly, or at least wavy. He shaved my hair completely off. I have photos of me sitting on my little three-wheeled rider with fuzz for hair. It didn't work. I've had straight brown hair all my life.

Mother thought it would be a treat to take me to my first movie at age four. We walked to the theater to see a Temple movie. Mother paid 9¢ for me and maybe 15¢ for herself.

I was afraid of the big, dark theater. I held Mother's hand as we went in. The music was loud. The only music I had ever heard was from our radio, and it wasn't loud. The movie came on, and people were doing crazy things that I couldn't understand on the big black and white screen.

I saw Shirley Temple with her dimples and sausage curls. Her face was so big, it filled the whole screen as the loud music blared. I had never seen such a big face. I was frightened and buried my face in Mother's shoulder. I cried and cried. Mother tried to console me and get me to stop crying, but I kept on. Finally, very reluctantly, she carried me out. She couldn't understand why I was so upset—it was only a movie, she said. I don't remember her ever taking me to a movie again.

About that time, Mother read *Gone with the Wind*. When the movie came out in 1939, Mother left me at home with Daddy and went to the theater to stand in a long line to see the movie.

Kasson notes that people had become concerned about the influence of movies on children and youth even before the Great Depression, and two studies were published on the subject in 1933.[37]

Henry Forman, in *Our Movie Made Children* said:

> The mirror held up by the movies is gazed into by myriads of adolescents and even young children in their secret thoughts, in their broodings, their daydreaming and fantasies—they want to be like the people in the movies.[38]

---

37 Kasson, 126

38 Forman, Henry J. *Our Movie Made Children*. The MacMillan Company, New York, New York, May 1933. Page 141. As quoted in Kasson, 126.

And Herbert Blumer, in *Movies and Conduct,* said:

> If we consider play as a kind of acting, movies made per-
> formers out of most children. ...we may see Shirley Tem-
> ple as leading a vast throng of child actors, imitating the
> little girl who began her own career parodying adults in
> Baby Burlesks.[39]

WE DON'T ARGUE IN FRONT OF THE CHILDREN.

The Depression continued until 13 million men were out of
work. One in five people lost their jobs. The increase in crime that
started in the 1920s continued into the 1930s. It was a new world.
Organized crime took over in Chicago, and Al Capone was a famous
crime boss.

Daddy tried to pay off his debts as best he could. Every so often
we would drive to North Philadelphia, where Henry Ferris owned a
large, semi-detached Victorian brownstone that had been turned into
apartments. Henry and his wife, Edna, lived on the second floor in the
back, and rented out the rest of the house. We would walk up some
steep steps to the apartment in back. Henry was parsimonious, and
the apartment was small and stuffy. He was short and rotund, with a
paunch and a bald head. His wife was thin and mousy.

Daddy would give him a check and we would have a short visit.
I'm not sure if Daddy ever paid off the whole amount. He would have
done so if he could; he was that kind of person. The *callow* youth had
become more mature and skeptical, but he was still a dreamer. He
tinkered with inventions in his spare time, but always kept his day job
at the Autocar. He worked an eight-hour day Monday through Friday,
and a half day on Saturday. He made about $25 a week.

One evening I lay in bed listening to my parents discuss whether Daddy should give money to an acquaintance called Kerfut. They
always referred to him by his last name. Every once in a while, Kerfut
came around with his tale of woe. He couldn't find a job, he said, and

---

39 Herbert Blumer, *Movies and Conduct.* New York, MacMillan, 1933, p
17. As described in Kasson, 127.

things were really bad. On this occasion, he'd asked Daddy if he could borrow $20 until he could get back on his feet. Of course, $20 was out of the question, as Daddy made only $25 a week, but they were discussing whether or not to give him $10. In 1937 the Depression was still deep, and people helped friends who were less fortunate and didn't have jobs. They wanted to help Kerfut get a fresh start, but they were afraid he might use it for drink.

Daddy had a kind heart. He had experienced poverty himself with the loss of his business, and he was grateful for his solid job. They finally decided they would help him, what they called, "get back on his feet."

I am always surprised when I hear someone say, "We don't want to argue in front of the children." My family lived in such a small space, I usually heard whatever my parents were talking or arguing about. If they lowered their voices, my ears perked up. All the more reason I would want to hear what they were saying.

LAURA & HARRY JODREY

Laura and Harry Jodrey

I was not yet three when Daddy's youngest sister, Laura, came to Ardmore and married Harry Burton Jodrey in May, 1937. They stayed with us while they looked for work. We had a couch without arms that could be opened into a bed. Mother called it a *lounge,* which is what they called them in England. Laura and Harry stayed with us, sleeping on the lounge, until Harry got a job and they could get an apartment. They eventually moved back to Ohio and bought a hardware store in Georgetown. They raised a family of five, and stayed there the rest of their lives.

Bea with Aunt Bea at Cairnwood

My mother made some of my clothes from cut down hand-me-downs that Aunt Bea, her sister who worked for the Raymond Pitcairn family, gave her from the Pitcairn girls. The girls were older than me, and their clothes were made from fine fabrics. When I was four or five, I remember she made me two little suits from worsted serge. They had boleros and pleated skirts, and were identical except that one was light green and the other tan. They were my favorite outfits. She made me a sailor suit with white braid trim. She made

Halloween costumes, spring coats, and winter coats for me. I never had a store-bought dress until I was in my twenties.

~

Aunt Elsie and Dwain

Daddy said she disciplined her dogs better than her son.

Aunt Elsie & Dwain

Aunt Elsie was always a stickler for cleanliness and afraid of germs. She would carry a cloth with her, soaked in Argyrol disinfectant, to wipe off door handles before touching them. Mother was prone to sanitizing things too, but not as thoroughly as Elsie did. In those days more communicable diseases were incurable, so people were more careful to avoid catching them in the first place. Being nurses, Mother and Aunt Elsie were well aware of all those diseases. There were no antibiotics, and sulfa drugs were just coming into use.

Elsie loved opera and had season tickets to the *peanut gallery*. She had a fast and emphatic way of speaking, and Daddy didn't like her much. He thought she took advantage of Mother. Shortly before Mother and Daddy married, she married Roy Barnes, who was tall but slight of build. Daddy didn't like him much, either. Daddy called him "cantankerous." Roy had a bit of George Raft in him, in both looks and character. Raft was a heavy-lidded movie star who usually played a gangster. Roy didn't talk a lot, but when he did, he was complaining that his life wasn't going well, and he was figuring out ways to "beat the system." His attitude was sullen and vindictive.

Elsie and Roy lived in an apartment house on Germantown Avenue. Their son, Dwain, was born on March 4, 1933, about a year and a half before me. He would be their only child, and Elsie had great aspirations for him. She fussed over him because he had asthma. She washed her hands often, and sterilized anything he might touch. But she didn't keep him under control. There was a sandbox at the Germantown apartment, and I have a photo of Dwain and me playing together in the sandbox.

Dwain and Bea playing in the sandbox
at the Germantown Ave. apartment
June 1936

Little Dwain

During the Depression, Elsie and Roy were on Relief (welfare) for a short time. My parents struggled as well, but they believed in making do and not taking handouts.

Aunt Elsie's family moved to an apartment on Alden Road, and Dwain went to the Bryn Athyn elementary school. Roy was a working-class man, and obviously felt uncomfortable in that social milieu. He seemed plagued by a sense of inferiority. When Dwain misbehaved, Roy egged him on. It was his way of "sticking it" to the community.

Sometimes Aunt Elsie invited us there for Sunday dinner. We would be greeted by two slobbering Airedale dogs, who nearly knocked me over, as I wasn't very big then. Aunt Elsie reined them in, and Daddy said she disciplined her dogs better than she disciplined her son.

No more flippery or flappery!

The Great Depression lasted from 1929 to 1941. Born in 1934, I witnessed aspects of the period through a child's eyes. As I look back now, my memories are influenced by the photographs of the time, which were black and white and grey. This is something of a metaphor for the era. Color didn't enter photography until after World War II. But men actually did wear grey suits and hats and grey button-up sweaters and jackets, with scruffy black or brown shoes. Women wore long dresses. No more flippery or flappery! Life during the Depression was serious business.

Edward Hopper, a Depression-era painter, expressed the loneliness and separateness of people in *Night Hawks*. The painting depicts several people at a circular lunch counter, sitting as far from each other as possible, a white-capped soda jerk behind the counter, and darkness outside. Grant Wood from Iowa depicted life on Midwest farms in many paintings, the most famous being *American Gothic*, in which a dour farmer stands beside his daughter, holding a pitchfork, with an arched window behind them. Dorothea Lange's iconic photograph of the Depression is *Migrant Mother*, in which a woman with a despairing look on her face sits with her children around her. My own mother often reminded me that "Life's no bed of roses."

Radio and movies were important to people during the Depression. Movies provided some escape from the grinding trials of real life. And our president, Franklin Delano Roosevelt, spoke to us on the radio at home with his "Fireside Chats." The radio was a recent acquisition for most people, and the president's soothing, confident voice coming into the living room as an invited guest did much to assuage their anxiety. Someone was looking out for us and making things better. His famous phrase was "We have nothing to fear but fear itself."

❧

DEWEY & ALMA

Daddy had a friend, Dewey Burnett, who was tall and lanky and had a slight southern accent. He was pleasant and outgoing. I think he worked at the Autocar in a different section from Daddy.

Mother's friend Alma, from Erie, had worked at Cairnwood. Mother introduced them, and they married, but didn't have children. Dewey had stomach problems. He had an ulcer, and he drank a lot of milk, which was supposed to be good for the ulcer. The milk made him sick, but he drank it anyway because he thought he should. It was later determined that milk didn't help, and antibiotics are now given to kill the bacterium, Helicobacter pylori, that causes ulcers.

One Christmas, Alma and Dewey gave me a child's microphone. Dewey tried to get me to sing into it, but I was too shy. Whenever I was uncertain that I couldn't measure up to what was expected of me, I just stayed silent. But Dewey encouraged me to speak into the microphone, hoping, I think, to conjure up my inner comedian. I think I finally did speak into it.

Dewey seemed to like interacting with me, and I felt sorry that they didn't have any children. They lived in an apartment house that was a three-story converted Victorian at the other end of Spring Avenue. Eventually they moved to Erie, where Alma was from. Dewey, because of his ulcers, didn't live very long after that.

❦

Our Apartment at 248 East Spring Avenue

248 East Spring Avenue
Photo by Larken Rose, 2019

Our apartment was on the second floor on the right. Across the hall were the Corrs, and after they moved, Mrs. Glavin, Marguerite, and Elaine. I was four when Elaine moved in, and she was two. Under their apartment was a family store, a delicatessen with everything from sliced meat to candy bars. A family called the Martins lived in the apartment under us and ran the store.

Our living room had a window with a radiator under it. There was the lounge that could be slept on. Dewey Burnett made us a carved wooden rocking chair with arms. Daddy's chair had wider wooden arms and soft cushions on the back and seat. The radio had carved wooden feet and an opening in front with three wooden slats covering a brown cloth hiding the speaker inside. The old desk had a wooden flap that opened down to make a writing space. Daddy had built a bookcase to house a set of *The World's Greatest Literature* by Spencer Press from 1936. This was an inexpensive collection of the Classics that "every man" could afford to have.

The only contemporary "Art Deco" piece was a small round chrome table with a black glass top. That was the style of furniture at the time. I used to pull my small chair up to that table and draw pictures. Every few years we got to choose new wallpaper and paint. I got to help choose when I was old enough.

In the kitchen, we had a wooden ice box with upper and lower sections. Periodically the ice man came up the stairs carrying a fresh block of ice with metal tongs to put in the lower section. This kept our milk, butter, and meat cold in the upper section.

A cream-colored patterned oilcloth covered the wooden table. Two kitchen chairs were scarred from use. My high chair stood at the corner between Mother's and Daddy's chairs.

The kitchen sink was porcelain with curled piping underneath. Mother heated water and scrubbed clothes and diapers in the kitchen sink on a washboard made of corrugated metal. The washboard had wooden sides and an open handle at the top for carrying. She used a laundry soap, and had to rinse the clothes a few times, squeeze out as much water as she could, and carry them down the stairs to the backyard in a wicker basket. She hung everything on the clothesline outside.

On sunny or breezy days, they dried quickly and smelled fresh. When the clothes were dry, she took them off the clothesline and carried them back upstairs. She dampened them a bit, rolled them up and let them sit a while to even out the dampness. Then they were easier to iron with the heavy metal iron that she kept hot on the stovetop.

The stove was across from the sink, and it had a gas line. You turned on the gas and lit the burner with a match. In the corner was a built-in cupboard with glass sections. We could see the dishes stacked up and the cups hanging on little hooks. We had the Blue Willow pattern for the dishes, which was popular in England. Mother's family had had it also. Her father had brought it back from the Orient.

Most women still did their washing every Monday morning, ironed on Tuesdays, cleaned on Wednesdays, and baked on Fridays. This centuries-old schedule was built around the time required to get clothes and linens washed, dried, and ironed before Sunday. Cleaning the house and cooking food came later in the week. It became a version of the old nursery tune, *Here We Go Round the Mulberry Bush*:

This is the way we wash our clothes
Wash our clothes
Wash our clothes
This is the way we wash our clothes
So early Monday morning

(and so on through the week)

Mother swept the floors with a broom and used a carpet sweeper to sweep the rug. The carpet sweeper was a metal box with two bristled rollers inside on a long handle. She pushed it back and forth across the carpet, and the rollers picked up the dirt, which collected in the box. She would get on her hands and knees to clean the floors and bathroom fixtures with ammonia or Lysol liquid. The bathroom had hexagonal white tiles and white fixtures.

Every so often during the summer, Mother took the rugs out to the backyard, hung them on the clothesline, and beat them to get out the ground-in dirt.

The laundry man would come once a week or so to collect our sheets and shirts and bring them back laundered the next week. We did have that service.

When we needed a bath, Mother heated water in the tea kettle several times and poured it into the tub in the bathroom. Then she added cold water from the faucet. We did have running water, which was a treat for Daddy who used to pump water from a well on the farm.

The bedroom was barely large enough for my parents' double bed and my crib beside it. Daddy and Mother each had a bureau. One window looked out on the pebbled roof of the two-car garage, and under that window was the black trunk that Mother had brought with her from England. I used to sit on it and look out the window.

The other window looked out to the street. We had a small three-cornered closet built in to the corner of the bedroom, usually with the stuffing coming out. There was a mirror on the front side. When I was about three or four I would stare into the mirror and pretend I had an imaginary friend. I would talk to my reflection, and use my voice for her to talk back to me. I believe that an only child lives inside her head more than other children do; she creates her own imaginary life.

Mother had an electric sewing machine that she'd had since nursing school. It was the kind that sat on the table with a pedal down on the floor to make it go. She didn't have to use a treadle like her mother did. The radio and all the lamps were also electric.

We had a black "candlestick phone" consisting of a long upright metal tube as thick as a heavy candle on a round base with a rotary dial, topped with a bell-shaped mouthpiece. The long bell-shaped hearing apparatus was connected to the base with a wire, and there was a hook on the side to hang it on. I remember Mother calling Aunt Bea at Cairnwood, and later at Glencairn. She would pick up the receiver, and the operator would say, "Number, please?" Mother would say, "Bethayres 3-0," and the operator would connect her.

Some people had a "party line," which was less expensive. The trouble was you might pick up the receiver and find other people on the line, sometimes for hours. I think we had one early on, but later we had a private one-party line, so Mother could call in for work assignments. She was working private duty by that time.

New Technology

Inventors were still hard at work creating and improving things, and during the thirties and early forties new technology came onto the scene at a fast pace. Daddy took me to the Franklin Institute to share with me his passion for new inventions and mechanical things. Magical new things came into our apartment as well.

One new addition to our apartment was an automatic water heater. The new tank attached to the wall near the stove, the water tank in the kitchen, and the pipes that went to the bathroom. Then, lo and behold! Mother could light the heater with a match, and after it heated up, hot water would run right into the bathtub or the kitchen sink! No more heating water on the stove.

One day an electric washing machine arrived. It was a round metal tub with legs and a strange looking wringer—two rollers with a little space between. There was barely room for the machine between the sink and the chair at the table. This machine "does everything," the ads claimed. Mother took a while to learn how to use it. A rubber tube attached to the hot water faucet filled the tub with water. Then the clothes were added, along with granulated or powdered soap. The three-pronged agitator moved back and forth rhythmically, making a sloshing sound. When it was done, the water drained out through a rubber tube attached to the sink. Then fresh rinse water went in. After rinsing, Mother put each piece of clothing through the two rollers and turned the handle. The rollers turned and wrung out the clothes, which then went into the wicker basket to go outside. Some delicate clothes had to be washed by hand with Lux Soap Flakes. And there was always Ivory 99% Pure hand soap that made suds to wash the dishes.

Daddy read the want ads in the *Main Line Times*, and found a second-hand refrigerator for sale. A friend helped him carry it out of the house, put it into his truck, and carry it into our apartment. The ice box disappeared, though we still called the refrigerator an "icebox" for many years to come.

Later on, Mother got an electric iron to press our clothes, and a second-hand Hoover upright vacuum cleaner to replace the carpet-sweeper.

Mother was delighted with each new device, and Daddy was always ready to learn how to fix anything that went wrong. Roads were paved during the Depression, and even Daddy's old farmhouse was electrified in the early 1940s. Everyone was thrilled with this new technology. Nothing was made of plastic at this point. Plastics would not come into use until after World War II.

Since Mother did all the cleaning, I didn't notice when things got easier. Mother always wanted to get things done as quickly as possible, and didn't want to spend time teaching me to do chores. She did like teaching me to cook. When I was about three I had a picture cook book. It was lots of fun. There was a picture of a bowl and a picture of two eggs beside it, and a cup half filled with sugar. There was milk, flour, a spoon, a spatula, and so on. I would figure it all out and make the batter and put it into the cupcake pan—also pictured in the book. Mother would bake it for me.

NO LUCK WITH ANIMALS

I was given a little turtle for my birthday. I think his back was painted with different colors. He was the first living animal I had ever had contact with. I played with my little turtle and watched him slowly work his way across the patterned ersatz Oriental rug. He stood out in stark contrast to the light red parts, but sometimes he disappeared into the curves of brown or red. He was shy, and sometimes he would hide in his shell.

I forget what I named him. I fed him a few seeds of turtle food every day. I dropped it into his hexagonal glass bowl when I wasn't playing with him.

One day I couldn't find him. He was lost. I looked all over for him, and Mother tried to help. I got worried. I was walking around in my leather shoes, and I heard a crunch. To my horror, when I picked up my foot, there was my little turtle, crushed dead. I cried. I never got another turtle. And this was a foretaste of my later encounters with animals. I learned that tragedy could occur without knowing.

A few years later I saw a cat hiding in the tall grass growing around a telephone pole. I reached into the weeds to pet him, and he scratched me. I went upstairs, crying. Mother was upset, worried that the cat could be carrying some disease. She didn't know if she should take me to the doctor. She rubbed the scratch with antiseptic. My relationships with animals never got very far.

HORN AND HARDART'S

Horn and Hardart was a restaurant chain in Philadelphia, the first food "automat" in the United States. Prepared food waited in little glass cubicles along the wall. We would put a nickel in the slot, turn the handle, and pick out a piece of cake or pie. Hot foods were served cafeteria-style. We waited in line, sliding a tray along, and a woman behind the counter served out the hot foods. Mother and I would go there often for lunch after we had been to Strawbridge's,

Lits, or Gimbels. We both liked the vegetable soup. Men would come in to keep warm and have a cup of coffee, sometimes reading a newspaper or just staring into space.

There was one on Lancaster Pike in Ardmore where Mother, Daddy and I would go on special occasions. We usually got turkey, mashed potatoes, and peas. We liked apple pie and vanilla ice cream for dessert.

Parsimony

People were parsimonious. They saved their string by wrapping it up in a ball to reuse. A "rag man" from Ethiopia came around occasionally, to ask people for their old rags. He would sell them to someone else. That's how he made his living.

Mother shopped at the corner store down the street. She would take a bag with her. At the store, all the merchandise was behind the counter. You went to the counter and asked for what you needed. They had canned goods on the shelves, and some fresh produce in bins up front. Meat and fish would be in the ice box. Mother would carry the bag home with me in tow, or pushing me in a stroller.

She shopped at least twice a week. She wanted to be sure she got fresh flounder. We often had fish on Friday, when the grocer got in fish for the Catholics, who were required to eat fish on Fridays instead of red meat. There were a lot of Catholic Italian and Irish immigrants in our neighborhood. Sometimes she would get a small piece of chicken already cut up. Some people bought the whole chicken. It was already dead but whole.

Most people didn't have cars in those days. A huckster came to sell us vegetables in season. He would park his truck across the street and the neighbors would come out to buy his produce. Mr. Shaddhi came from the Middle East to try to sell us Oriental rugs, but we couldn't afford to buy any.

❧

MOVIES

People liked slapstick comedy with silly situations. W. C. Fields was a favorite, and was deadpan funny. He often played a drunk (which I think he was in real life). In those days being a drunk was considered funny. He was heavyset and middle-aged and smoked a cigar which he used as a prop. Fields was from Philadelphia and often made fun of Philadelphia. He said things like, "First prize was a week in Philadelphia. Second prize was two weeks."

Musical comedies were uplifting and fun. Busby Berkeley had a raft of girls tap dancing on stage in unison. Fred Astaire and Ginger Rogers did graceful ballroom dancing in their movies.

❧

THE GOLDEN AGE OF RADIO:

The Martians are coming!

Everyone had a radio now. Families gathered around the radio in the evening, as they would gather in front of the television many years later. From the early 1920s into the 1940s was radio's "Golden Age," when broadcasting included dramas, soaps, thrillers, Westerns, gossip shows, and news. These "Old Time Radio" shows are now preserved on the internet for younger generations to discover.

In the 30s, the radio soap operas *Ma Perkins* and *Stella Dallas* came on in the afternoon. In the evening, we listened to the comedians Jack Benny and Fred Allen, and *Amos 'N' Andy*.

The sitcom *Fibber McGee and Molly* introduced the character of Throckmorton P. Gildersleeve. In the 40s, this character would get his own show, called *The Great Gildersleeve*.

Lamont Cranston was *The Shadow*. "Who knows what evil lurks within the hearts of men. The *Shadow* knows."

Kate Smith sang on the radio through the 30s, and sang "God Bless America" during WWII.

John Gambling started his morning program, *Rambling with*

Gambling, with Irving Berlin's song, "Oh How I Hate to Get Up in the Morning."

Walter Winchell had a ticker behind him. The staccato "tick, tick, tick" emphasized the urgency of what he was about to say. He told us about the war and what famous people were doing in their private lives. Lowell Thomas also gave us serious news.

Henry Aldrich said *"Com-*ing, Mother!" after his mother called, "Hen-reeeeeee! Henry *Al-*drich!" in the teenage sitcom *The Aldrich Family*. [40]

Our Gal Sunday was a soap opera about an orphan girl who married a British aristocrat.

We heard advertisements for Wheaties and Corn Flakes; for Ivory 99% pure, Camay, and Lifebuoy soaps, and Lux Soap Flakes for washing clothes by hand; and for Chesterfield, Camel, and Walter Raleigh cigarettes. The company gave out coupons for Walter Raleigh cigarettes, but they weren't as good as the others. Gillette razors used the slogan, "Look sharp, feel sharp, be sharp," which I got teased about in high school.

One balmy evening in October 1938, people were listening to dance music on their radios. The music was interrupted from time to time by a series of news bulletins. Sirens blared and screams emanated from thousands of New Yorkers who were supposedly under attack. My parents and I were listening as well. We didn't know if we should be frightened. Mother went to the window and saw neighbors gathering outside. We went down to see what was going on.

"Do you know what is happening? Are we being invaded?" someone said.

We were alarmed. Others were skeptical. "It's only a radio play," one person said.

Others weren't so sure. "It sounds like we're being attacked!"

Everyone milled around for a while. Then someone checked the radio. The program was over. It was only a radio play after all, created by the well-known actor and future filmmaker, Orson Welles. He created the program from H.G. Wells' horror story, *War of the Worlds*, in which Martians take over the Earth.

---

40 en.wikipedia.org/wiki/The_Aldrich_Family

In the 1940s, there was *Duffy's Tavern*, "where the elite meet to eat," with Archie the proprietor speaking.

Inner Sanctum Mystery was a show based on mystery novels.

Dorothy Kilgallen and Dick Kollmar began broadcasting *Breakfast with Dorothy and Dick* from their apartment in New York City in 1945. They chatted about current events and celebrity gossip.

Our Miss Brooks with Eve Arden aired in 1952.

APHORISMS

People drew on a lot of old sayings to pull them through hard times. During the Depression, I heard a lot of these. The operative words were:

Keep a stiff upper lip
(keep your emotions well hidden, your sorrows inside)

Keep your nose to the grindstone
(keep working and don't complain)

Make do
(do the best with what you have)

The early bird gets the worm
(get up out of bed)

Don't cut off your nose to spite your face
(don't harm yourself in anger, or in seeking revenge)

A stitch in time saves nine
(nipping a problem in the bud saves a lot of work)

Absence makes the heart grow fonder

Grin and bear it

Out of sight, out of mind

A penny saved is a penny earned
(Benjamin Franklin, Poor Richard's Almanac)

Waste not, want not.

(Also Ben Franklin)

Mother had her own set of favorites: "Life's no bed of roses," she often told me, and "Money doesn't grow on trees." (I didn't think it did.)

Daddy would say, "Hold your horses!" He meant, don't be impatient—I'll be there in a minute.

Émilé Coué de la Châtaigneraie published his work *Self-Mastery Through Conscious Autosuggestion* in the United States in 1922.[41] The mantra-like saying, "Every day, in every way, I'm getting better and better," was called the "Coué method." Some American newspapers quoted it differently, "Day by day, in every way, I'm getting better and better."

It's hard to realize, unless you lived through it, how different our values were. It wasn't until the 1960s that you would say, "I love you" before hanging up the phone. In the 1960s "letting it all hang out" and telling people your inmost thoughts and feelings was a radical idea. During the Great Depression, the war, and even into the 50s, that was not acceptable at all. You were expected to keep your feelings to yourself and *make the best of it*.

We had a collective responsibility to keep everybody happy.

Pencils 10¢

One day, Mother and I were on our way to Strawbridge and Clothier in Philadelphia to buy fabric to make clothes. We got out of the subway car underground, and went up a few steps to cross over to the other side through a dark, damp passageway that never saw the light of day. The subway train rumbled beneath us as it went on its way. An old man sat in the passageway with his back against the wall. He had no lower legs. His pant legs were folded underneath his thighs. In his hand he held a cup with three pencils in it, and a note attached, "Pencils 10¢." I looked at him as we were passing. He had a vacant expression in his rheumy eyes.

"Mother, can I have 10¢ to buy a pencil from him?" I asked.

---

41 en.wikipedia.org/wiki/Émile_Coué

She gave me a dime, and I walked back, put it in his cup, and took a pencil. He grunted, "Thank you."

"Don't take the pencil," Mother called out.

I was puzzled. *Why not?* I thought as I walked toward her. Then I realized what she meant. I walked back and put the pencil back in his cup.

THE CHILTON BOOK

It was a luxury every couple of years for Daddy to buy a new book on automobiles. We would drive into Philadelphia, turning down side streets, then turning into a large courtyard paved with cobblestones. We parked in front of a large brick building. Daddy went in, and Mother and I stayed in the car. There was nothing interesting for us to see. Daddy came out with his fat compendium about cars. For Daddy, it was like a Christmas present. He couldn't wait to get home to read it.

The Chilton Book was the definitive book on automobiles and their parts. There were some photographs and ink drawings of car parts. Cars weren't as reliable then as they are now, and sometimes Daddy would be called to help out a friend whose car had broken down. I remember one man had a broken axle and was stuck on a bridge.

MARY GREGORIA
We weren't supposed to talk about that

Mary Gregoria was my first friend. She lived next door to our apartment house with our side yard/backyard between us. Her parents were from Sicily, an island south of Italy, and they didn't speak English at all. They attended St. Colman's Catholic Church. When I asked Mary where her father worked, she said he worked for the city. I asked her what he did, but she just said he worked for the city. I think he was a garbage collector but she didn't want to say so.

The Gregorias had three girls: Mary was my age, Teresa was older, and Dolly younger. A son, Anthony, came along later. I remember Mrs. Gregoria holding him in the rocking chair on the front porch.

Mary's home was a three-story semi-detached house probably built in the early 20th century. There was a front porch with a couple of rocking chairs. You walked into a hallway with stairs ahead. A small living room was on the left and a dining room opened into it. The living room had a three piece "suite"—an overstuffed couch and two overstuffed chairs covered with a prickly dark maroon fabric. Crocheted doilies graced the arms and backs. The dining room had a bay window with lace curtains, a dining table and chairs, and a picture of Jesus on the wall. There were no other prints on the walls, no rugs on the floor, and no books—not even in Italian.

The parents slept upstairs in the front room. They had a big double bed with a carved dark wooden headboard on top and a smaller carved footboard at the bottom. The three girls had the middle room, which was sunny with a bay window. The only furniture was a double bed, a single bed, and a large chifforobe. (a combination of wardrobe and chest of drawers). Mary took a discarded wooden orange crate, draped it with some flowered material, and used it as a bedside table. I would have liked to do that too, but there wasn't room for a crate in our small bedroom. Mary and her sisters washed their hair in a utility sink in the laundry room behind the kitchen.

The kitchen was the heart of the house. There were always good fragrances from Mrs. Gregoria's Italian cooking, although I didn't think the smells were so great at the time. I was used to the smell of boiled potatoes and chicken. Mrs. Gregoria rolled out dough on the dining room table and sliced it up into one-inch bands to make pasta.

The older people ate Italian bread, but the children wanted to be American and ate the doughy white Friehofer or Bond breads. They ate lots of pasta, and called the tomato sauce "gravy." Once in a while, Mary's father had a load of grapes delivered to their basement. The grapes were fermented into wine, which he stored in barrels. The basement always had the pungent smell of fermenting wine. We weren't supposed to talk about that.

A boarder named Johnny lived in the back room upstairs. He came and went, and wasn't there often. It was "hush hush," and we kids were not supposed to know he was there. Or, if we did know, we were not supposed to tell anyone.

Mary Gregoria didn't have any toys, so I shared mine with her. Aunt Nora gave me a new doll every Christmas. I let Mary play with my "last year" doll. Mary came to my apartment to play card games and board games. We played fish, Parcheesi, Rook, and slap jack. I had Tinker Toys, which were round blocks with holes and rods to connect the blocks and construct things.

I had a scooter, a tricycle, and eventually a bicycle. My mother took me down town to the Men's YMCA for swimming lessons once a week in the summer. Although Mother grew up near the water, she never learned to swim. My parents wanted me to have all the advantages that they had never had. They valued books, education, and activities for me, while Mary's family valued living in a big house.

Mary and I walked to the park to swing on the swings and slide down the sliding board. We walked to a golf course one time and saw a golf ball lying in the weeds. We thought it was just lost or forgotten so I picked it up to carry away. "Hey, you kids, what are you doing?" a man yelled. He scared us. I dropped the ball and we ran away as fast as we could.

Mary's mother was heavyset and moved slowly. She never tried to talk to me, nor did she look at me. I was just one of the kids running around. She would sometimes get after the children, shouting in her language that I couldn't understand. To my knowledge she never spoke any English and Mary always had to translate for me.

One day she was standing at the dining room table cutting long slices of pasta with a large kitchen knife. Mary and Dolly started going after each other and calling one another names. Mrs. Gregoria burst out at them in rapid Italian, gesticulating with the knife in her hand and looking ferocious. On the other side of the table, I recoiled in horror. Mary saw my face and started laughing. She said her mother wouldn't hurt anyone. It was the Italian way.

Mother thought Dolly, the youngest sister, had had some disease like measles, which left her unsteady on her feet with weak eyesight. She was two or three years younger than us, and she was always tripping and skinning her knees. Her knees were always scabby with one injury or another, and she was always picking the scabs off and bleeding. She was always crying. I didn't want to play with her—I didn't know how to play with her. So Mary and I would run and hide, and Dolly would try to find us and cry. I think her mother told Mary to let her play with us, and I think Mary would have, but I was the bossy one in our relationship.

The Joyce family lived in the other half of the semi-detached house next to the Gregorias when we were all very small. There were six children in that family, and Mary Joyce was our age. The two Marys came up to our apartment to play. Mother would often make cookies, and give us two or three to eat. Mary Joyce would always save one to take home to her mother, which impressed my mother a lot.

The Depression had deepened by 1937. Mr. Joyce had a job in a factory as a welder, where sparks would fly around. He was going blind and thought he would lose his job because of it. He would have to go on Relief. They couldn't afford the rent in that house, so they moved to a smaller house in Narberth on Woodbine Avenue. I was sorry to see Mary Joyce move. Mother and I did visit the Joyces several times after they moved. Mother used to give Mrs. Joyce some of the clothes that I had grown out of, for which she was very grateful.

The Driscoll family lived directly across the street from us. There were four or five adult children and their mother. They kept to themselves and didn't go out to speak to others in the neighborhood. To us neighborhood kids, they were mysterious, but they didn't seem to mind if we ran around on the large grassy area between Spring Avenue and their house. We didn't abuse the privilege. After their mother died, they all continued to live in the house, except one son who got married and moved away.

Mary Gregoria and her siblings were all born in the United States, but they were still learning how to be American, so they deferred to me. Mary assumed responsibilities and motherly duties at an early age. Sometimes I would walk up to Lancaster Pike with her to pay the electric bill. She would go on errands for her mother and sometimes intercede for her with a salesman because she could speak English. She and her sisters had to clean the house. Teresa, who was several years older, wasn't around very much, and Mary was the one who helped her mother.

Because her mother didn't know the ways of shopping in America, Mrs. Gregoria gave Mother some money to buy Mary a white dress a few weeks before her first Holy Communion. Mary was seven years old. The three of us took the trolley to 69th Street. We walked up the hill to Penney's and picked out a pretty dress, and a pair of white shoes at Becks.

The Sunday of Mary's Communion came, and afterwards she and I were running around on Driscolls' lawn across the street. Suddenly, demons came into my head and I started running after Mary, pulling at her dress and trying to tear it. She was disbelieving.

"What are you doing?" she cried out. "This is my new Communion dress!"

I stopped before I could do any damage. Mary ran home crying. I don't know why I did it. Imaginary BLACK SPOTS swirled around the hem of my dress.

Sometimes I would go to Confession with Mary. I would sit in the pew while she went into the booth to confess her sins to the priest. In this case I should have been the one going to Confession.

One day we were in the 5&10¢ store. Mary saw a fake green glass ring that was being sold for 10¢. She looked around carefully, slipped the ring off its holder when no one was looking, and took it. I was shocked that she would do such a thing, but I never saw her do it again.

Mother and Daddy purchased a new patterned rug, and threw the old threadbare one in the backyard trash. Mary and Teresa came over and took it to their house. They were a thrifty family. Later on I saw the rug in one of their rooms.

Margery Stewart and her family moved into a house on our street a few houses down from Mary's. Her father was a policeman, and she had a younger brother. Margery's parents had light skin with a slight African-American cast. They were called "colored" in those days, but her family could pass for white. Margery was a little younger than we were, but came to play with us and we welcomed her.

I remember people talking about the Stewarts being "colored," and I had a feeling they thought they were not as good as the rest of us because of that. I thought it was unfair for people who had recently came to this country for a better life to look down their noses and feel superior to those whose families had been here for centuries and were emancipated from slavery less than 100 years before.

The Stewarts moved a year or two later. We were sorry to see Margery go. I realize now that when it came time for her to go to school, Margery probably would not have been allowed to go to my school on Wynnewood Road. The "colored" children went to Ardmore Avenue School.

On the other side of Grandview Road and Spring Avenue, on the corner where the orange school bus used to stop, lived an older couple. They had a son with Down syndrome. He would walk between them up the road almost every day.

Mother Taking Care of Me
Good Intentions and Scars

Mother liked taking care of me, and tended to be overly concerned about my health. She knew I would be her only child and I was precious to her. I think the losses in her family and her mother's family made her vigilant. She whisked me into bed at the slightest sniffle. She took my temperature and bundled me up in blankets if I had a fever. I liked being catered to, and especially liked the toast and jam delivered on a bed tray.

Mother knew all the latest theories in modern medicine, and followed them to a T. She loved using her nursing skills and knowledge to care for me, and she also used them to care for herself. She took a sleep aid to fall asleep, and a little phenobarbital to calm down. She often reminded me of the time she fell asleep on night duty and could have been expelled from nurse training. She had to be careful to stay awake then and now she had to be careful to get enough sleep.

I remember Mary calling up to an open bedroom window from the sidewalk below. "Can Be-Be come out to play?" she shouted.

Mother called out the window, "Be-Be is sick today."

"Oh, Be-Be is always sick," Mary called back, disheartened. I don't remember Mary ever staying in bed sick. If she had a cold, she would walk around with a dripping nose.

Every once in a while, I would have croup. My throat would be sore and dry. My breathing had a roaring sound like the fog horn of a tugboat at sea. Mother would heat up a kettle of water and let me breathe the steam.

We took a trolley car to see our dentist, Dr. Kane in Philadelphia. He had a waiting room with highly polished Windsor chairs and a glass fronted cabinet containing the plaster of paris molded figures his son, about 10 or 11, had made and painted. His office had a big window which fronted out onto a street bustling with activity. Outside, people were lined up to buy vegetables from Brown Brothers produce market. At first horses pulling a cart, and then a few years later, trucks, would be coming in with vegetables and fruit. Throngs of people came in and went out.

I would get cavities filled. I tried not to think about the pain and was pretty stoic. They didn't use Novocain in those days.

SUPERFLUOUS ORGANS

Mother and Daddy thought their little genius should start kindergarten at age four, but my tonsils squelched that project a few weeks in. I was enjoying kindergarten. We had milk and cookies, and took naps on cotton warp-faced repp mats. But I got a sore throat, and Mother took me to Dr. Rodenheiser. He decided I should have my tonsils out. Tonsils were considered superfluous and could come out as a matter of course to prevent sore throats and throat infections.

Mother told me I would have ice cream afterward. I was so happy I jumped up and down on the couch and kept repeating "I'm going to have my tonsils out, I'm going to have my tonsils out! Goody! Goody! Yeah! Yeah!" Mother allowed me to dissipate some of my enthusiasm. Normally she didn't let me jump on the couch and "break the springs." Sure enough, my throat was sore afterwards, and I was given a scoop of ice cream every day for several days.

I went back to kindergarten at age five.

The following summer, I had a stomach ache. Mother was immediately anxious that it could be appendicitis. She knew that Mrs. John Pitcairn and her daughter, Vera, had died of appendicitis. She put me right to bed. I had grown out of my crib by this time, and my inventive father had taken it apart and fashioned a new structure. With a larger mattress—*Voila!* I had a "youth bed."

Dr. Rodenheiser came to the apartment the next day. He and Mother asked me where the pain was. But by then, I didn't have any pain. She kept saying anxiously to the doctor, "It might be peritonitis, a burst appendix." She suggested that I got it from lying on the wet grass while playing at Markleys' on Grandview Road.

The doctor poked around my stomach asking me where the pain was. I didn't have any pain, and didn't know what to say. I felt sure nothing was wrong, but Mother and the doctor did not agree. I just lay there obediently. Daddy said that nobody on either side of the family had ever had a ruptured appendix.

But I was whisked off to Delaware County Hospital (where Aunt Nora was the head dietitian) to have my appendix removed. The appendix, like the tonsils, was considered a superfluous organ. I remember lying on the operating table with a tan-colored half dome over my face. It looked like corrugated rubber. Ether came through it. I looked at it for a few seconds, breathed a couple of breaths, and I was out.

I woke up in the children's ward and was offered a glass of orange juice by the children's nurse, Miss Sellers. I told her I liked tomato juice better. Miss Sellers had a vivacious voice and a kind, loving manner toward children. She gushed and fussed over us. When I told her that I liked tomato juice, and oatmeal more than Cream of Wheat, she took my wishes into account.

The only adult in the ward was a man down at the end next to the window. He listened to the radio all the time. I remember hearing, "Let me call you sweetheart, I'm in love with you." Across from me was a girl with typhoid fever, which you get from drinking bad water. Next to her was a girl with undulant fever, which you get from drinking bad milk. One girl had head lice, and had to have her hair shaved off.

After two weeks, the big day came when the doctor came in to take off my bandage and remove the sutures. I had a scar on my stomach and little points up and down beside it where the thread and needle had sewn me up. Finally I got to go home. Miss Sellers gave me a little doll, and gave me an effusive and affectionate goodbye. I liked Miss Sellers a lot.

Back at home, Mother put me to bed and waited on me. In those days, it was recommended that you not exert yourself for a long time after an operation, so Mother kept me in bed until I was crazy with boredom. When she thought I needed some fresh air, she carefully helped me down the stairs, put me in the stroller, and went for a walk. I think this went on for about six weeks. At night when I was still confined to the bed, I would go to sleep and dream of running around and playing. Then I had a startling dream of baby bottles floating around out in the universe. I kept trying to catch one and I couldn't do it. I finally caught one and held onto it. But then it too floated away.

When I was allowed to walk around the apartment again, I used a crayon to draw a scar on my dolly's belly with little dots beside it. I wanted my doll to have a disfigurement just like mine. I showed it to Mother. She laughed. I wondered why she laughed. She thought it was cute.

Aunt Nora told Mother there was gossip going around the hospital about Miss Sellers running around with a married doctor. Several years later, Miss Sellers killed herself with an overdose of pills.

When the heart suffers for what it has lost,
the soul rejoices for what it has gained.

—a Sufi saying

Unfortunately, my extended convalescence probably allowed adhesions to form inside my abdomen, and many years later I would have an ectopic pregnancy. This is when the embryo attaches to the inside of a fallopian tube instead of going to the uterus as it should. If not removed, it eventually breaks the tube, and the mother can bleed to death. Today, patients get up out of bed the day after an appendectomy to prevent adhesions from forming. While trying so hard to do the right thing for me, Mother had done the wrong thing, and I was unable to bear children.

But, as a result of this misfortune, my three wonderful children came into my life by way of adoption.

QUARANTINE

When we were sick with an infectious illness we had to be quarantined. Many serious diseases could not be well treated or cured. A Health Inspector would come around and post a large yellow sign on our door, which had to stay there until we were no longer contagious.

Polio caused a lot of fear. I wasn't allowed to go to a public swimming pool because the disease could be transmitted through water. (The YMCA, where I later learned to swim, had a heavily chlorinated, indoor pool, and there was no active polio epidemic at the time). There was no vaccine then, and polio broke out regularly in different parts of the country. The disease would paralyze your limbs, often for life, as it did to President Roosevelt. He had contracted polio at age 39, and remained paralyzed below his hips. He used a wheelchair in private, but the extent of his disability was concealed from the public with the cooperation of the press. With crutches, steel braces, and great effort, he could "walk" a short distance to a podium, where he could stand and hold on while he spoke. He presented a jaunty demeanor, and the public did not know how much he suffered.

We saw people walking around with braces on their legs. Sometimes at the 5&10, Mary and I saw a lady about 35 years old who wore a skirt down to her ankles. Everyone else was wearing skirts to their knees then. She had a limp, and used crutches, and we could see braces below her skirt. One of the sales ladies told us she'd had a bout of polio. We heard about a few cases on the radio too.

I saw the results of other common illnesses also. Connie, a first-grade classmate, wore her platinum blonde hair long to cover the empty sockets behind her ears where she'd had mastoid surgery. Diphtheria left you with a heart condition. Measles could leave you with a hearing problem. Chicken pox left you susceptible to shingles later in life. Mumps gave you swollen glands in the neck and could make you sterile. Whooping cough is self-explanatory.

The usual diseases were measles, mumps, and chicken pox. I had measles and chicken pox, but not mumps. Whooping cough and rheumatic fever were not so prevalent, and I never had them. Mother thought she'd had smallpox as a child, as she had some pock marks on her back. But smallpox was rare now with vaccinations. There was also tuberculosis, which Mother's father, Herbert, had died from. You had to be careful to not be coughed on.

So Mother kept me indoors, or close at hand.

THINGS WE ATE

Mother bought flounder, which had to be fresh. Despite growing up in a fishing town known for its succulent oysters, Mother never ate oysters, or any kind of seafood except flounder.

She would make little hamburger patties for me, and gush over them as she as she tried to persuade me to eat them. We all liked mashed potatoes, and we often had boiled carrots or green beans. Daddy liked making dried beef the way they did on the farm. Often when Mother was cooking, he would say, "We used to do it this way on the farm," and he would show her how his mother made the gravy with flour and milk. It was one of his favorite foods. I liked it too. For dessert, we had custards and Spanish cream.

GAMES AND TOYS

When I was small, Daddy brought home the two little magnetic dogs. He also gave me a small thick book with figures of a man and woman dancing. Their positions changed slightly on each page, and if you thumbed through very fast, they moved and danced. I also had a wooden acrobat held together by two sticks. When you squeezed the sticks together, the acrobat would jump around and flip upside down.

When I was older I had a yo-yo. I had a jump rope with a wooden handle at each end. Mother had a set of ivory Mahjong pieces. They had colorful Chinese characters carved into oblong pieces about one and a half inches long. I would put them on top of each other and watch them fall down. I wondered what the mysterious characters meant, and how to play the game. It was very popular in the 1920s, but I don't remember Mother playing it at all. It was relegated to a children's toy by the time I was a small child.

Daddy taught me how to play some games when I was older—Parcheesi, dominoes, checkers, and Chinese Checkers. I played a game called "Authors." I had a deck of cards, each with a picture of a famous author. There were four names at the bottom. You were to choose which one was the correct name of the author. I learned the names of James Fennimore Cooper, Mark Twain, Rudyard Kipling, Robert Louis Stevenson, Henry Wadsworth Longfellow, Nathaniel Hawthorne, Louisa May Alcott, and others.

In front of the store where we played
Photo by Larken Rose, 2019

Children went outside to play. Mary and I played on the wide area of concrete outside Martin's store. We drew squares with chalk on the concrete and played hopscotch. We jumped rope, and when there were three of us, we did double Dutch with two ropes. I spent a lot of time throwing a ball against the brick wall of our apartment house and catching it.

In the fall, flurries of wind brought the colorful leaves twirling down from the trees to dance on the lawns and sidewalks. Several of us took turns being buried in piles of rustling leaves on Mary's front lawn. One would lie down, while the others piled all the leaves they could gather on top of her. Then suddenly she would jump out of the pile with giggles. We would scatter away, laughing.

Sometimes the wind snarled like someone was whistling and weeping deep down in a well. We bundled up in our heavy coats and walked against the wind, but we didn't go far.

Mother, Daddy, and I would go to Willow Grove Park. Daddy would go on the rides with me, but Mother was too fearful.

THE CONVENTION CHURCH

When I was three or four years old, I went to the Convention Church at 22nd and Chestnut Street with Mother. Ardmore was part of the Main Line, the area through which the main line of the railroad took businessmen and shoppers east from Paoli to downtown Philadelphia. Mother and I took the train downtown to church, unless Daddy was coming, and then he would drive.

Mother had friends in the Convention as well as the General Church. I believe Mother and Aunt Elsie had gone to the Convention church on Chestnut Street when they were in nurses training. I sat with Mother in a pew near the front. There were not many people attending, and they were mostly old. The minister was Reverend Richard H. Tafel, Sr. As he preached, I sat quietly looking at the beautifully carved mahogany choir stalls. I must have studied them hard; I can still see them in my mind's eye today.

After the church service, we would all gather in a back room to socialize. I just stood around. There were mostly women. One was a friend of Mother's named Dagny Hansen. I had never heard the name Dagny before and I thought it was an interesting name.

An elderly lady, Mrs. Hansen, was Dagny's mother. Once

during the summer, she invited us all out to her home near Fox Chase. She had a nice house surrounded by a large green lawn. I remember her as a white-haired lady with soft features and a crinkled neck rising above the white lace collar of her lavender dress. We sat in lawn chairs drinking iced tea, with colorful flower beds all around us.

CHAPTER FOUR:
STARTING SCHOOL

Bea in living room

FIRST GRADE

Dick and Jane

I went to first grade in 1940 at Wynnewood Road Elementary, a public school in a two-story building near the park, about a half-mile walk. Mary went to St. Colman's Catholic School, so I could only see her on weekends or after school.

I was excited to be in first grade. We started the school day with one of the children reading a passage from the Bible, usually a Psalm. We then said the prayer. We then rose and pledged allegiance to the flag.

The teacher gave us books that were handed down from one first-grade class to the next. We covered them with oaktag paper. Our book was a first reading book called *Dick and Jane*, and we learned using the phonic system. I loved learning to read. We would take turns reading *Dick and Jane* out loud. One day when it was my turn to read aloud, I came across the long word "grandfather," and was completely baffled. I tried to sound it out, but I couldn't, so the teacher had to tell me the word.

My parents had given me a blackboard for my birthday, and Daddy affixed it to the wall in our living room. Every day after I came home from school I would write the letters I had learned on the blackboard with white chalk. We started with cursive writing and learned printing later. For cursive writing, we used the "Palmer Method," keeping our arms flat on the desk with our pencils between thumb and forefinger. It was a very awkward method, and was soon abandoned.

I wore glasses in first and second grade. Then I decided I could see just as well without them and tossed them aside. I didn't wear glasses again until I was 28.

The boys wore corduroy knickers that went below the knee and long, dark knee socks. All the girls wore dresses. You could tell which girls were only children by their pretty dresses. Jane Williams was always neatly dressed in a different starched dress every day. Carolyn Durant had sausage curls that her mother must have curled every morning. She wore a different pretty dress every day, freshly-starched, usually with fashionable puffed sleeves. Her brown curls were topped with a big bow of grosgrain or satin ribbon to match the color of her dress.

My idea of happiness when I got home from school was eating a Delicious apple with shiny red skin and crunchy meat. I would look out the window at the street below and the vista up Grandview Road. I liked to see the orange school bus dispersing older students.

My classmate Jane Williams was as shy as I was, and as carefully dressed. She was also an only child. One afternoon, she invited me to her brand-new house on the other side of Wynnewood Road. It was a small house, but everything was new and beautifully decorated. Her room was decorated in pretty pink with ruffled curtains and matching bedspreads on the twin beds. I was surprised that she had two beds in her room. It seemed like a waste when she slept in only one. We were both so shy, I don't think we spoke to each other hardly at all.

For God so loved the world

In the summers after the first, second, and third grades, I went to day camps put on by Baptist or Presbyterian churches. They took children of all religions. They read Bible stories to us, and we drew, colored, and painted pictures. We sang songs and played games—the usual things in a summer school for children.

The camps were within walking distance, which was good, as Mother didn't drive then. I remember one young teacher reading to us from the Bible. She was very pretty and small, and had a pocketbook made of white beads. I remember another teacher saying, "For God so loved the world, that He gave His only begotten Son, that whoever believes in Him shall not perish, but have eternal life."[42]

When a teacher at Wynnewood Road School would ask me what my religion was, I would just say "Christian." In elementary school, I couldn't explain the intricacies of Swedenborg's doctrines.

Second Grade

I was happy to return to school for second grade, carrying my school bag and lunch box. We covered a new set of handed-down books with oaktag paper. I loved workbooks in which I could answer the questions by coloring in the appropriate places.

Walking to school in the fall, I would kick and scatter piles of leaves, feeling triumph over nature. On rainy days, I wore my brown boots, and a rhythmic succession of drops pelted my raincoat as I

---

42 John 3, verse 16

sloshed through puddles of water. I walked slowly, holding my little flowered umbrella over my head while the sky poured down the audible "dot, dot, dots." I watched the rivulets of water run down the slope of my umbrella. I lingered and enjoyed the downpour, sometimes putting back my umbrella and tilting up my face to catch raindrops in my mouth. Wet green grass shimmered as I walked up Grandview Road.

In the winter when snowflakes fell, I trudged through fallen snow in my boots, kicking up against crusty banks in some places. If there was an ice slick on the uneven pavement, I'd glide across like a sled runner, sometimes toppling over. At home, I would try to make a snowman.

But spring was best of all. The sun was bright and longer lasting. The ominous clouds and the cold of winter dissipated. The air was soft and gentle. Color came into the picture, especially yellow. Violets and tiny wildflowers peeped out from under cover. Dandelions sprouted the brightest yellow in the universe on the grassy strip between sidewalk and curb. Buttercups, forsythia, and daffodils added their own yellows to the riotous welcome of spring.

The first time I went to the library, Mother walked me there. Miss March, the librarian, welcomed us. The first thing I noticed was the large engorgement at the base of her neck. Later Mother told me she had a goiter. You got that if you didn't have enough iodine in your diet. Iodine came from fish and seafood, so people who live inland are more likely to get a goiter. Now salt makers are required to add iodine to the salt we all use.

After this introduction, I was allowed to walk to the library by myself. I went alone or with Mary. I loved going there. Walking down Spring Avenue, I would look up the narrow street on the left. That was where the "colored" people lived. There were row houses with stoops on both sides of the street. I was told that most of the people who lived there worked for the upper middle class and wealthy people on the Main Line. Some of my classmates' families had maids.

I loved reading books, and second graders were allowed only four at a time. I would read them all as soon as I got home, and had to wait until the next day to get more. I went every day, and Miss March checked out more books for me. I read every one of the *Flicka, Ricka, and Dicka* books. I also read about *The Five Little Peppers and How They Grew*. I read the *Bobbsey Twins* series when I was a little older. Every one of the cardboard covers was well worn. I liked the pictures of children frolicking and having fun.

MY FIRST EXISTENTIAL CHOICE

One of my friends from second grade at Wynnewood was Anna Mae Mattis. She invited me to her home, which was near the school but in a different direction from mine. It had been whispered that her mother was very sick and dying. They thought it was lung cancer, but people didn't talk readily about those things. I tiptoed into the living room with Anna Mae and met her mother, who was sitting in a chair on the other side of the room. There was another lady there also. I believe Anna Mae's mother smoked. In those days, people said that smoking had nothing to do with lung cancer. Mother always thought otherwise.

They had just finished decorating Anna Mae's bedroom, and she took me up to see it. She had a pink flowered chintz bedspread with matching curtains, and a little vanity with a mirror. It was beautiful and just right for a seven-year-old girl. It was the center room in the semi-detached house.

I don't think I ever invited her to my apartment. I can't remember. Usually I went to my friends' houses, where it was more fun to play. But we both liked going to the library, and one day as we were walking home with our books, we met Mary Gregoria heading to the library by herself. Anna Mae and Mary didn't know each other.

"Be-Be, walk back to the library with me," Mary begged as she started walking backward.

"I'm with Anna Mae," I said.

"Come on, Be-Be, come with *me*," Mary insisted.

"If you go with her I will never speak to you again," said Anna Mae.

There were several rounds of this—Mary insistent, Anna Mae firm, and my own mind in turmoil. I stood there feeling torn. I felt comfortable with my good friend Mary. Anna Mae was a new friend. I faced my first existential choice, and I chose wrong. I left Anna Mae and went with Mary. Anna Mae never spoke to me again.

Peggy Burns was another friend in second grade. She lived in a town house on Montgomery Avenue. We would practice our spelling words by asking them to each other. One of the words was *bottom*. Our mothers had spanked us on the *bottom* when we were naughty, and we thought that word was hysterically funny and would laugh uproariously every time we came to it in the list. We finally gave up when we had a good knowledge of how to spell the words, and switched to a game of Parcheesi.

One day I came home from school and found several ladies with my mother talking about a terrible thing that had happened in the neighborhood. Mr. Ryder, who lived down the street on Spring Avenue toward the park, had shot himself in his basement. Everyone was shocked, and people wondered if he had financial problems. His wife said that no one knew why he did it.

CHRISTMAS

I was beginning to be suspicious

A few weeks before Christmas, Aunt Bea invited us out to Bryn Athyn for Sunday dinner and to see the annual Christmas Tableaux at the Assembly Hall. At Glencairn, a large tree was set up with beautiful decorations, and a Nativity scene with large figures. It was a gracious way to introduce the Christmas season.

Mother made all her Christmas gifts. Each year I could help a little more. We made satin clothes hangers by wrapping wire hangers with cotton batting and wide satin ribbon. One year we made calendars. We cut a pretty photo from a magazine and pasted it on heavy cardboard. Underneath the photo, we pasted on a small calendar. Another year Mother had a pattern for bedroom slippers, or *scuffs*, made of quilted cotton. We made pencil holders out of felt. Mother made pincushions.

Mother would write out Christmas cards and I would lick the 3¢ stamps and affix them to the envelopes. We would walk with them to the post office.

Mother liked to dress me up in pretty clothes that she made herself. She liked to dress up my dolls too. She made them little coats and hats from a silky material. She sewed lace around the hats and coats and embroidered pink rosebuds on them. On Christmas Eve, I would hang my stocking and prop up my dolls under the tree. The next morning, lo and behold, my dolls were all dressed up in brand new clothes.

I was curious about Santa Claus and asked a lot of questions. "How does he know what each child should have?" I asked. "How can he get all around the world in one night?"

When I was six, I was beginning to be suspicious, but I dismissed my doubts. I wanted to believe in Santa Claus. Mother took me to Strawbridge's in Ardmore to sit on Santa's lap and ask for a gift. I knew there was no chimney in our apartment house except the one that went outside from the furnace next to the coal bin. Fireplaces in the living room were for rich people. Mother equivocated the best she could. Daddy smiled and held his head back. I sensed they were keeping a secret from me, and I was determined to find out what it was.

I remember a dark winter afternoon near Christmas time. The air was cold. Mother and I were walking along Lancaster Avenue amidst blustery wind and intermittent snowflakes. There were twinkling lights and garlands of evergreen decorating the light posts. Christmas music came out muffled from behind store windows.

There were advertisements for the movie *Miracle on 34th Street*. The Salvation Army man was out ringing his bell bundled up with ear muffs, hat, and heavy gloves. He stood in front of his red bucket, jingling for a donation of money to help the poor. We walked into Kresge's 5&10 to buy some Christmas wrapping paper and some red and green construction paper to make chains. We made these at school also, to decorate our classroom.

Mother and I took a little run around in the FAO Schwarz toy store. This was a branch of the top-notch New York store that carried exotic and very expensive toys. It was a whole store filled with toys just for children! There were child-sized stoves and sinks. There were huge Steiff stuffed animals and small cuddly ones. There were many games and books. Mother and I walked around quietly so as not to be noticed. We knew we wouldn't be buying anything, and we thought the store clerks probably knew it, too. They would occasionally ask if we needed help, and we said we were just looking.

One year, a week or so before Christmas, I peeked into a closet and saw a large box with a picture of a globe on it. It was tucked in the back under some clothes. Sure enough, the globe appeared under the tree on Christmas morning as a gift from Santa Claus. I was about seven or eight years old, which seems pretty old to find out the truth about Santa.

My aunts were the ones who occasionally gave me exotic toys for Christmas. Aunt Bea gave me a set of marionettes. Snow White and the Seven Dwarfs were beautifully crafted out of wood and painted bright colors. I figured out how to work the strings, and I put on a play for the neighborhood children. They were all wide-eyed with excitement. Dolly laughed loudest.

On Christmas Day, we would go to church and hear the Christmas story and sing Christmas carols. We would go to Horn and Hardart for Christmas dinner afterwards. When Mary and I were old enough, we went to see Maureen O'Hara in *Miracle on 34th Street*. After Christmas, we would roll up the ribbon and fold the wrapping paper, taking care not to tear it so we could use it again next year.

❧

NEIGHBORS IN THE BUILDING
We're all going to freeze to death!

Early on, the newlywed Corrs moved into the apartment across the hall from us on the second floor. Tommy and Mary Corr were both 19 years old and expecting their first child. Tommy was a milkman. After their second child was born, they moved to a twin house not far away.

Later on, Mother and I went to visit Mary and the children. The house had a bare floor with no rugs. The furniture was basic: an overstuffed couch and two overstuffed chairs. The room smelled of urine and dirty diapers. Mary was holding a child on her lap and smoking. Another child was playing on the floor, and another crawling around. I didn't know how to play with small children, so I sat beside Mother and listened to their conversation. Mary was a very friendly lady with a nice smile. I liked her, but I knew I didn't want to live like that.

Mrs. Glavin, who moved in when the Corrs left, was old and thin with a permanently worried look on her face. She wore baggy dresses and always had an apron on unless she was going to church. She wore her gray hair coiled up in a school-marm bun at the back of her head. There was a definite "old ladies' style" in those days. Only "loose" women dyed their hair. Old ladies wore 1930s style dresses, cotton stockings, and black, Cuban-heeled, lace-up shoes. The dresses were usually a dark color with a crocheted collar or lace, and sometimes crocheted cuffs on the sleeves. That would be their best Sunday clothes. Everyday "house dresses" were usually of washable cotton, possibly with an apron tied around the waist.

The men had one, possibly two, good suits for work or church. They wore a white shirt with a detachable collar. The collar got laundered more often than the shirt did.

Mrs. Glavin had a slight Irish brogue. I think she must have come over from Ireland as a child in the late 19th century. Many immigrants came from Ireland for several decades after the disastrous potato famine in the mid-19th century when a blight wiped out most of the potato crop for several years in a row. Potatoes were the staple of their diet, and many people died of starvation.

In the winter, Mrs. Glavin always seemed to be cold. She would tuck her hands into the opposite sleeves of the worn-out sweater she always wore. If something awful happened, she would say "Praise be to God" and cross herself.

Mother and Mrs. Glavin communicated a lot. If coal wasn't delivered on time for some reason, Mrs. Glavin would say, "We're all going to freeze to death!" Mother always concurred in her dire predictions. Both came from the "Old Country," where *life was no bed of roses*. For those coming from the Old Country and its hard times, a dour view of life was almost built in. The English paradigm was to "keep a stiff upper lip" and "muddle through." Mrs. Glavin was Irish, but I think she had the same idea.

Immigrants like my mother, my aunts, and Mrs. Glavin accepted struggle as the norm. They were eager to put into practice the hard work ethic of the Old Country. Hardship was to be overcome, and the light of hope at the end of the road was always in focus. Everyone believed they would have a better life eventually.

Mrs. Glavin's daughter, Marguerite, worked at Eiler's sporting goods store as Mr. Eiler's secretary. I was always interested in clothes, and noticed what people wore. Marguerite was always stylishly dressed. In summer, she wore brown and white spectator shoes. During the war, skirts were shorter to save fabric for the men and women serving in the war. During the Depression, skirts had been long. But women had more propriety now than in the Roaring Twenties. During World War II, women rolled up their hair in the front to achieve a pompadour.

Stockings had seams down the back, and women would often turn around and ask a friend if their seams were straight. Before the war, silk stockings were giving way to a new, thin material called nylon. But when the U.S. entered the war, nylon was diverted from stockings to parachutes and other war materials. Women tried painting their legs with a flesh-colored cosmetic leg paint, and drew a line down the back to look like a seam. The problem was that during the heat of summer, the paint would run. So that idea didn't last long, and it became acceptable for women to go without stockings during the summer.

Marguerite's last name was Arenz, and Elaine's last name was Arenz, too. It was whispered (and I believe it was proven) that Mr. Arenz was a bigamist who had deserted his family shortly after baby Elaine was born. We never saw him. I don't think Elaine ever saw him. No one talked about such things in those days; it was considered shameful. Every once in a while, Elaine's paternal grandmother would visit from New York. She was a heavy, rotund woman who breathed heavily every time she walked up the stairs.

It was shameful to have a baby out of wedlock, and the appearance of propriety had to be kept up. The Ten Commandments and Christian principles were taken very seriously in those days. When it came time for Elaine to marry, her illegitimacy was a concern for her future in-laws, who were prominent business people.

PASSIONATE KISSES

The Martins, who lived in the apartment below us, and ran the store below Mrs. Glavin and Marguerite, bought a house and gave up the store for some other endeavors. Martin's store became Pizzi's store, and we had a succession of tenants in the apartment below us, who stayed for a few years each.

I remember the new store owner. One time we went in to buy a pound of something, and his scale was broken. He held up a pound of flour in one hand and Mother's request in the other and figured out about a pound. He asked Mother to do the same to make sure he was correct.

Eventually the corner store became more of a convenience store, selling candy and soda. It got to be a hangout for young male friends who wanted to socialize. Occasionally they became too noisy, and Marguerite in the apartment over the store had to call the police.

One of the people who lived in the lower apartment was a young woman with a two-year-old daughter. Her husband was a Merchant Marine who wasn't home much. She was tall and slender with honey-colored hair down to her shoulders. She would have been beautiful, but her face was pockmarked from acne. Her husband was tall, sandy-haired, swarthy, and muscular. One time when he had just come back from a long trip, she invited me down to play with their two-year-old daughter. The husband embraced her, and they looked deeply into each other's eyes. They stroked each other and kissed passionately. My parents never did anything like this. I was supposed to be playing with their daughter, but I was transfixed. They didn't seem to notice me watching them.

I'm sure my parents loved and depended on each other, but they never showed any outward affection, at least not in front of me. They kidded around and had fun.

The woman with honey-colored hair took taxis a lot. Mother and Mrs. Glavin would watch from their upstairs windows as the taxi came to pick her up. They marveled that she had money to take a taxi. Neither of them had ever been inside one in their lives. As Mother said, "We went on 'Shank's mare.'" In other words, they walked.

An older woman, Mrs. Henzie, lived below us for a while with her two teenage daughters. She was divorced, which was uncommon at the time. I think she was the first divorced person I had ever met. She had a good job in a factory, and used to stop at the "tap room" on her way home. Her younger daughter, Dodie, was tall and thin.

Mother was working private duty cases for people on the Main Line at this time. During the summer when we were out of school, Dodie would "watch" me when Mother was working. I used to do a lot of coloring in a coloring book while we sat on the steps and talked. I did the children's clothes in bright colors. I couldn't figure out what color to make the skin.

"What color is flesh color?" I didn't have *flesh color* in my box.

"It's light orange," she said. I was surprised, but I tried it and it looked pretty good.

Another couple came later. I think they had one small child. I remember being upstairs in our bedroom with Mother when we heard knocking on the floor from below. Mother told me to be quiet. We listened. "Tap, tap, tap," it sounded again from below. The lady downstairs was lying in bed tapping with a broom handle. She was having a miscarriage and she knew that Mother was a nurse. Mother went down and took care of her.

Neighbors knew that Mother was a nurse, and she was often asked for help or advice.

Mary Boyle lived in a house down the street. She was 16. She had to stay in bed with two broken legs from an automobile accident. She smoked and listened to the radio to pass the time. From time to time we were told that her legs were not healing as fast as they should, and people were worried. Later it was discovered that it was bad for people to stay in bed too long.

THE GENERAL CHURCH

Oh Come, Let us Adore Him

My family began attending services at the General Church Advent Society's church, on the second floor of the Presser Building at 16th and Chestnut Street. The Presser Building was a music school with studios for different musicians. The concert hall wasn't used on Sunday mornings, so our church group rented it for Sunday services.

Before the service the children would run around, up and down the long halls. Sometimes there were musicians in the studios upstairs, practicing their instruments. I remember a soprano singing scales at the top of her lungs. She was loud. Our childish energy could scarcely be reined in, and occasionally someone would come down and tell us, "Please do not make so much noise!"

Our minister, Reverend Homer Synnestvedt, was elderly and portly. He wore a long white robe with a blue stole. He had a white beard, and would have made a good Santa Claus if he had worn a red suit. He was dignified with an affable manner and was jolly with children.

We children would sit together in the big hall to listen to the lessons given by the minister. Then we would file out and go to the back room for Sunday School. One Christmas, I remember standing in the front row at church next to my cousin Dwain. We were about six and seven. He was bellowing at the top of his lungs, "Oh, Come

Let Us Adore Him!" pouring his whole heart and soul into the song. I would remember that wistfully in later years.

Some members of the Advent Society had joined the church as adults, and since Mother had gone to school in Bryn Athyn, they considered her more knowledgeable. She taught children's Sunday school there for many years.[43]

Sometimes after church several couples and their children would go together to Horn and Hardart's for Sunday dinner. We usually got chicken with mashed potatoes and gravy. Daddy and I got apple pie with vanilla ice cream for dessert.

STAINED GLASS AND A SMALL DEAD FOX

Sometimes we went to the Bryn Athyn Cathedral for church, and I sat with my parents in the pew. I was too shy to go to the children's area, so I sat through the adult portion of the service with my parents. I looked up at the beautiful stained-glass windows high in the clerestory. The windows on the lower level were grisaille clear-glass with leaded separations. I wondered why the more beautiful ones were not on the lower level where you could enjoy them. I learned later that in medieval times the worshippers were not to be distracted. The Bible stories were to be learned and aspired to, to

---

43 Some of the Parishioners at the Advent Society in Philadelphia:
Donald and Provida Fitzpatrick, and son Don
Ted and Myra Carroll and daughter Ann
Herman and Ruth Gloster and two children
Billie and Harry Furry and son Bob
Doris and Al Kingdon and son Bill
Emily and Carl Soderberg, daughter Emmy Lou, and son John
Eliot Cranch and his wife
Arlene Glenn Archer, who had a glass eye, and her husband
Colleen Starkey, who had a withered arm
Arthur and Marjorie Williamson and their five children
My aunt Elsie Barnes and her son, Dwain. I don't remember her husband, Roy, ever going to church.

look up heavenward. The grisaille was decorative for peaceful contemplation.

I was distracted, however, by the ladies' hats. In those days, men left their hats outside on the coat rack, but ladies wore their hats into church. They wore felt hats decorated with artificial flowers, or straw hats in the summer. There were large brims and small brims. Some hats just covered the crown of the lady's head, and some had a veil covering half of the lady's face. I remember that Mrs. Furry wore a small dead fox around her neck, with beady glass eyes.

When the organ played, we stood up, and I would try to sing some of the songs I knew.

IMPENDING WAR

"September 1, 1939"[44]

—W. H. Auden (1907-1973)

I sit in one of the dives
On Fifty-Second Street
Uncertain and afraid
As the clever hopes expire
Of a low dishonest decade:
Waves of anger and fear
Circulate over the bright
And darkened lands of the earth,
Obsessing our private lives;
The unmentionable odour of death
Offends the September night.

---

44 W. H. Auden, *Another Time*. Random House, 1940. Copyright © 1940 W. H. Auden, renewed by the Estate of W. H. Auden. First and Third Stanzas. Entire poem seen in *Wall Street Journal*, "Notable and Quotable" http://www.poemdujour.com/Sept1.1939.html

Exiled Thucydides knew
All that a speech can say
About Democracy,
And what dictators do,
The elderly rubbish they talk
To an apathetic grave;
Analysed all in his book,
The enlightenment driven away,
The habit-forming pain,
Mismanagement and grief:
We must suffer them all again.

In 1939 Raymond Pitcairn moved his family from Cairnwood into their new castle home on a hill just above the Cathedral. Raymond and his wife, Mildred Glenn Pitcairn, combined their names and called their new place "Glencairn." From the Glencairn tower, you could see the city of Philadelphia 16 miles away. Their new home would house many ancient and medieval artifacts that both John Pitcairn and his son Raymond had collected on their travels.

A large room with a high ceiling and stained glass windows would be used for concerts and church events like the Christmas Sing. The whole community was invited to the Christmas Sing, to sing Christmas hymns and listen to well-known musicians and singers invited by the Pitcairns.

It is better to remain silent at the risk of being thought
a fool, than to talk and remove all doubt of it
—-Maurice Switzer[45]

Aunt Bea would often invite us for Sunday dinner after church

---

45 Switzer, Maurice. *Mrs. Goose: Her Book.* New York. Moffat, Yard, 1907. Quote Investigator chooses Maurice Switzer as the top choice for originating this saying, which has been attributed to both Abraham Lincoln and Mark Twain. https://quoteinvestigator.com/2010/05/17/remain-silent/ by Garson O'Toole

in the servants' quarters at Glencairn. The first time I heard classical music was sitting in "the help's" living room before dinner. Four or five girls waited on Raymond, Mildred, and their children in the big dining room. The girls were often relatives of the family, or young adults whose families were members of the Church. Some of them worked there until they got married or went back to school. I would sit at the table and not say a word.

Years later, Jane deCharms, one of the girls at that table, told me she felt so sorry for me having to sit there with all the adults. I told her I didn't mind at all. I was more comfortable listening to adult conversation than talking to children I didn't know. I enjoyed hearing about the scandals and problems of adults in everyday life, and it was easier than groping for interesting conversation with my contemporaries.

I was comfortable being a fly the wall. Only when adults asked me questions to include me in the conversation did I become uneasy. I didn't know what was expected of me, or what to say. I was a serious and deliberate child. In front of adults I wanted to know exactly what I was expected to do before I did anything.

At times, I sensed that they expected me to be light-hearted and spontaneous, or when I was very small, to amuse them with a cute malapropism or two. I had seen other children do this, but I would have been extremely embarrassed if I'd done so myself inadvertently. Years later I heard a saying that would have suited me fine. "It is better to stay quiet and have others think you're a fool than to open your mouth and confirm it."

Daddy was also quiet at Glencairn. He just sat and listened. He may have been the only man at the table. Daddy was mild mannered and hesitant of speech. He wasn't familiar with many of the social graces, which he learned by watching others. For instance, he learned to stand up when a lady walked into the room or pull out a chair for a lady to sit down. He always held the door open for others to go in.

I didn't feel shy when Mother carried me into the kitchen to say hello to Lena, the buxom African-American cook. She had a hearty laugh, and always commented on my big brown eyes. Ashleys have penetrating brown eyes that people remark upon. "You have your mother's eyes," Lena would say.

In springtime, on the way home from Bryn Athyn, we would stop and pick some honeysuckle that grew beside the road. We would put it in a milk bottle full of water and enjoy the fragrance for a few days.

Toys and Peacocks

Vera, the youngest Pitcairn daughter, was three years older than me. She wanted to show me her dollhouse and her big beautiful bedroom, which I wanted to see. I followed her to her room, but clammed up as usual and only answered direct questions, fearful I would say something unacceptable. I gazed in wonder at the dollhouse with its Lilliputian kitchen implements, and beautifully upholstered furniture and draperies, all perfectly made to scale. She carefully picked up each delicate piece of furniture and the tiny silverware and plates and cups on the diminutive dining room table.

We went outside to the playhouse where they kept riding toys and small cars with pedals. We drove the cars around on the macadam path. I saw assorted other riding and pushing toys. Peacocks strutted their iridescent turquoise plumage across the green lawn.

That morphed into a cactus obsession

—Tryn Clark

Usually after Sunday dinner, we all went up to Aunt Bea's room. Our footsteps echoed as we climbed the highly polished stairs. Aunt Bea had a nice room over the porte-cochère. It was light and airy, with windows on each side of the room. On the left was a big, beautiful walk-in closet, which I admired. All sorts of hat boxes and clothes were carefully organized in there. At Christmastime, it was full of colorfully wrapped gifts. The bathroom was straight ahead, and up two steps to the right was her bedroom.

Aunt Bea had a wealth of knowledge about homeopathic medicine. She read the *Materia Medica*, an authoritative source for homeopathic remedies. She dispensed sugar pills from little vials to the Pitcairn children and many of the help as well. She could be a little crusty, which can be the case with some who have a soft interior. She took care of the Pitcairn children and eventually the grandchildren. Her charges called her the "General." She was strict but fair. Twice weekly she made flower arrangements for the house.

Arthur, Marjorie, Caryl, and Roy Wells were all siblings in a large family. Their father was an honorary Colonel from Kentucky. Arthur studied succulents in the School of Agriculture at Penn State, and this study "morphed into a cactus obsession," according to a relative, Tryn Clark. Olive and Donald Rose were a sister and brother from England. Arthur Wells married Olive Rose, and his sister Marjorie married Olive's brother, Don. The Roses had twelve children, who were sometimes referred to as "a dozen Roses."

Caryl Wells was Mother's friend, and Olive Wells was Aunt Bea's best friend. Olive and Aunt Bea shared a common interest in England and people who still lived there. Aunt Bea would go to Olive's house in the afternoons to drink tea, knit socks, and discuss the events of the day and happenings in England. They had knitted wool socks for soldiers in the Great War (World War I) in which Arthur's brother Roy had served. A member of the Pitcairn family told me that he remembered Aunt Bea walking up the hill to the house with two of the small children tugging at her skirts, reading a letter telling her that Roy had been killed in the war.

MY COUSINS IN WIVENHOE

Every year around the Fourth of July, the newspapers would count how many Civil War veterans were still alive. By 1938, there were very few. By 1939, the blue summer sky was cloudy with rumors of another war. Adolf Hitler's menacing voice came over the radio. He spoke in German, so we couldn't understand what he was saying. His shrill, emphatic voice was funny as well as scary.

In 1938, Neville Chamberlain, the British Secretary of War, had signed the Munich Pact and told his countrymen that he had secured "peace in our time." He was wrong. Britain and France declared war the next year in September, when Germany refused to withdraw troops from Poland. For eight months, most of the action happened at sea, and this period was dubbed "The Phoney War." The Phoney period ended with Germany's invasion of Belgium, the Netherlands, and Luxembourg in May, 1940.

On Sundays up in Aunt Bea's room, she and Mother discussed their brothers in England who had been through the Great War and were now facing war again. Daddy and I just listened. All their grandparents were gone now, and their sister Annie had died also. Herbert was a postman in London, and Felix lived with his family in Kent.

Aunt Bea was the one who corresponded with the relatives in England, and was closest to Charlie, who still lived in the family home in Wivenhoe. Charlie had met a nurse named Emily Coles while they were both serving in World War I. After the war, they married, and Charlie became a plumber. Emily was diabetic, and they didn't have children right away, so they adopted the daughter of Charlie's cousin Jack Roper, who had a large family. They named their adopted daughter Ursula. But after a few years, Emily gave birth to two boys of her own: Tony in 1927 and Michael in 1930. During the 30s, Charlie added an indoor bathroom to the family home.

When the boys were about six and eight years old, Emily's diabetes went out of control, and she had to go to a sanatorium in London for a few months. After her discharge from the sanatorium, she must have been craving sweets. As she walked to the train station to return to Wivenhoe, she stopped at a pastry shop and ate some pastries. She collapsed and died on the spot.

During the 20s and 30s, Aunt Bea had sent money to Charlie to pay off the mortgage on the Ernest Road house. But when she went over there expecting the mortgage to be paid in full, she was surprised and upset to find that Emily had taken all the checks and spent the money on other things.

After Emily died, Charlie did not think it was proper for Ursula to continue living with them, and she went back to live with her birth parents. But she helped Charlie with the boys, and a neighbor named Iris became Charlie's full-time housekeeper. Ursula told me years later that Charlie was very hard on the boys after their mother

Glencairn, the Pitcairn's new home. Photo by Stephen Conroy, 2019

Arthur and Olive Wells   Uncle Felix with Kathleen, Pauline, and Peter
with their two daughters

died. She thought he felt powerless to change his own life, and struck out in anger at his sons. Michael, the younger one, fared better than Tony, the elder.

Wivenhoe was vulnerable to attack, on the east coast just 50 miles from London. The coastline was being mined, and food was scarce and rationed. Aunt Bea was sending packages of necessities to her brothers and their families, who were grateful for the food and clothes. The British government was sending children who were in harm's way to America for the duration of the war if they had relatives to take care of them. Tony and Michael were eligible for this program, and Aunt Bea suggested that they come and live with us. She would help pay for a larger apartment.

I was excited. I would have two older "brothers," and maybe even my own room! The adults began preparing for the event. Mother and I walked to both Roach Brothers and Crosiers Real estate offices to look for a new apartment. We looked at several apartments, mostly in converted three-story houses. I hoped we would get one of those, or one like them up on Spring Avenue near Alma and Dewey.

I believe that Tony and Michael were set to come on the next ship when we got shocking news from Aunt Bea. The ship just ahead of theirs had been torpedoed by the Germans on the high seas. Everyone on it drowned. The British government decided it was too dangerous to send children over, and stopped the program. So Tony and Michael remained in England, and we went on living in our one-bedroom apartment at 248 Spring Avenue. I was very disappointed.

Tony would become an apprentice to a bookbinder after finishing school at the age of 14. Many years later, he expressed regret that he did not come to the United States as a child. Michael did well as a salesman for a Dutch tulip company.

We followed, somewhat, the careers of the two English princesses. Margaret was a little older than me, and Elizabeth a couple years older than that. The princesses worked to boost the morale of the English people as they endured the war.

In the summer of 1940, Germany had defeated France. The German Air Force, the Luftwaffe, began test bombing to destroy the British Air Force. In September, they waged a campaign to destroy the military and industrial areas of Britain. London docks were continuously bombed for four months. Beginning in September 1940, German planes bombed London for 57 consecutive nights. In November and after, there were raids by German Messerschmitt fighters on Birmingham, Coventry, and major port cities.

On December 7th, 1941, we drove out to Bryn Athyn for church and had lunch with Aunt Bea. We were up in her room conversing as usual when someone knocked on the door. She came in and told us, "The Japanese have attacked Pearl Harbor. We are at war."

⟪❧⟫

MOTHER'S CONVERSION TO HEALTH FOOD

I've always admired off-beat and outrageous people;
they make life more interesting for the rest of us.
—Beatrice Pitcairn

Mother's friend Dr. Caryl Wells graduated from the Girls Seminary in Bryn Athyn in 1915, and went on to study at The Philadelphia Orthopedic Hospital and Infirmary for Nervous Disease. In 1931, she graduated and became a naturopathic doctor. She ran her practice from her second-floor apartment in a 19th century brownstone row house on Spruce Street in Philadelphia. She did colored-light treatments and colonic irrigations. Mother started going to Caryl for treatment of her migraines and other problems, and sometimes took me with her.

If Daddy didn't drive us there, we would go on the trolley. We walked up a long, steep set of stairs. The stairs were long because the ceilings were very high. Caryl's apartment was filled with clutter: the tables and floor were piled with books and paraphernalia for the treatments she gave. She had different colored plates of glass about 8x10". She would decide which color you needed for your particular ailment, and insert the glass plate into a device that looked something like a lantern for a light show. She plugged it into the wall and focused the warm colored light onto the part of your body that was giving you trouble. She gave me a treatment once. She decided yellow was the right color for my "condition." I lay on her chiropractic table with the yellow light focused on my exposed belly for about 20 minutes.

Caryl persuaded Mother to give up allopathic (standard) medicine, and stop taking phenobarbital. She also told her to give up white flour and white sugar, which she called "vicious" foods, and switch to whole grains. Mother was already using some homeopathic medicine, as were Aunt Bea and many people in Bryn Athyn.

Mother and Caryl read Swedenborg's Writings, and they would

sometimes read the same passage and compare ideas. They both liked finding parallels with their own experiences and incorporating new ideas into their Swedenborgian frame of thought. Caryl had a high and wheezy voice, especially when she was excited about something she had read that agreed with other things she had experienced or read about. I remember them reading *Apocalypse Explained* and *The Animal Kingdom*, both books by Swedenborg. They would talk on the phone for long periods of time, discussing the latest discoveries in health foods and natural methods of healing. Mother could become talkative when it came to her own special interests. She was so thrilled with her discoveries about health and nutrition that she wanted to spread the word.

I remember Caryl talking a lot about "correspondences." Swedenborg used the term "correspondence" to mean a connection between a natural thing and a spiritual thing, so that spiritual things were represented by natural things. This was an important concept in his revelation of the spiritual meaning of Biblical stories. Birds, for instance, corresponded to "Things spiritual, rational, and also intellectual."[46] Caryl had several birds in cages in her apartment because she liked their correspondence.

> He who draws wisdom from God is like a bird flying aloft enjoying a wide and extensive view, and directing its flight to whatever is required for its use[47]

I think Mother used to take a little wine at Holy Supper, and when we went to Glencairn. But after her conversion to health foods, I never saw her drink alcohol of any kind again. As sometimes happens when one converts to a new religion, my mother, upon discovering the value of health foods and eschewing standard drugs, became a rabid proselytizer. She wanted to share the good tidings about raw and natural foods. She threw out all our white flour and white sugar. When we got ration stamps for sugar during the war, Mother gave all our sugar stamps to neighbors. No more sour balls

---

46 Swedenborg, *Arcana Coelestia*, #40
47 Swedenborg, *True Christian Religion*, #69

or lollipops for me.

One day Caryl told us she had a boyfriend, a Greek seaman named Louis Kostas. She called him "Louie." Caryl was in her forties then, and Louie was in his sixties. His wife had died, and he had a grown family back home in Greece. Caryl's apartment was so cluttered that the only place that she and Louie could do any "courting" was sitting on the toilet seat, where she could sit on his lap. I remember Mother and Daddy laughing about that.

Caryl married Louie in February of 1941, and bought a row house in West Philadelphia. By that time she had 35 birds flying around her apartment. In her new home, the birds were given their own room upstairs.

Louie did most of the cooking, making good Greek food with lots of garlic. He took Caryl to Greece to meet his family, and his relatives came from far and wide to meet her. She was disconcerted when he took her gold watch off her wrist and gave it to his brother. Then he took off her gold bracelet and gave it to another family member. His family in Greece was quite poor.

Louie Kostas was about 97 years old when he died in 1974, and Caryl stayed in their Philadelphia home for the rest of her life, as her neighborhood changed around her. Most white people moved out to the suburbs, and her neighborhood became African-American. She got along well with her neighbors, but often young men would sit on her porch and harass her, telling her she did not belong in *their* neighborhood. But she stayed, and she drove Emmy Lou's mother, Emily Soderberg, to church in Bryn Athyn. Emily was in the same kind of neighborhood, and did not want to move either. Eventually Emily's children persuaded her to move after a break-in landed her in the hospital for two days.

As a shy person myself, always trying to do the acceptable thing, I've always admired off-beat and outrageous people. They make life more interesting for the rest of us.

Though Mother and Caryl remained friends, we moved on to Dr. Adolph Bimmler as a physician. His office was in a tall brownstone house in West Philadelphia. The second floor was turned into a waiting room, an office, and a treatment room. Dr. Bimmler and his wife Frieda, who worked with him, had come over from Germany where they were trained as naturopaths. Before the war, Germany was considered a leader in scientific progress and in areas of human health.

The Bimmlers had a daughter, but I never saw her. I think she was a lot older than me. I would sit in the waiting room while Mother had a treatment, which took about an hour. I would soon tire of playing with whatever toy I'd brought, if I'd brought one. I would examine the pictures on the wall. One or two people might come in and sit down, and I would stare at them. When I was older I realized that staring wasn't a polite thing to do. But I especially liked to look at fashionable women, observing their dresses and shoes. But there weren't many fashionable women there—it was mostly older women.

One day I was the only one there. At that point my legs weren't long enough to reach the floor and they stuck out straight in front of me. I noticed to my horror that my socks didn't match. Both were white, but one had a red pattern around the top and the other had a blue pattern. I kept trying to roll them so that the tops wouldn't show. When I went out onto the street and onto the trolley with Mother, I was afraid everyone would notice my unmatched socks!

Later on I went for an evaluation and possibly a treatment. Dr. Bimmler had a big machine. He strapped something to my arm. He turned on the machine to get the lights going so he could evaluate my condition. I don't remember what kind of treatments he gave, but I don't think he had the same kind of light machine as Caryl. I think he may have been a chiropractor too.

I think it was Dr. Bimmler who told Mother she should go on a cleansing diet. One weekend we bought a wooden crate of oranges. The three of us went on the cleansing diet. We ate nothing but oranges all weekend to cleanse our systems. By Sunday, Daddy and I had to eat something else for sustenance.

◦ ⁓ ◦

MOTHER LEARNS TO DRIVE

Sometime around 1942, Daddy decided Mother should learn how to drive. She would be able to drive herself to work, and it would give her more freedom. Daddy knew people in the used car business, and he could always get a good deal on a car. I pleaded with Daddy to get one with a "rumble seat," which was a two-person bench seat in the back where the trunk would be. It looked like so much fun to sit there with the wind blowing in your face, looking all around unobstructed. I wanted to see what the world would look like as I was bouncing around. I kept on pleading, "Please, Daddy, let's get a rumble seat."

Daddy said no.

"Please, please get a rumble seat! I want a rumble seat!" I shouted out. "Please, pleeeease ..."

Mother said I was *determined* (decided, resolute).

But Daddy was adamant. "No!" he said emphatically. He'd had a rumble seat before. "Once you've had a car with a rumble seat you'll never buy another," he said. "If you're sitting there when it rains, you get all wet. If the back is closed, the rain leaks around the edges. And you can't communicate with the driver."

I cried and pouted. Daddy tended to crush people's romantic dreams. That day he crushed mine. Rumble seats went out of style a few years later.

Daddy was always partial to Plymouth. He drove a black Plymouth, and he got Mother a dark blue Plymouth coupe for $200. He also got a nice second-hand car for Aunt Bea, which she drove for years.

Mother's coupe had two doors and a ledge in the back behind the seats. I lay across the ledge and watched Mother learn to drive. In those days, stores were closed on Sundays, and the deserted parking lots were a good place to learn to drive. Mother grasped the knob on the gearshift pole and tried to synchronize her left foot on the clutch pedal. When she got it wrong, the car lurched forward, stalled out, and stopped. It was a jerky ride.

I watched and learned. I was sure I could do better. Sometimes Daddy let me sit behind the wheel and drive a little. I had to stretch to see out the window, but I knew then that I wanted to drive as soon as I was allowed. It was a long wait until I was 16, but I got my license as soon as I could.

Mother eventually mastered the manual transmission, and was able to drive herself to her work at the hospital. She liked her new freedom, and I did, too. We could go more places now. We drove up to Lancaster Pike to Mrs. Higgins' Bakery to buy a loaf of Mrs. Higgins' Original Oatmeal bread. I'm nostalgic for the delicious taste of that oatmeal bread, made with real oatmeal. It's the best bread I've ever had. We also went to visit Mother's friends and drove to Bryn Mawr Art Center.

Mother didn't want to drive downtown, so we still took the subway to Martindale's Health Food Store for soya burgers and vitamins. We drank carrot juice, and Mother bought a juicer so she could make her own carrot juice. She also juiced celery, cabbage, beets, and spinach. A little green book by a Dr. Walker in Arizona told her which juices were good for various ailments.

We ate oatmeal for breakfast. Mother soaked the oats overnight and cooked them up in the morning. We sweetened it with raw sugar or honey. We ate lots of chicken and lentils for protein. Mother heard that dandelion leaves were good for you, so we would go for a walk and pick the dandelions growing in the strip of grass between the street and the sidewalk.

Sometimes when we were in Philadelphia, we'd go to Horn and Hardart's for lunch. The vegetable soup warmed us in the winter. Mother walked briskly, and I had to trot along to keep up. Then I could put a nickel in the slot and spin the glass door of the compartment and take out a piece of pie. Other times we had raw beet and carrot salad at Martindale's.

Mother and some friends of the same mindset would drive together to Great Valley Mills out beyond the suburbs of Philadelphia. They would buy freshly milled whole wheat flour and unbleached white flour. Daddy always liked the chocolate cake Mother made for him before converting to health food. She now made it with unbleached flour, raw sugar, and carob powder in place of chocolate. They switched from coffee to Postum, a product made of wheat with no caffeine. Daddy had grown up with everything fried in lard, and I don't know if he liked these changes. But he never complained, and ate whatever Mother served.

An Amish Food Market was set up on Suburban Square near the Suburban Movie Theater, across from Strawbridge and Clothier. The Amish people came from Lancaster every Saturday to sell their wares. We browsed around and bought some of their tasty food.

Mother canned tomatoes at home. I remember a large pot on the stove with glass jars rattling around, being sterilized by the steam. She also made yoghurt, saving the culture from one batch to add to the warmed milk for the next. I didn't like it much, but the yoghurt had a stronger flavor than it does nowadays.

With butter in short supply, the stores sold white oleomargarine. It came with a little bag of artificial yellow coloring that you had to mix in to achieve the look and feel of butter. Mother wisely avoided it. It looked horrible to me whenever I encountered it at someone's house.

Everyone had a ration book with stamps and coupons inside. Children were allowed two pairs of shoes a year. Gasoline stamps were given according to how far you had to drive to your job, and Daddy walked to his job. We had to carefully save up coupons for our summer vacations in Ocean City or Ohio. We traded our sugar stamps for something else, or gave them away.

Mother listened to Bernarr MacFadden on the radio, and later Carlton Fredericks. She attended J.I. Rodale lectures. He was a proponent of eating natural foods. Dr. Diehl, a friend of Mother's, complained of ulcers. Nothing he took for them did any good. Mother told him to drink cabbage juice. He was skeptical, but tried it anyway. To his great surprise his ulcers went away.

Mother and I rode bicycles together, and went for walks. She encouraged me to take deep breaths to get more oxygen into my system. She heard that goat's milk was more healthful than cow's milk. She found a man in Lancaster County who sold raw goat's milk, unpasteurized, straight from the goat.

We took our own containers and made the long drive out to rural Lancaster County. We turned off onto an unpaved road and drove for a while. Another dirt road went up a steep hill. At the top of this bumpy road full of rocks and stones was an old, crumbling farmhouse. A dog was barking, and the wooden front porch was piled up with discarded furniture and household goods. The *goat man* came out to meet us. He didn't invite us into the house. We stood and waited for him to fill our containers. I wondered how sanitary the goats' milk could be. Mother, who was always so fastidious in matters concerning health, didn't seem to care. It was *natural*, straight from the goat!

We all drank goats' milk for a while, but I didn't like the taste. It wasn't what I was used to. I don't think we went out to the goat man's place more than two or three times. It was a long way to drive.

CHAPTER FIVE:
WORLD WAR II

It was the job of motor transport to deliver the goods,
and American wheels and axles
never let us down.

—General Dwight Eisenhower[48]

In the early part of the war the Autocar Company advertised that the workers could take evening classes at Haverford College. Daddy signed up right away. He took a class in physics. I remember him coming home thrilled and animated about the things he had learned. He told us about a new substance for cleaning clothes. They were doing experiments with a new chemical that broke the surface tension of the water. A duck was then put into the water, and could not stay on top. Daddy thought the duck looked surprised as it sank into the water. This new chemical would be called "detergent" and would replace soap, which was made from lye, to cut the grease.

During the war Daddy got a more important job at the Autocar plant as a "troubleshooter." He was called to different work places to fix things that were going wrong. He got a raise, I believe to $35.00 a week.

Daddy's family in Ohio were mostly Republicans. Daddy said that at the Autocar someone would go around and collect money for the Democratic Party. Part of the union dues he paid were sent to the Democratic Party. I didn't think that was fair. I don't think Daddy voted.

The Autocar company had three shifts. The workers took turns, working for two weeks on each shift. Daddy hated the graveyard shift because he couldn't sleep during the day. On the middle shift, his supper hour was about 8:00 p.m. Mother and I would go to

---

48 www.autocartruck.com/history/ "1940s, V for Victory"

Horn and Hardart's and buy a chicken pot pie for him. Sometimes we would get one for each of us. We would go home and heat up a pie in the oven, and drive to the Autocar. Daddy would come out and eat it in the car. Mother and I ate ours at home. I remember them being very delicious.

Throughout the war, Daddy earned extra money by fixing people's refrigerators in the evenings or on Saturdays. He went to some large estate homes on the Main Line, and must have done a good job. He got plenty of business by word of mouth.

From time to time Mother and I would visit a real estate office, usually the Roach Brothers. I would be excited at the thought of them buying a house. Mother would be shown photos of some suitable places. She would dither and be skeptical. Finally, the constraints overwhelmed the desire and we would leave.

There was always a worry. What would happen after the war? Daddy might lose his job. Buying a house would lock us down in one place. Why be locked down with the whole world out there? Who knows what could happen? Mother was fearful by nature. She was never quite sure she was standing on firm ground.

Everyone was being told to put up black curtains and close them at night so bombers couldn't see where to drop bombs. People worried that the Autocar truck factory, on the street behind Ardmore Avenue, could be a bombing target. "Autocar supplied over 37,000 armored half-trucks, all-wheel-drive prime movers, and standard production models, including the Model U, for the overseas war effort."[49]

Victory Garden

I was abashed!

The county commandeered vacant lots to be used for Victory Gardens to grow produce. The vacant lot where Daddy and I had picked black-eyed Susans was now given over to Daddy to grow veg-

---

etables. Daddy loved it. He dug up the ground, tilled the soil, planted seeds, and added fertilizer. I went with him to "help." He planted tomatoes, beans, corn, lettuce, watermelon, and cantaloupe.

I shared Daddy's sense of wonder as the first tiny leaves peeked out of the rough soil, and the plants grew up. Soon there was a tiny green striped ball that would grow into a large watermelon. I went with Daddy every night after his work. We watered the garden if it hadn't rained, or pulled weeds. Daddy staked up the tomato plants as they grew taller. Each day brought a new wonder.

In August, the tomatoes were drooping from their vines. Cucumbers hid on the ground under their leaves. Corn grew while no one was watching, and swayed majestically tall. The watermelon, striped with dark green bands, grew larger. I loved watermelon and couldn't wait until it was ripe. The warm sun shone its blessings on Mother Earth. The rain would come sometimes just in time to revive the wilting plants.

We picked the large, ripe tomatoes and ate some for dinner. They were delicious. Mother canned some in Mason jars for the winter. We walked to the garden in the evenings after supper. We pulled out weeds and Daddy loosened the ground after a rain. The luscious watermelon was full grown. "Let's pick it, Daddy!" I said.

"We have enough to carry home right now," Daddy said. "We'll pick it tomorrow."

The next evening we walked to the garden, ready to bring the watermelon home. I looked around. It was *gone*. I was *abashed*—astonished, confused, confounded and disconcerted!

Daddy's "dander was up." It had never occurred to us that someone would steal it! But Daddy tried to put a good face on the situation. "We have another one coming up," he said. The second one grew, but not as big as the first. And we picked it sooner. I learned that there are bad people in the world who would steal watermelons.

Mother was not a gardener. She would can vegetables, but wasn't interested in growing them. She would make flowers from chenille or crepe paper, or paint them on china, but she never grew any. Once I had asked her to buy me a 10¢ pack of flower seeds, which I planted by the backyard fence. I stuck my finger in the ground for each seed, and covered it with dirt. But Mother didn't tell me to water them. I waited and watched all summer, and they never came up.

But the farmer in Daddy was still there. He was matter-of-fact about it, but I could see the enthusiasm for growing things that he did not express in words.

It's good to eat a little bit of dirt

Since so many men had gone to be soldiers, the factories had a shortage of workers. Women were enlisted to work in factories for the first time. Norman Rockwell created a poster of a smiling girl wearing a bandanna around her head called *Rosie the Riveter*.

We heard that people were suspicious of German-Americans during the war, but our German friends were good people and loyal Americans. Adolph Bimmler, the naturopath we went to, and his wife Frieda were German-Americans, as were the Greens, down the street from us. The Greens had two sons, Horace and Herman. I think they were both in the Army. One was overseas, and one was married to a nurse named Polly. They also had a boarder who was a radio operator.

Mary and I used to go visit Mrs. Green. Neither of us had a dog, and we loved playing with her little black cocker spaniel, SuSu. She always gave us a couple of her homemade cookies. If a cookie dropped on the floor, she would pick it up and eat it. She said it was good to "eat a little bit of dirt."

At Christmastime, she got out her Christmas carousel from Germany. It was large, with about five tiers of carved animals and crèche figures. There were candles on the bottom tier, and wooden reflectors set at an angle on the top one. She would light the candles, and the whole thing would twirl around. Neighbors would come over to see it.

Mrs. Green was born in the late 19th century, and grew up in the Frankford section of North Philadelphia. She kept in touch with her old girlfriends from school, and they got together once a year to keep in touch. She was a great fan of Franklin D. Roosevelt. She told us how desperate she and her husband had been during the Depression, and how F.D.R. saved them and the country by giving people relief and jobs.

"He's wonderful," she said. "He saved us. We would have lost our home and everything if not for President Roosevelt. We love him."

Roosevelt continued his *Fireside Chats* through the war. He had a New York accent, and didn't pronounce the "r" at the end of a word. He always spoke in a calming tone, and it was comforting to hear that he was taking care of us and everything would turn out all right.

Some people had maps on their walls to follow the progress of our soldiers in Europe. They used pins with different colored heads to show where the Allies were in relation to the Axis.

SONGS SUNG DURING THE WAR:

Let me call you Sweetheart, I'm in love with you
Let me hear you whisper that you love me, too
Keep the love light glowing in your eyes so blue
Let me call you Sweetheart, I'm in love with you
                    By Leo Friedman and Beth Slater Whitson
                              sung by Bing Crosby, 1934

Mairzy doats and dozy doats
and liddle lamzy divey
A kiddley divey too,
wouldn't you?
                    By Milton Drake, Al Hoffman, and
                              Jerry Livingston, 1943

I'll be seeing you in all the old familiar places
That this heart of mine embraces, all day through
In that small cafe, the park across the way,
The children's carousel, the chestnut trees,
the wishing well,
I'll be seeing you in every lovely summer's day
In everything that's light and gay
I'll always think of you that way

I'll find you in the morning sun, and when the night is
new
I'll be looking at the moon, but I'll be seeing you ...
Music by Sammy Fain, lyrics by Irving Kahal
Sung by Bing Crosby, 1944

Don't sit under the apple tree with anyone else but me
Anyone else but me
Anyone else but me
No, no, no, no
Till I come marching home
Music by Sam H. Stept
Lyrics by Lew Brown and Charles Tobias
Sung by Glenn Miller, and the Andrews Sisters
(lyrics were adapted for wartime)

Things We Didn't Have

Post-it notes, TV, video games, DVDs, computers, internet, anything made of plastic, drip-dry clothes or electric dryers, cell phones, wrist watch phones (those were for Dick Tracey in comic books), detergent, ball point pens, CDs, or tapes.

At school we used pencils, but the old desks still had built-in inkwells. We were graded on our handwriting. We went to the library to research things. Toys were made of wood or metal. We could buy kits to cast our own toy soldiers from lead.

There were no supermarkets, and no exotic foods from faraway places. There were no plastic bags, trash bags, or plastic food containers. The township collected food garbage separately from other trash, and it was fed to pigs. We stored our leftover food in Mason jars.

There was no McDonald's—the only takeout was White Castle or Chinese. White Castle's founders invented fast food as we know it. When they opened in 1921, people were afraid of ground beef. Upton Sinclair had described America's meat-packing industry in stomach-churning detail in *The Jungle*, published in 1906. White Castle fought back with a super-clean image, including windows through which customers could watch the fresh meat being ground up.

Women, when they dressed up, didn't wear pants. Even around the house they wore skirts or house dresses. If you went out, you wore a hat, gloves, and stockings.

Men were more modest as well. Back in 1934, Clark Gable caused a sensation when he removed his shirt in the movie *It Happened One Night* with Claudette Colbert. People were shocked that he had nothing on under it! Men always wore cotton undershirts with thin straps over the shoulders. The "T" shirt came into vogue with World War II, when the military issued a more substantial, short-sleeved undershirt that became popular with everyone.

THE SEASHORE

The whole house smelled of vinegar

Mother and Bea on the beach

Daddy got a two-week vacation every summer, and most summers we went to the beach in New Jersey, usually Ocean City. Planning for the seashore was exciting. Then there was the long drive down the Black Horse Pike. I would sit there quietly until I saw evidence of the bay.

We had to cross the bridge to get to the shore. I would be watching the seagulls glide around, and sniffing for that first whiff of salt air wafting off the ocean, ready to fill my lungs with it. We cranked the windows all the way down, and the ocean air infused us with a sense of wellbeing. Few cars had air conditioning in those days. If we were stalled in traffic going over the bridge to the beach, we could hear music from the other cars. We didn't have a radio in ours. But we would sit in the car savoring the restorative breeze and the lilting music punctuated by the screech of seagulls telling us that we had arrived.

We would be there for two whole weeks! After growing up in landlocked Ohio, Daddy appreciated being on the edge of the country. We had to drive through Ocean City to get near the beach, and then drive around more, looking for signs advertising Rooms For Rent. The town was full of neat, white, freshly painted clapboard houses with well-kept lawns. Some were old Victorians with cupolas and wide porches or wrap-around porches. High-backed wooden rocking chairs sat on the porches, or maybe white wicker ones. Flags flew in the soft breeze.

We usually went to several places before we found the right one at the right price. Mother would be the one to go in and look. When we found one agreeable, we would carry in the suitcases. I, of course, wanted to go to the beach right away. We would walk to the beach from our room, usually two or three blocks. At our usual place, the large mast of a sunken ship was buried in the sand. Our feet plowed through resistant white sand and caught between my toes in my rubberized beach shoes. I carried my bucket and shovel, and Daddy carried our towels. We never got an umbrella, as Daddy wanted to lie in the sun and get a tan. Mother wore a hat.

After we spread our towels on the beach, I would run into the ocean to thrash in the water and dodge the waves. Daddy liked to wade in the water, and stand in the waves, holding my hand as we jumped over incoming swells. When I was small, he took my hand and led me in. After I had swimming lessons I could go in by myself.

When I tired of that, I'd concentrate on making an acceptable castle in the sand. I had to outsmart the ocean as it rose up and threatened to demolish my castle. But defying the thrust of nature was part of the thrill. Waves came sliding over the sand with white foam caps bubbling on top. The water in perpetual motion was mesmerizing.

Mother would play in the sand with me, and help me construct

Bea, a boy, and Jeanne Fyfe at the beach

Bea, Ocean City, 1939   Bea and Dwain, Seaside Heights, 1936

a castle with wet sand as the ocean continuously filled in our holes. Mother was fearful of the water, and never did more than walk along the sand at the edge of the lapping waves, getting her feet wet. She had never learned to swim. Daddy would lie on his towel on the sand, getting a tan.

The sand was fire-hot at noon when we walked back, hot and tired, to have lunch. Often there was a shower outside behind the house for washing off sand. Mother would cook something on a hot plate, or in a little kitchen, depending on what we had. Maybe once or twice during the whole trip we would go out to a restaurant. Mother would usually complain about the food being too greasy or too salty. Daddy ate anything that was put in front of him with gusto. I picked at strange foods that I wasn't used to and left it half uneaten. We all

115

liked Horn and Hardart's food best, but I don't think there was one at the shore.

Ocean City had a boardwalk where we could stroll after supper and look into the shops. Sometimes, a slather of fog would come over the ocean. Sometimes rain came in, fast and forceful. When the rain was over, there was a calm, wet tranquility. The air was cleansed and we could go back outside.

Once Aunt Bea rented a place on the bay from her good friends the Raymond Cranches. They were Beryl's parents, but I don't remember Beryl being there. I think Mother and Daddy and Aunt Bea shared the rent, or Aunt Bea rented it and invited us as her guests. I would stand on the dock and watch the waves lapping against the pilings, the neighbors' boat rocking in the water, and other boats going by. A man would take six or seven children out for a boat ride every morning from the dock next door. One morning, he asked me if I wanted to go with them. I really wanted to go, but I was too shy and said, "No, thank you." The boat hummed off without me.

On some of our trips, we got a room in a house and ate our meals with the owners. One of the more memorable ones was a house that smelled of vinegar. When we sat down to dinner with the elderly owners, the food tasted awful, as if everything had been cooked in vinegar. I didn't eat anything.

One year Daddy decided to try a different beach. We went to Sea Isle City, up the coast, a much smaller beach town with no boardwalk. We'd rented a very small, free-standing wooden cottage. It was dark inside, with one window and a strong, musty smell. We had to bring our own bedding and towels. It was cold and rainy that year. I don't remember the beach. I don't remember the ocean. All I remember about that vacation is that it was freezing cold. At night as I lay on my cot, the thin mattress crackled. It was stuffed with straw. As the cold wind pushed through the cracks in the boards, we hunted for blankets. There weren't many, so we pulled the two hooked rugs off the floor onto our beds for warmth. We still couldn't get to sleep. It was so cold and rainy! Other years, we tried some other beach towns. Seaside Heights was one.

One year we went to Ocean City and we invited Marguerite and Elaine down for a few days. They enjoyed soaking up the sun, but I don't think either of them ever learned to swim. I was a little older and my breasts were just beginning to form. By that time I was designing, or at least having some input into the clothes Mother made for me. She'd made me a two-piece bathing suit in blue and white checked cotton. The top had straps in the back and on the shoulders. I went into the water, was hit by a wave, and my top came almost all the way off.

I was so embarrassed. I thought everyone could see me. I quickly tied it back on. I had a lot of clothes that summer. Marguerite commented that I never wore the same outfit twice, and she was probably right.

The silvery sparkle of waves in the brilliant midday sun. The softness of the waves, forming and reforming, shaping themselves into larger waves, and crashing, with white foaming edges. The sensation of endless forming and reforming and the ineffable promise of infinity. The smell of salt water on our bodies. We were encapsulated in a wonderful experience that we all loved and were sorry when it was over.

TRIPS TO OHIO

A Day on the Farm

Oh, how one wishes sometimes to escape from the meaningless dullness of human eloquence, from all those sublime phrases, to take refuge in nature, apparently so inarticulate, or in the wordlessness of long grinding labor, of sound sleep, of true music, or of human understanding, rendered speechless by emotion!

—Boris Pasternak, Doctor Zhivago

117

Daddy's eyes brightened when he reminisced about life on the farm. He would smile and toss his head back when he talked about his childhood.

Every three or four years, we made the trip out to West Union, Ohio, on Daddy's summer vacation. During the war, we had to save our government issued stamps to make sure we could purchase enough gas. One year Daddy said we might have to buy some gas on the "black market." I was shocked. Daddy was always a law-abiding citizen. But it turned out we didn't have to do that.

The Pennsylvania Turnpike opened for service in 1940. The new highway stretched 160 miles from Carlisle to Irwin. There were seven original two-lane tunnels, but the road got so much more traffic than expected, plans were soon underway to widen or bypass the tunnels.[50] With the Turnpike came Howard Johnson's motor lodges and restaurants at the rest stops.

I remember our first trip on the Turnpike. We breezed along so much faster than before, through Pennsylvania and past the Monongahela River. For a short time, our road wound through the mountains of West Virginia before the Ohio landscape opened up and the road became flat and straight. As the miles rolled by, I was content to be going somewhere. Very few cars passed us on the other side of the road.

Driving in a triumvirate, usually two of us paired up and left the third one alone, instead of all riding together in the front. When Daddy drove, Mother always sat in the back. Daddy joked that he was the chauffeur and Mother the grand lady. When we travelled, I sat up front with Daddy. Sometimes when I was still small enough, I would stand, holding onto the dashboard in front of me. Nobody even considered seat belts in those days.

I thought that Daddy was the more rational of my parents, and that I was more rational, too. We had a silent agreement. One time we were driving along after stopping for lunch, and I noticed the hem of my dress caught in the door. In our 1938 Plymouth, the front-door hinges were in the front, and the back-door hinges were in the back. So the back doors opened the opposite way. We weren't going fast yet, so I opened the front door a little and pulled my dress in. We were going a little faster when Mother opened her back door, and the wind blew

50 www.paturnpike.com/yourTurnpike/ptc_history.aspx

it wide open.

"Don't open the door like that, Dorothy," said Daddy, a little frustrated as he pulled over to the side.

Mother looked hurt. "Well, Beatrice opened her door, and you didn't say anything," she said.

The roads had a mirage effect; when the hot sun hit the macadam, it looked like there were pools of water on the road ahead. We didn't have a radio to entertain us on the road. Although the built-in Motorola car radio was introduced in 1930, the majority of cars didn't have radios until the 60s. [51] We relieved the boredom by looking for Burma-Shave signs. They were few and far between. They were a series of small signs, each one bearing a small piece of the whole message:[52]

NO LADY LIKES / TO DANCE / OR DINE / ACCOMPA-NIED BY / A PORCUPINE / BURMA-SHAVE (1938)

THE QUEEN / OF HEARTS / NOW LOVES THE KNAVE / THE KING / RAN OUT OF / BURMA-SHAVE (1939)

PAST / SCHOOLHOUSES / TAKE IT SLOW / LET THE LITTLE / SHAVERS GROW / BURMA-SHAVE (1939)

A PEACH / LOOKS GOOD / WITH LOTS OF FUZZ / BUT MAN'S NO PEACH / AND NEVER WUZ / BURMA-SHAVE (1939)

IT'S BEST FOR / ONE WHO HITS / THE BOTTLE / TO LET ANOTHER / USE THE THROTTLE / BURMA-SHAVE (1940)

WHEN YOU DRIVE / IF CAUTION CEASES / YOU ARE APT / TO REST IN PIECES / BURMA-SHAVE (1940)

---

51 "When the Car Radio Was Introduced, People Freaked Out," Bill DeMain, January 3, 2012. *mentalfloss.com*/article/29631/when-car-radio-was-introduced-people-freaked-out

52 *The Verse by the Side of the Road: The Story of the Burma-Shave Signs and Jingles.* Frank Rowsome, Jr. Drawings by Carl Rose. The Stephen Greene Press, 1965. Penguin Books USA, 1990

WILD / DASHES / FROM THE BY-WAYS / CAUSE CRASHES / ON HIGHWAYS / BURMA-SHAVE (1941)

SHE KISSED / THE HAIRBRUSH / BY MISTAKE / SHE THOUGHT IT WAS / HER HUSBAND JAKE / BUR-MA-SHAVE (1941)

DON'T STICK / YOUR ELBOW / OUT SO FAR / IT MIGHT GO HOME / IN ANOTHER CAR / BURMA-SHAVE (1941)

SOLDIER / SAILOR / AND MARINE / NOW GET A SHAVE / THAT'S QUICK AND CLEAN / BURMA-SHAVE (1941)

LET'S MAKE HITLER / AND HIROHITO / LOOK AS SICK AS / OLD BONITO / BUY DEFENSE BONDS / BUR-MA-SHAVE (1942)

SHAVING BRUSHES / YOU'LL SOON SEE 'EM / ON THE SHELF / IN SOME / MUSEUM / BURMA-SHAVE (1943)

WITHIN THIS VALE / OF TOIL / AND SIN / YOUR HEAD GROWS BALD / BUT NOT YOUR CHIN / BURMA-SHAVE (1943)

Occasionally we saw MAIL POUCH TOBACCO painted in huge swaths of red on the side of an unpainted barn.

Ohio was hot and humid in summer. We would have at least two windows open. The wind roared and whipped our hair as we cruised along two-lane roads between fields of alfalfa and wheat. Occasionally there was a leafy tree, and we could stop and eat our picnic lunch in its shade. Occasionally we'd go through a small town. I saw a Pep Boys sign with the three Pep Boys on it. I started to tease, "Daddy, there are only *two* Pep Boys, Mannymoe and Jack."

"No," Daddy corrected me, "It's three: Manny, Moe, and Jack."

"No, Mannymoe and Jack!" I said.

"No," Daddy said, "It's Manny, Moe, and Jack."

I said again with more emphasis, "It's *Mannymoe* and Jack!"

I sensed that Daddy was becoming irritated, but I knew I could outlast him. I goaded him for a while. Finally Daddy fell into silence, and then it was no fun. So I became silent also.

Mother said I was *willful.* (Governed by will without yielding to reason; obstinate; perverse; stubborn)

After the Pep Boys episode, Daddy was quiet. I looked out the car window again at the fields of wheat bordering the dusty highway. Black and white cows grazed in fields. Some were brown and white. The still, calm landscape settled my mind into horizontal vistas. Predictable yellow fields of corn stretched to the horizon. A white clapboard farmhouse appeared every now and then, set back on a long driveway, giving scale to the landscape.

We stayed mainly on macadam roads, but occasionally took a dirt road. Sometimes we'd see a farmer with a horse and cart to remind us that someone really did take care of all this. We had the freedom to drive on an endless road with the scenery on either side just for us, the soft colors of nature's grains: alfalfa, wheat, and corn. They grew along one after another in clear procession, all reaching for the clear blue sky. The sun's warmth and glow made them grow.

The farmer hoeing his field has a special relationship with nature. A cloud drifting overhead could cast an aura of gloom, but might also bring much needed rain. The sun could scorch the earth and render it dry and infertile, but its friendly light was needed to make the plants grow. The Yin and Yang of Chinese philosophy. Clouds moved and reformed. But we moved at a faster clip, and could outrun them all. We were at peace with the world.

A hill ascended from the Ohio River, and a trickling stream meandered down beside the winding road. Near the farm, the dirt roads were dusty in a mostly hilly landscape. The Sharp farm nestled between two hills.

We always stayed with someone in Daddy's family. I remember Daddy kidding Mother about the old wooden privy in the backyard, saying it would make her feel right at home. Mother was not amused; that's what she'd escaped from. But by the time I was aware of those things, everyone in the family had indoor plumbing and electricity.

Coming through the countryside, we had passed some dilapidated, falling-down farmhouses. Some of these were being replaced with Sears Roebuck kit houses, and Daddy's old homestead was one of them. A brand-new kit house stood near the old collapsing farmhouse. Daddy's sister Anna Lou had just moved in there with her husband Earl and their children. The poverty and want of the 1930s was being replaced with the new and modern. Daddy was happy that things had improved in Ohio since his teens. He had not been able to go to high school, but his younger siblings had that opportunity.

I don't think Mother liked going to Ohio very much. Daddy's sisters were laid back and not very talkative, unlike the loquacious Ashleys. Words were few, well thought out and precise, crystallized into little droplets to be dispensed at the appropriate time. Mother had no commonality with Daddy's sisters, and was never at ease with them. They fried a lot of food in lard, and Mother's digestive system couldn't take it. She believed her stomach problems came from the bacon fat she ate as a child. She didn't like the bulky feather bed we slept on either.

Mother loved the bustle of city life, the security of unknown people following the same paths, the easy access to trains and trolleys for shopping, classes, and lectures. For her, the solitude of fields stretching out in all directions held a threatening emptiness. Birds that fly, cows that moo, and pigs that squeal were better in children's books. Mother wouldn't have been a good fit for Ohio, telling everyone they should drink vegetable juice and give up white sugar. They'd been eating their own way for many years—deep fat frying in lard, and cooking vegetables until they were limp and pale green.

But Daddy enjoyed his two weeks in Ohio. He was animated as he laughed and talked with his brothers. Daddy's older brother Henry married a woman who had a farm, and farmed for the rest of his life. Raymond worked for the railroad, and his wife, Essie, was a schoolteacher. Every summer they went to an Indian reservation with their church group. Essie taught the children and Raymond fixed equipment. Raymond and Essie had four children, and all their names began with the letter "E": Ethelyn, Everett, Edward, and Erma.

THE TAMME SISTERS

On one of our trips, when I was about seven or eight, Daddy decided to look up his two elderly aunts, two of the Catholic Tamme sisters who had shunned his mother Magdelena after she married his Methodist father. I guess he figured he might as well let bygones be bygones, since a lot of time had passed. But this was the only time he ever did that.

He called them on the phone, and they invited us to come for Sunday dinner. After several attempts, we finally found the house, isolated on a paved country road. The old white Victorian clapboard house had a wrap-around porch in front, and a round cupola on one corner.

The two sisters sat on the front porch. One was a widow, and the other had never married. I don't remember how they greeted my father, but I don't remember them embracing, or even shaking hands. They were as laconic as the Sharp family.

We each sat down in one of the white wicker rocking chairs with large arms. I sat on the edge with my legs dangling in front. At the other end of the porch, a dead chicken was hanging from the rafters by its feet. I looked with horror at its wide-open mouth. Its eyes stared at me in rebuke as if it was screaming as it was being murdered. I surely hoped we wouldn't be eating it for dinner.

We were strangers connected through the labyrinth of genealogy. The aunts spoke in their soft Southern Ohio accent. There were silences between sentences as everyone reconfigured their thoughts to remark on a long forgotten time, to forge a common bond with the past. This had to have been hard because there had been no interaction between their families since before Daddy was born.

I had noticed before, that sometimes when there was an awkward lull in a conversation with people we didn't know well, the adults would zero in on me, hoping for some light-hearted banter from the child. But much to my relief, the aunts didn't do that. They ignored me, and I was grateful. Eventually one of them asked if I wanted to go around and see the backyard. I went around to see. There was brownish grass, cut short, and some bushes and brambles beyond. Stretching around this on all sides was farmland. I went back to sit on the porch and listen to the adults grope for conversation.

One of the ladies got up, pulled the resentful chicken down from the rafter, and went into the house. After about two hours of waiting, it was time to go in for dinner. I was very hungry. The dining room was sunny, with a bay window. The furniture was serviceable, the sturdy dining table covered with a white tablecloth.

I had sensitive taste buds. I knew what I was used to at home. If I went somewhere and tasted something that was cooked in a different oil, or tasted different in any way, it wasn't appetizing to me. But after the long wait for dinner, I was ready to eat anything.

My worst fears were confirmed. The whole chicken, minus the head with its vacant eyes, was lying there on a platter. The chicken that I had perceived staring at me from the rafter got her revenge. Her meat was too tough to eat. I chewed and chewed to no avail. I couldn't swallow a bite. I knew I shouldn't, but when no one was looking, I spit out the invincible flesh into my large linen napkin.

The rest of the sinewy bits I carefully spit out onto my fork and buried under the mashed potatoes on my plate. But I was hungry and I did eat most of the mashed potatoes and all the watery, overcooked string beans.

It was finally time to leave. We never visited the aunts again. I think they died soon after that.

Aunt Ida

We always visited Daddy's eldest sister Ida, who had come to help Mother when I was born. Ida was 38 when she married Charles Washburn, a widower with two young children—John and Doris, who were eight and six at the time. They were older than me. She never had children of her own. They had a little house in West Union.

Aunt Ida was calm and placid, rocking back and forth in her rocking chair. She started each sentence with "I reckon," as she described the changes in their small town since our last visit. Daddy had a slight southern Ohio accent, but he didn't use their vernacular. He'd made an effort to change some of his word usage, such as not using "was" for "were." He never said "I reckon." He would laugh when something *struck his funny bone*. When he got angry, he'd *got his dander up*. He *had a hankerin* for things he wanted. He didn't take the Lord's name in vain. When he was exasperated, he would say, *for the love of Mike!* or *for Pete's sake!*

Aunt Ida didn't drive or have a car, so we took her around with us to visit relatives. On Saturday night, we stood in the downtown

Raymond and Essie Sharp
and their four children

Everett Sharp

Aunt Ida Sharp

Aunt Marie and Maxine

square while musicians played fiddles, harmonicas, and accordions—the "Ole Time Music" that Daddy loved.

Daddy's sister Marie lived in the medium-sized town of Blanchester, Ohio. She had two daughters, Maxine and Joanne. Her husband was a writer for the local newspaper. When Maxine was 18, she got an internship with a Republican Party delegate from Ohio. During the summer of 1948, she came to the convention in Philadelphia during which Thomas Dewey was nominated to run for the presidency. Philadelphia hosted conventions for three parties at once during a sweltering heat wave in June.[53] But Maxine did not come to visit us.

My cousins were mostly boys, and mostly older than me. They were usually out doing something when we visited, so I sat with the adults, observing and listening, which I liked best.

Back at home after one of our trips, I thought about how lonely life on the farm must have been, so isolated from other people.

"What did you talk about on the farm?" I asked Daddy.

"We didn't talk, we had to work," Daddy replied.

I pressed further. "What did you talk about at the supper table?"

Daddy drew his head back. He had a twinkle in his pale blue eyes and an impish grin on his face. "We talked about our work," he said.

One sensed that Daddy had a deep well of feeling, but had never learned the words to express it.

GOING TO THE MOVIES

My mind entered movie land and stayed there for several years.

After our fiasco with Shirley Temple, I don't think Mother ever took me to a movie again. But when I was old enough, I began going to the movies with Mary Gregoria. We may have been as young as six when we started. At about eight or nine, we were walking to the Suburban Movie Theater in Ardmore every Saturday. The Suburban had the movies we liked. In those days, the children's price for a movie ticket was 11¢ on Saturday. I became a great movie fan.

We saw a full Western movie first. Gene Autry and Roy Rogers were the "singing cowboys." Autry would sing as he rode his horse, and all the good guys followed along. Roy Rogers sang while riding his palomino, Trigger. The Westerns would come to a satisfactory

53 www.ushistory.org/gop/convention_1948.htm

conclusion. The heroes would defeat the bad guys and ride away as the sun set over distant mountains.

Next we would see a serial. That would be a 15-minute story, usually a mystery, that left us hanging so we'd have to come back the following Saturday to see what happened next. It often ended with the hero about to be pushed off a cliff, or a woman tied to a railroad track. We would see the train chugging closer and closer, and the episode would stop there. The woman was always rescued, but we had to come back the next week to see.

After the serial would be a cartoon or a short "Our Gang" episode. Then there would be the Pathé News of the day about the on-going war. We watched and listened intently as the announcer spoke of bombs dropping on Germany in his authoritative voice, and we saw soldiers going into battle. *The March of Time* was a newsreel series that had been a radio show through the thirties. Westbrook Van Voorhis, the "Voice of Doom," described the soldiers' progress in his stentorian voice.

After the news, we would see previews and coming attractions for the following Saturday. Then finally, the lion roared and the Feature began. I was excited to sit down in a movie seat and be transported into another world. New places opened up to my imagination in movies like *Home in Indiana*. I loved seeing the sophisticated lifestyles, the grand houses, and the pretty clothes.

For 11¢, we were kept entertained for a long afternoon.

Early on, Mary and I saw *The Girl of the Limberlost*. I remember the girl being sucked into quicksand, going down and down, screaming. It frightened me. I think she was rescued at the last minute. After that we saw *The Phantom of the Opera*. That movie scared me so much, I had nightmares for several nights afterwards. We saw Elizabeth Taylor in *National Velvet*. In that one, a small white Scotty dog was mistreated and later died. I cried and cried in bed for several nights.

Children internalize and become part of the stories more than adults, I believe. We didn't just watch the movies; we became part of the movies. We participated in them. Around the fifth and sixth grades, my mind entered movie land and stayed there for several years. The movie screen didn't reflect real life; it enlarged life. It bored an imprint into my psyche. It floated in my mind when the film was long over. It picked the top off real life, as if picking a perfect flower from a mass of ordinary ones.

Musicals were my favorites, or comedies in modern dress. I didn't like swashbuckling films in old-fashioned dress, but Mary and I usually went to see those anyway. I saw Betty Grable and Harry James in *Springtime in the Rockies*. I had a warm glow for a long while after that. *The Road Series* was fun. The movies were a combination of adventure, romance, and comedy, starring Bob Hope, Bing Crosby, and Dorothy Lamour. We saw *The Song of Bernadette* with Jennifer Jones, 1943; *Leave Her to Heaven* with Gene Tierney, 1945; and *The Best Years of Our Lives* with Frederick March, 1945.

We saw *The Thin Man* series with William Powell and Myrna Loy as Nick and Nora Charles, sophisticates who exchanged smart repartee. No one Mary and I knew spoke like that. The movies brought us words and ways of speaking that, as children of the working class, we had never heard before. We were absorbed into a world of beautiful homes and scenery. The pictures from the screen were much more enduring than the static pictures in our children's books. We were enchanted by the music, the dancing, the singing, and the light-hearted tone of the comedies. The figures on the screen were real. Folks walking around us seemed like fake imposters, stodgy in their assigned places, stick figures waiting to come alive.

During the war, I saw a movie that took place in war-torn Europe. A woman was escaping from somewhere with only the clothes on her back. The heel had come off one of her shoes, and she had to limp along for a long time. Finally she and her male escort came to an abandoned stately home. She went in with an air of delighted anticipation. She walked up the stairs into the master bedroom. She opened a closet door and saw dozens of pairs of shoes laid out on the racks. Ecstatic, she tried to put one on. It was too small. She was crestfallen. I could feel her disappointment in the accompanying music, which played a large part in conjuring up the proper emotions.

Good movies have an afterglow that leaves you joyful, sad, or moved long after the scenery, faces, and dialogue have drifted from memory. Movies were fun and exciting and showed me a world outside my own experience.

In *On the Town* (1949) Frank Sinatra, Gene Kelly, and another sailor danced around on the deck of a ship. They stepped up and down from different platforms, singing, as three beautiful girls smiled at them, ready to go out on the town. The movie was based on the Broadway musical produced in 1944, and it made war look like a good time. That was what the people needed to see when there was so much carnage overseas. I especially liked tap dancing, with two people together to reinforce the enjoyment.

In the movie theaters, ushers carried flashlights and led customers to their seats in the darkness. There was a candy counter, but Mother forbade candy and I wasn't given money to buy any. I got a job as an usher when I was a teenager. I thought it would be great to see all the movies for free. I lasted only two days. It was boring to stand there and watch the same movie over and over again.

LEARNING TO SEW

One of my greatest pleasures was going downtown to Philadelphia with Mother to Strawbridge's fabric section. We would take the elevator up to the 4th floor. We would say hello to Artol Soderberg, Emmy Lou's uncle, who was a floor manager, if we saw him. We entered a colorful world of fabrics—bright floral cottons, chambray, Swiss dimity, dotted Swiss, heavier wools for winter coats, and shiny satins for dressing up, which we never needed. Rayon was coming into vogue, but we didn't like it. It was inauthentic.

We would go to the pattern section and look through pattern books. We bought only Simplicity or Butterick patterns. Vogue was too expensive, but I liked to look through the book to see the latest fashions.

I perused ads in the *Inquirer* and the Sears Catalogue to find things I liked. We never ordered clothes from the catalogue, but we compared the prices to the cost of our fabrics and patterns. We didn't buy clothes that we could make ourselves. Daddy often helped as well. Usually some time around July or August, Daddy and Mother would get busy cutting out and sewing up a new winter coat for me, and sometimes one for Mother, as well as other clothes for us.

Mother taught me to sew and how to use a sewing machine early in my life. I would pin the pattern onto the fabric, and sometimes cut it out myself. Mother would sew the pieces together, but later on I could do that, too. She showed me how to put in a zipper and make buttonholes. She taught me terms like gathering, pleats, inverted pleats, dirndl skirt, on the bias, interfacing, hemstitch, binding, and pinking shears. I learned the names of fabrics like tulle, muslin, satin moiré, and taffeta silk.

❦

THIRD AND FOURTH GRADES

The BLACK SPOTS were surrounding me again.

In September of 1943, I turned eight and went into third grade. Elaine, who lived across the hall, started first grade. I was invited to her birthday party in October, along with Mary and a few other children. Elaine was turning six.

Mother and I went to the 5&10 to get a few small gifts for her birthday. We got four things: a card with two decorative barrettes, and two other cosmetic things which I thought she would like. We thought we needed one more thing, so as an afterthought, as we were walking around, I saw a "school companion," which was a cardboard box containing pencils, an eraser, a small ruler, and other classroom necessities.

On the day of the party, Mary didn't have a gift to give. I thought Elaine would like the pretty things best, so I gave Mary the "school companion" to give her. We went to my apartment to wrap them up, and then across the hall to Elaine's for the party.

Elaine opened gifts and thanked people. When she opened Mary's gift, her face lit up with excitement. "A school companion! Just what I wanted for first grade!" she said. She showed the school companion to everybody. Later she told Mary it was the best gift she got.

I always loved going back to school. I loved the smell of the oaktag paper and the ritual of measuring, folding, and making pockets for the covers of my hand-me-down books.

I was an eager student in the early grades and caught on to things quickly. When the teacher asked a question, I tried to be the first one to put up my hand, and I shook it back and forth to show the teacher how smart I was. The teacher began to look annoyed. She ignored me and picked other students. I had a flash of insight. It wasn't nice to try to get ahead of everyone else. After that I kept quiet and waited my turn.

We would each read a passage from the Bible. As I was insecure, I usually read a passage well worn by others. We would say the prayer in unison. We would stand to pledge allegiance to the flag. I don't remember if we sang.

Every once in a while we would go individually into Miss Schwartzlandre's room. She would check our health and make sure we had good posture.

Everyone had to save their tin cans for the war effort. We third graders would go around with a little red wagon and pick them up from driveways. I went with a third-grade friend to gather cans. On a nice day, the tin sparkled in the sunlight and we took turns pulling the wagon. We had to remove all the paper and smash the can down flat. My friend's mother took us to the assigned place for pick-ups. Days later we would go back to pick up newspapers, which were heavier.

Across the street at the Dougherty house there was a celebration when their older son decided to become a priest. This was a wonderful happening in an Irish Catholic family. We went over there to congratulate him. Most of the Catholics had large families and it was a special joy to all when one would renounce the world and become a priest or a nun, devoting their life to God. On the way home, I thought there was something sad about dedicating your life to God and never having a family or children.

The Dougherty family had several children older than me, but occasionally I went over there to play their piano. That is, I banged away, pretending I knew how to play. I had the vague feeling that my playing wasn't altogether pleasant or enjoyable for them to listen to. I wanted to take lessons, and I begged Daddy to get us a piano.

He said, "No. There's no room in the apartment for a piano, and it would annoy the neighbors."

I was sullen.

When I got to fourth grade, however, we were encouraged to learn an instrument. We could take lessons from the school instructor, Mr. Natecki, and join the school orchestra. Though Daddy had refused to get me a piano, he encouraged me to learn the violin. He thought of the "Ole Time Music" in West Union Square. I knew that what I would learn wouldn't be exactly "Ole Time" fiddle music. I remember learning "The Blue Danube Waltz" and "Humoresque."

I took violin lessons and played in the school orchestra when I was ready. Mother drove me to Mr. Natecki's house to continue my lessons in the summer.

I got an allowance every week, and Mother also paid me to practice my violin. That agreement didn't bode well for me as a violin player, but later I developed an appreciation for music. Mrs. Shutte, our classroom music teacher, also instilled in us a love of music. I remember her reading to us a story about Brahms, and how he grew up to be a composer. We then put our heads on our desks and closed our eyes as she played Brahms Lullaby on the Victrola. I don't remember anything about Brahms' life, but Brahms' Lullaby takes me back to that classroom.

Daddy brought home a wooden ice cream maker. I was excited. He put a block of dry ice into the device. A cold cloud rose up from the ice cream maker. He put cream and milk into the upper part, and maybe brown sugar or raw sugar. Then he turned the crank. You had to turn it until the mixture froze into ice cream. Daddy turned and turned the crank. He let me have a turn turning, but I didn't last very long. All I wanted to do was eat it! We may have made ice cream one more time. But the ice cream maker ended up on a top shelf, and was eventually discarded. It was so easy to walk down to the corner and buy ice cream.

One day I was trying to learn to roller skate on one foot. I was skating down the sidewalk from the end of our block to the area in front of the store, edging around on one foot and trying to keep my balance, when the rollers of that skate encountered an uneven meeting of concrete squares.

I went down hard on the concrete, and my right arm hurt a lot. As I tried to get up, I noticed my arm looked crooked. I went inside, crying, to show Mother, and she pronounced it broken. We walked quickly to the trolley, then took a bus, and walked further to the doctor's office. He worked the bone into place, telling us about a new technique for setting broken bones. Then he put a cast on it, which I wore for about four weeks.

I didn't try roller skating again for a long time.

BLACK SPOTS

I don't know why I did it. A boy a couple of years older than me said something I didn't want to hear. As he was walking away, I picked up a small rock and threw it at the back of his head. That evening he came around to our apartment with his parents to tell my parents. None of the four adults could understand why a mild-mannered child like me would be so aggressive.

I said I was sorry. I didn't know why I did it. The looming BLACK SPOTS descended quickly, landing on my shoulders. I was ashamed and held my head down. After they left, Daddy had a flash of anger in his eyes and tightened his lips into a fine line. He raised his voice as far as it would go (which wasn't very far) and reprimanded me. He seemed almost bewildered that I would do something so wrong.

A new family moved into the last house on our block. They were from Italy and didn't speak English. They had a daughter named Gemma. I had never heard that name before. She sat on the porch and rocked in a rocking chair. Mary said her mother wanted her to be friends with Gemma. We approached Gemma a couple of times, but since we couldn't communicate (especially me) we didn't want to play with her. I think eventually she was integrated into the Italian groups.

One day in the heat of summer, I was sitting in a chair and put my feet on the windowsill of the open window. I sat that way for a while. The next day Milton Markley teased me. "I saw your feet out the window yesterday," he said.

I was taken aback. Putting your bare feet out the window was vulgar.

"I didn't put my feet out the window," I lied.

"Yes, you did," he said, "I saw them out the window."

"No," I said, tangling myself up in the lie.

Of course, my feet were smaller than anyone else's so it had to be me. Milton had caught me in a lie. I was ashamed, so I ran up the stairs to my apartment with BLACK SPOTS sticking to my clothes again.

From the time I was a baby, I'd looked up at the cracks in my ceiling as I was falling asleep, my imagination turning the lines into rabbits, landscapes, and barking dogs. As the years passed, my imagination had more and more to play with as the cracks became longer and more numerous, and the water spots spread wider. Then pieces of the cracking plaster began dropping onto my bed when it rained, and water dripped onto my blanket. Mother asked the landlord to fix it. Then she became alarmed that it was a health risk, and called the Board of Health. It wasn't a fit place to live in and unhealthy for her child, she said.

A workman came, and the ceiling was repaired so smoothly that my imagination had nothing to work with. No more animals or castles appeared in it. It was just a smooth white expanse.

DADDY'S INVENTIONS

Ah, but a man's reach must exceed his grasp,
or what's a heaven for?

—Robert Browning

Daddy always admired bright, well educated people, and would have liked to be one himself. Daddy lived in his own world. He had a sense of wonder about the world, and an eagerness to learn about it. He loved reading about new mechanical inventions, and seeing the latest technology like the newly designed cars that came off the assembly line every year.

He took me to the Franklin Institute downtown, and tried to share his enthusiasm for machines with me. It didn't work. I was bored and would have rather been in Strawbridge's fabric department. I always liked riding on the huge steam engine in the back of the museum, though. When I was little, I called it the "choo-choo train." I don't believe we ever went to the Art Museum, which was nearby. That would have been alien territory for all of us. My parents said they "wouldn't understand it."

Daddy tried to show me how a car worked. He opened the hood of the car and explained each thing enthusiastically. I think he would have liked to have had a son. Since I wasn't interested, I still don't know how a car works.

Daddy would tell the old story of an engineer who was called to fix something on a ship. The engineer looked around and found the problem. He took a hammer and pounded the pipe a few times. The problem was fixed. He sent a bill to the Commander for $500. The Commander, surprised at the price, sent a letter back asking for an itemized account of the job. The engineer replied, *$1.00 for hitting the pipe with a hammer. $499.00 for knowing where to hit.*

Daddy had the spark and determination to keep going. He avidly read *Popular Mechanics* to keep up to date. He got excited when he encountered a new invention he had learned about. Near the end of the war he read about an invention the government had in mind for downing planes. He was triumphant. He had thought of it long before and sent the idea to the government. Probably many inventors had the same ideas at the same time.

I never paid much attention to Daddy's inventions, but the one I remember was a "Sterile Air Machine." He worked on that for a long time. He gave it to a friend, Mr. Furry, to test. Mr. Furry put fruit into it and it lasted four or five months without going bad. He was amazed. Today, sterile air is important in the processing of many food products.

Daddy wanted to apply for patents. Several times we went out to Bryn Athyn to see Mr. Raymond Synnestvedt, who was a patent lawyer. Mother and I would sit in the car until Mrs. Synnestvedt invited us in.

I would type letters to the patent office in Washington. We had an old black L.C. Smith typewriter with gold lettering. It stood up high and you had only finger power to work the keys. I used the "hunt and peck" system, and looked forward to the day when I could learn to type properly. I remember debating whether to sign letters with "yours truly" or "sincerely yours." I had fun doing it. The three of us were working together.

Inventors, like little flowers that perk up in the grass, shouldn't be stepped on. The country needs people with new ideas to move forward. They form a pyramid on which others can stand.

He who has imagination without learning
has wings but no feet.

—Joseph Joubert[54]

My cousin Everett was able to get the kind of education Daddy would have loved to have, and do things Daddy would have loved to do. Everett studied engineering at Purdue University and worked for the General Motors Automobile Company

---

54 See: quoteinvestigator.com/2018/08/19/imagination/

in Detroit, inventing devices to make better cars. Later he formed his own company, creating inventions and leasing them to other companies. He sold and leased his inventions all over the world, and traveled to Japan and South America to visit car companies.

Everett and his wife, Rosemary, lived in a large Victorian house in a suburb of Detroit. Sometimes people who were interested in his inventions came to see him in Detroit, and Everett would take them to the opera. He said that after growing up on a farm near a small town, it was hard for him to learn the customs and protocols of the countries he went to, particularly Japan.

I never saw Everett and Rosemary's home in Detroit. I saw them only at Sharp reunions in Ohio. But Rosemary told me that every square inch of the house and garage was cluttered with books and parts of Everett's inventions.

Everett and Daddy became good friends in later life.

⟨swirl⟩

MOTHER AND DADDY

Mother and Daddy got along well. Mother was loquacious when she wasn't shy, and Daddy was quiet. He depended on her to talk when they were together in a social situation. She depended on him for solidity and fixing things that were broken. He would measure and cut fabrics for a coat, for instance, which had to be precise. And of course he kept the cars in good repair. At the supper table, they laughed at people's foibles and the goings on in the neighborhood. They discussed their own situation, which required serious thought.

Neither were much interested in current culture or style. Mother still wore her stockings as she had in the twenties. Daddy finally abandoned his high laced-up shoes for the low-cut ones. High shoes weren't needed now that there was central heating. He quit wearing his workman's cap, too.

They kidded each other a lot. Daddy would tease Mother about her cooking. "That's not the way we do it in Ohio," he would say.

They didn't argue so much as bicker. When they bickered I

usually sided with Daddy. He usually seemed to have the more reasonable position, and Mother would often succumb and say, "Well, I don't know."

Mother and Daddy were both dreamers. They'd both had a spotty formal education and both were eager to learn new things. Mother was more neurotic. She was happy and affable at times, anxious and nervous at others, often driven by her fears. Daddy had a quiet common sense. He was described as "bashful."

It's often the case that we don't value what we grew up with. Both of my parents had big families. Daddy's was taciturn and happy, Mother's was contentious—but they were families. Several times during my childhood, I asked Mother if I could have a sister. All my friends had sisters—why couldn't I have one? Mother demurred. "You'll have to ask your father," she would say.

I think she would have liked to have another child, but she and Daddy had grown up in big families that never had enough money. They wanted to give me all the opportunities they never had, instead of the uncertainty and struggle they had endured. So I remained an only child. I had no brothers or sisters, but I felt secure.

Besides, I think Mother, on occasion, considered me a *handful* (as much as one can control or manage).

Fifth Grade

Around fifth grade, I began to reflect and see the humor in our lives. I think I had Daddy's sense of humor, which saw the ironies in everyday situations. I drew a picture of our tiny bedroom with our very small closet so full that the door wouldn't close. It was close quarters in there with things piled into every available space. Stuff was piled up on Mother's old black trunk in front of the window. Things were squashed so tight in the bureau drawers that they could barely close. Daddy's bureau was neater than Mother's. He had a radio on his side of the bed near the window. He had rigged up a table on the window with space for a clock. There was a narrow path around the beds. Daddy had found a second-hand youth bed to replace the one he'd fashioned from my old crib. But I could just about fit into it now. I laughed at the situation the way someone would laugh at an incongruity that must be attended to.

THE PLANTER PEANUT

My parents enjoyed making Halloween costumes for me, and we were a good team. In fifth grade, I was looking at the Planter Peanut on the front of our peanut butter jar, and decided to be the Planter Peanut for the Halloween party at school.

Daddy constructed a costume of paper-mâché on a thin, wire base. Mother found some wrinkled, peanut-colored fabric, which Daddy glued to the base. I wore long black stockings, a monocle, a black top hat made of cardboard, and a black walking stick. I won a prize for that costume.

NANCY DREW

Mother and I went to Leary's second hand book store in Philadelphia to buy interesting or out-of-print books. She read *Anthony Adverse* by Hervey Allen, and I read it later. I used *Book of Knowledge: The Children's Encyclopedia* to look things up for school work.

When Mother and I went to the downtown Strawbridge's store, I was allowed to go to the book department and pick out one book. In fifth grade, I was reading all the Nancy Drew books I could. I perused the selections and carefully chose one that looked interesting that I didn't already have. Mother paid the $1.50 for it and I started reading it as soon as we got home. I liked Nancy Drew. She was 16, and drove her own roadster with the top down. One time she drove 50 miles all the way to the shore. I was impressed with her independence and derring-do. She would solve mysteries. I remember her father was a lawyer. I don't think she had a mother.

Overcoming is an important motivation. It is a strong force. It propels most literature, especially children's literature. To fantasize that one is a princess. To aspire to win the race with the hare. The struggle is more interesting than the achievement.

We can't say that in front of the children

At the supper table, Daddy would talk about his coworkers. I remember him telling us about their illnesses. One man's wife had a terrible disease that made her skin like leather. Some of them stopped at the tap room on the way home from work. Daddy didn't approve, and never went with them. He thought his father had gone a little too heavy on the liquor at times, and he didn't drink much himself.

Occasionally we would visit the McIntyres on a Sunday afternoon. There were two brothers and two sisters in the house, always coming and going. There were boxes of Corn Flakes and Wheaties and coffee cups on the dining room table. I think they were partying the night before and Daddy's friend was just waking up. He was lying on the couch listening to the ball game on the radio (The Athletics at Shibe Park). His brother was sitting in a chair reading *The Philadelphia Inquirer*. "They're a bunch of rummys," Mother would say later.

Edna, the McIntyre who was Mother's friend, came to our apartment once, later on. I can still remember how agitated she was. Her sister Anne and her husband had separated, and they were both alcoholics. He couldn't hold a job. He would go on a bender for several days, and come back remorseful. He would take his two boys, about seven and ten, out to the drugstore for milkshakes. She was at her wit's end and didn't know what to do about it. She talked to Mother for a long time, telling some unfortunate stories. I remember Mother saying that the sugar in milkshakes could make the kids into alcoholics. I never found out what happened to them.

I was exposed to this kind of adult conversation throughout my childhood. Mother used to tell me about her hospital cases and her friends' problems. When I was older, people would say, "We can't say that in front of the children," or "We mustn't let the children know about that." Sometimes I wondered what ruinous travesty was done to my psyche by hearing so much about ongoing life.

CHINTZ AND TEARS

One day I heard Mother talking on the phone to a nurse friend from the hospital, who was now retired. For a few months, I'd been hearing conversations about this friend's daughter-in-law wanting her to sell her house to her son. Mother's friend had planned to leave the house to her son when she died, but it seemed that his wife wore the pants in the family, and was pushing for her to sell it to him now. Mother's friend did not consent to this for a long time.

But this day, she was very upset on the phone. She had finally consented to sell the house to her son, with the proviso that she would continue living there. But some time after this, they asked her to leave. She was now renting a furnished room from another friend.

Mother and I went to see her. She had a second-floor bedroom in the colonial stone house. We went upstairs and found her sitting in an armchair as plump as she was. The chair cover, curtains, and bedspread were all chintz with pink roses. She was in tears, and she looked unhealthy. Her legs were swollen—she may have been diabetic. I sat on her bed and Mother sat in a straight chair while they talked.

She wiped her eyes with a handkerchief as she told us the whole story all over again. I envisioned little bubbles of sorrow filling the air. She was in an alien place now, where she didn't fit. Her whole life had been turned upside down.

"I can't believe she did this to me," she kept repeating. "I can't believe she could do this."

We couldn't believe it either. I was shocked that people could be so mean.

Ice skates

That winter, some of my friends from school were going ice skating at a local pond. I wanted to learn to ice skate too. Out came the want ads section as we looked for skates. Of course, I wanted the white figure skates like the other girls. Daddy clipped out the section for skates.

One Saturday we made the rounds. Since I wasn't full grown, the pickings were limited. There were nice white figure skates at the first house we went to, but they were too expensive. Since Daddy and Mother had never skated, I'm not sure they knew the difference between hockey skates and figure skates. At the next place we went, the skates for sale were black hockey skates that were way too big for me, but the price was right.

The next day after school I carried my skates up to the pond. I had several pairs of wool socks Mother had given me to wear with the skates. I had never ice-skated before. I took off my shoes and put on the socks and the skates and wobbled out onto the ice. I slipped and fell immediately. The skate blades stuck way out in front and I had a hard time maneuvering. After about half an hour of trying, my feet were cold so I took off my skates and walked home.

The skates were big enough that I could use them for a couple of years. I found out that you shouldn't stuff your skates with too many socks because it makes your feet feel colder.

John Dewey Ruins Painting Class

Mother signed me up for a painting class at Bryn Mawr Art Center, a large Victorian home on Montgomery Avenue that had been converted into an art center to teach painting. I ascended the creaky stairs to the children's art room. The teacher put a record on the phonograph, and music filled the room. We were expected to paint a picture inspired by the music.

But I was confused. I didn't know where to begin. I made an attempt at painting sky and grass, and then I sat there, and sat there—not knowing what to do. I couldn't coax the muse out of her slumber. I felt uneasy. I wanted to be told what to do. I wanted to be given a specific problem and some direction. I didn't feel I had the necessary imagination to paint a picture with just the inspiration of music. Many children would love the spontaneity of it, but I didn't.

That was the only painting class I ever refused to go to. I hope Mother got her money back.

The art center was probably inspired by the educational philosophy of John Dewey, who had come into vogue in the 1930s. When Mother and Daddy went to school, they learned their lessons by rote, repeating things until they remembered them, and following directions. But telling children how to do things was the old-fashioned way. John Dewey thought that every child had a creative spirit that could be crushed by the boring repetition of facts, and that children learned in the act of doing things.

He was also an atheist who believed that the moral aphorisms in my parents' schoolbooks were obsolete. Philosophical pragmatism rejected moral absolutes and embraced uncertainty, provisionality, and the continuous testing of hypotheses through experimentation. Pragmatism held that "the function of thought is to guide action, and ... truth is preeminently to be tested by the practical consequences of belief."[55] Or as John Kaag put it, "Pragmatism holds that truth is to be judged on the basis of its practical consequences and its ability to enrich human experience."[56]

---

[55] Merriam-webster.com, Pragmatism

[56] John Kaag, "The Philosopher and the Thief," *Browsings, The Harper's Blog,* March 6, 2014. See: John Kaag, *American Philosophy: A Love Story*, Farrar, Straus and Giroux, 2017

JANET VOLLMER AND BLACK BEAUTY

Tears are a distillation of all melancholy vapors
rising from the human heart.

—E.B. White, 1931[57]

Bea on a pony, 9 or 10 years old

Janet Vollmer was always the smartest girl in my class. I sat behind her in fifth grade. She would always get 100. As hard as I would try, I usually got 90 or 95. Janet liked horses, so I thought I should like horses too. In fact, I probably would have been too scared to ride a horse. I got on a pony once to have my picture taken, but that pony didn't go anywhere.

I borrowed *Black Beauty* from the library. When I got to the place where the owner mistreats the horse by piling too much weight on his back, I got upset and started to cry. I dreamed about it when I went to sleep and never finished the book.

Janet invited me to her house once. I remember it as a stately colonial home. Inside in the foyer there was a circular staircase with a wide window looking out onto the front drive. Janet had a beautifully

---

57 Unconfirmed

decorated bedroom with her own en suite bathroom. She had two younger brothers. When it was time for me to leave, Mrs. Vollmer came out to say goodbye. I'd like to think that I shook hands with her and said, "Thank you for the nice time," but I probably didn't. I wasn't trained to do that. I was used to friends drifting in and out of each other's houses.

JEANNE FYFE

Jeanne Fyfe was a friend who lived up on Grandview Road. She was chubby, with straight blonde hair, and a little older than me. Jeanne lived in a small house with her parents and her newly married sister and her husband. He was 4F (medically or physically unfit for military service), but had some kind of job helping the defense. Housing was scarce during the war, and families had to double up.

Jeanne came to our apartment in the evenings, and Daddy taught us how to play pinochle. Once Mother and I went to the shore overnight with Jeanne and her mother, to Asbury Park. The four of us also took a boat across the river and went to Woodside Amusement Park in New Jersey.

MOTHER'S AMBITIONS

Dreams are fragile,
often come unbidden,
alight for a while,
and then disappear into thin air.
White puff balls
bouncing around in the ocean until they sink.

—Beatrice Pitcairn

After getting chiropractic treatments for a while, Mother decided she wanted to be a chiropractor herself. She heard about lectures given by a chiropractor in Philadelphia called Dr. Thompson.

She began going downtown to attend those lectures once a week. I saw Dr. Thompson once or twice. He must have been charismatic. His students raved about him and were thrilled with his teaching. He was a Catholic, and married with five children.

Eleanor was a pretty student about 30 years old with dark blonde hair that she wore in a pageboy style. She lived in a small apartment on the first floor of a Revolution-era brick row house on a narrow cobblestone street in Philadelphia. Mother often went there to study with her, and she was a pleasant lady. She often left with Dr. Thompson after class.

One day Mother got a phone call from one of the other students. Eleanor had hanged herself in her bedroom. Mother was very upset. She and I went downtown to meet the other student and the three of us went to Eleanor's apartment. We went into the gloomy living room, where her brown stuffed armchair sat in its prominent place as it always had. We peeked into the bedroom, where she had hanged herself. The three of us stood around, silently absorbing the fact that Eleanor was not there and never would be again.

Mother got busy at the sewing machine making dresses to wear to New York City where she was going with a friend to a chiropractic convention. They stayed several days at the New Yorker Hotel. She came home buoyant, telling me about the things she had learned.

She was planning to sign up for a course in chiropractic and get a license. She investigated schools. There were two in the Midwest—one in Davenport, Iowa, and one in Lincoln, Nebraska. But she needed a high school diploma to enroll. She took correspondence courses, and I remember her studying in the evenings, and lying in bed, reading the required books. She had to go somewhere downtown to take a test, which she passed.

She gave chiropractic treatments in our apartment on a black Naugahyde table that folded up when not in use. Mary Corr, who used to live across the hall from us, was one of Mother's patients. Mother told me later that Mary was embarrassed because she didn't have any underpants on when she came for her treatment. Mary had five or six children by that time, and underpants were expensive.

Mother wanted a house where she could run a chiropractic business. So we three dreamers went on a Sunday afternoon drive, looking at houses for sale. A twin house would be good. The living room could be the office, and the dining room a treatment area. There would have to be a garage in the back for Daddy's workshop, and I would have a room of my own! We found some twin homes that should have been in our price range, but Daddy, like a wild bird, was still afraid to commit to anything permanent.

Mother sent away for information and was excited about going to the school in Nebraska. But she hesitated. I kept waiting, expecting her to go. She soon stopped talking about it and never mentioned it again.

❧

At the local magazine store, I perused the section that had books on house plans. I looked through them carefully. I bought one and spent a lot of time looking at it and imagining myself living in each one. I also spent a lot of time drawing my own plans for houses. It was a lot of fun.

❧

ASPIRATIONS

Mrs. Boericke played the piano for our church services at the Presser Building. She was a very proper, elderly lady. When I'd taken violin lessons for a year or so, she asked me to play for the Christmas Service. I sawed away at "O Little Town of Bethlehem" as best as I could.

We girls took turns putting on a white robe to light the candles. One day in the cold of winter, Emmy Lou slogged across the stage wearing large brown galoshes that showed below her white robe. She was also chewing gum. Mrs. Boericke got after her on both accounts.

But the Advent Church eventually had to leave the Presser Building. For a while, the society rented a building in West Philadelphia. Morley Rich was our pastor then. He and his wife, Stella, moved into a row house on Gratz Street. Then a large semi-detached house was purchased in Frankford, North Philadelphia. The parishioners did the work of converting the first floor of the house into a church, and the second floor was the manse.

In those days many parents had aspirations for their daughters to be movie stars like Shirley Temple or singers like the Moylan sisters. The Moylan sisters were just a little older than me and sang in harmony on the radio. I went to the 5&10 and had some pictures taken in a studio in the back. Daddy sent a couple of them to Hollywood. Maybe I would be the next Shirley Temple—a Shirley Temple with straight hair. We never heard from anybody. So I guess I, along with hundreds of thousands of other children, wasn't movie star material.

Emmy Lou's mother was more aggressive than my parents. She had taken Emmy Lou, under duress, for piano lessons. That had lasted only six weeks. The teacher gave up on her because she played the music by ear. Then she'd had voice lessons for two years. Now her mother was anxious for her to participate in a children's talent show directed by Stan Lee Broza on WCAU, a Philadelphia radio station. Children sang or played instruments on this Saturday morning program. Emmy Lou was coerced into trying out for the show. She had a nice singing voice, and Mrs. Soderberg was thrilled when she was accepted. Emmy Lou was not thrilled. Her mother bought her a pretty pink dress. Her blonde hair was curled and a pink bow fastened onto her curls.

They went to the studio at WCAU. When it was Emmy Lou's turn, she walked up to the microphone—and froze. She stood at the microphone, unable to utter a sound. Finally she was ushered out and the next child took her turn.

When I was eleven, Mother began leaving me alone in the house at night. She alerted our neighbor Marguerite. She went to her classes, and Daddy worked in the garage below. I lay on my bed looking at the catty-cornered closet that was stuffed too full to close, thinking something was moving inside it. I was a little scared.

THE END OF THE WAR

Uncle Robert Sharp

Time, like an ever rolling stream,
Bears all its sons away;
They fly, forgotten, as a dream
Dies at the opening day.

            —Isaac Watts, based on Psalm 90

Daddy got the word from his sister Marcella of their brother Robert's death on one of the islands in the Pacific. Robert had been a gunner in the Army.

Daddy opened the window, lit a cigarette, and stared out the window. He put his arms on the sill and smoked the cigarette. He stayed there a long time. Mother and I didn't say a word, but tiptoed around quietly. At supper Daddy told us about Robert.

"He was a good sharpshooter," Daddy said. "That was his job in the army as a gunner. He used to shoot rabbits when he was a kid."

Robert died on April 19, 1945, and was buried in the National Memorial Cemetery of the Pacific in Honolulu. The government gave $10,000 to each family that lost someone in battle. Marcella received this money, and Daddy thought she should keep all of it. Rob-

149

ert, their youngest sibling, had lived with her for years after their parents died. But she sent each of her brothers and sisters about $1,000. The Sharps were kind and sharing people.

Roosevelt's health declined during the war years. Though he was reelected in 1944, he died in April of the next year. He did not live to see the Axis powers surrender to the Allies. In June of 1945, as I was finishing fifth grade, we heard on the radio that the war in Europe was over. We went out into the street and celebrated with our neighbors.

Roosevelt's successor, Harry S. Truman, presided over the victory in Europe and the dropping of atom bombs on Japan. In August, we heard that Japan had surrendered also.

My own private world felt uneventful and narrow, and I wanted to know what was happening in the wider world. My parents subscribed to *Reader's Digest*, and occasionally they bought the *Sunday Inquirer*. I read about the Nazi atrocities during the war, and I was horrified to learn that they had gassed people and used their skin to make lampshades. I also saw the horrible photos of Leon Trotsky lying dead in a pool of blood after he was assassinated in Mexico.

Man's inhumanity to man was shocking, and we felt lucky to be unharmed. The heavy burdens of war were now lifted from people's shoulders. We loved our country and wanted to bask in its security.

CHAPTER SIX:
POSTWAR

EXUBERANCE AND EXTRAVAGANCE

Chrysler 300 tail fins
Photo by Stephen Roadcap

INVESTMENTS

After paying the full amount of $18 over several years and pasting stamps into my savings bond booklet, I finally paid it all and cashed it in for $25.00. I was thrilled that I redeemed it for $25.00. My enthusiasm was deflated when I heard Barnard Baruch, a top financial person, say on the radio that savings bonds were a bad investment. I thought I was doing a good and patriotic thing for my country.

Daddy had invested a small amount of money in the stock market. He also had some G.E. stock. I remember him deliberating about whether he should sell the stock or buy more. He remembered the recession of 1921 after the First World War, and he feared another postwar depression. I don't know what he did, but in the long run he sure should have invested in more of it. But Daddy always took a cautious approach.

Workmen now had a five-day week, and Daddy worked on his inventions in the garage in the evenings or Saturdays. He had the use of the two-car garage in our building because no one else there had a car. He read technical books, *Popular Mechanics*, and *U.S. News and World Report*. He read self-improvement books such as Dale Carnegie's *How to Win Friends and Influence People*. He would have liked to become an "outgoing persuasive" as Dale Carnegie prescribed, but it wasn't in his temperament.

※

G.I. Bill and Beetles

Service men and women had come home, and many were going to schools and colleges on the G.I. Bill, with the government paying their tuition. Many of these people were the first in their families to go to college. Also the government was afraid there wouldn't be enough jobs for everyone. It was a great program for everyone involved.

Some returning servicemen brought back Volkswagen Beetles they had bought in occupied Germany.[58] I remember them saying they bought the Beetle for $1800, which was very cheap for a new car. Beetle drivers were a private club, and waved at each other as they passed on the road.

The stigma of the little car's Nazi origin fell away in the United States. The Beetle became enormously popular, and a symbol of peace and love.[59]

---

58 en.wikipedia.org/wiki/Volkswagen_Beetle#Wartime_production

59 Priscilla Page, "The history of the Volkswagen Beetle as it turns 80 years old," July 04, 2018, www.hagerty.com/articles-videos/articles/2018/07/04/the-history-of-the-volkswagen-beetle-as-it-turns-80-years-old

SIXTH GRADE

The future looks bright

Walking up Grandview Road in the Fall to school for my last year there, the colorful leaves crunched under my feet. Weeds and wildflowers grew on the corner lot at Spring Avenue and Sutton Road, where our Victory Garden had been. There was a rumor that a famous architect was going to build a modern house on that corner lot.

The pent-up desires of the war years were now let loose with exuberance. General Motors and other car companies switched over from war machinery to cars. The plants revved up to turn out new, colorful, happy cars for the populace. The new Studebaker was a configuration to be marveled at. People would stop to look when one drove by. The cars had tail fins, aping airplanes and suggesting that they had the speed of an airplane taking off. This trend would reach its zenith with the 1959 Cadillacs, which had "the tallest fins ever appended to a vehicle that didn't fly."[60]

People were happy and optimistic. New houses were being built. Our inalienable right to the pursuit of happiness was a possibility to be fulfilled. Like the new cars, the new houses had a new configuration. They were "split levels." The basement was on the ground floor, the living area half way up on the other side, and the bedrooms half way up again, on top of the basement.

The corner lot was mowed and dug up for construction. We kids, and sometimes adults, walked down to the corner to see a very strange house going up. It was a cube, and there would be one house in each section of the cube. A four-plex: four houses attached together. It was said to be designed by Frank Lloyd Wright. We had never heard of him, of course.

The new, modern style was flat roofs with no decorative features—a sparse, plain style influenced by the Japanese. As the house was going up, we watched and tried to figure out where things would

---

60 Paul Ingrassia, *Wall Street Journal*, Sat-Sun April 21-22, 2012

go. We saw plate glass sections going from floor to ceiling. Mary and I saw an inside balcony covering half of the room below. The kitchen would be tucked into the alcove under the balcony, and the bedrooms and bath would be above it on the balcony. The living room would have the whole two-story view out the window. We had never seen anything like it before.

Modern art was also strange to us. In magazines like *Life* and *Look* we saw paintings with splashes of color that looked like a small child's painting. We didn't know what to make of it, and a lot of people scoffed at it. One magazine had a competition between paintings done by a monkey and those of a modern painter. Who knew which was which?

Mother, Daddy, and I would plan outings to the Sears and Roebuck store all together on a Saturday. Daddy drove to the store on 69th Street, and went right downstairs to the tool section. Mother browsed around upstairs and often got socks for me. She always needed white stockings for her nurse's uniform. Other times we went to the Notion Department for needles and threads.

Mother and I would take the subway downtown to Strawbridge's. After the war, fabric was more available, and fashions changed accordingly. Short skirts and skimpy dresses with shoulder pads were out. French designers brought in long full skirts using copious material. The skirts were a full circle of material with a hole in the center for the waist. Stiff petticoats underneath widened the circle. Winter coats were almost ankle length. The designers were Christian Dior, Balmain, Schiaparelli, Lanvin, and Balenciaga in Europe. In America, Anne Fogarty is the name I remember.

We ascended the elevator to the fourth-floor fabric section and encountered a dazzle of colors and designs. I was elated, and Mother delighted in it as much as I did. We looked carefully through the fabrics, rejecting some and noting possibilities. Some were too expensive and we settled on second best. Then we looked through the pattern books. We took our time. I liked to think it through, picturing how a pattern would look made up in the fabric we chose. The "Gibson Girl" style was briefly revived after the war, and Mother told me that women wore *leg o' mutton* sleeves when she was a girl in England.

Mother and I had fun. At lunch time, we usually stopped at Martindale's Restaurant and Health Food Store for a raw beet and carrot salad, cottage cheese, or vegetable soup.

The perfect house

On the corner across from the new modern four-plex, a modest one-story house went up. It had two bedrooms and a bathroom, and was selling for $12,000. I pleaded with Daddy to buy the house. Surely by now he could afford it. We walked down to look at it. It would be perfect for us. I begged Daddy to buy it.

"Daddy, can't we please buy that house. Pleeeease!"

I kept after him. But he was worried that Autocar would not be making so many trucks now that the war was over. He joked about waiting until his "ship came in." And he was always worried about being "nailed down to a place." Other dreams and possibilities would stagnate and shrivel up. Perhaps Daddy's "hankering" to move back to Ohio kept him from committing to a house. But he knew that Mother would never want to live there, and I don't think he would have wanted to be a farmer again. He romanticized farm life, but he never forgot the hard work.

Miss Liberty

Aunt Nora took me to see the musical *Miss Liberty*. The ladies wore long dresses with hoop skirts as they did in the mid 19th century a la *Gone with the Wind*. I decided to be Miss Liberty for the school Halloween parade in sixth grade. Mother and I went downtown to Strawbridge's. I chose some red, white, and blue fabric. Daddy made the hoop. Mother sewed the dress. My patriotic outfit fit the postwar mood, and I won first prize.

❧

Aunt Nora

Alcoholics live on the wrong side of a crashing wave.
—Beatrice Pitcairn

Aunt Nora was taller than Mother, and wore more up-to-date clothes. I imagined that she went with a smart, sophisticated crowd that drank cocktails and smoked cigarettes. I wanted to be like her when I grew up. When she came to visit us, I used to count the number of cigarette butts in the ashtray after she left. Mother didn't approve of smoking.

Nora had a sunny room in the red brick nurses' building on the hospital campus, furnished with light blonde wood furniture in the current style. Her sewing machine occupied a prominent place. Like all the Ashley women, she sewed her own clothes. I remember a burnt orange wool suit she tailored with a long jacket and matching skirt. She wore fashionable shoes with open toes and cut-outs on the side, and a medium heel. She always looked handsome.

She traveled to interesting places. One time at our apartment, when I was about eight, she was telling us all about a Windjammer trip she had taken in Maine during her summer vacation. She was describing it all in vivid detail, telling us what she did every day. I was enjoying the story, but Mother got impatient. She got up and moved around as if she didn't want to hear any more.

"I'm not finished yet," Aunt Nora said, looking a little bothered.

I thought Mother's impatience was rude. She was probably just too busy to sit and listen. I wanted to hear the rest, and Daddy and I kept on listening.

But my sophisticated Aunt Nora had problems I knew nothing about. One day when I was about twelve, we were all driving home from Bryn Athyn. Aunt Nora was riding in the back with me. She asked me about school. I told her I didn't like History (though in later years I loved history). Aunt Nora began telling me about the sentries in England who guarded the coastline from enemy invasion during a war. They would ask, "Who goes there, friend or foe?"

"We were afraid of invaders," Aunt Nora said. "Who goes there? Friend or foe?"

She'd had too many drinks and she kept repeating herself. She kept telling me that I should study history. "We children played the game," she said in her slight English accent. "'Who goes there, friend or foe?' We children would say."

She told me that when she was a child, an oarsman would row her across the river to see her grandmother in Rowhedge. The oarsman would say "Who goes there?" in jest. Or maybe the man at the station on the other side said it quite seriously. I'm not sure. She may have had it muddled.

I thought her tipsiness was quite funny at the time. But late one summer night, we got a phone call. Aunt Nora had been arrested for drunk driving at the seashore in Stone Harbor. She was calling from Cape May Courthouse, and she needed us to come and pick her up.

We drove down the next day with Aunt Elsie and Dwain. I was excited because something was happening! But the adults were grim-faced and didn't say much. Dwain amused everyone by naming every single car he saw coming or going on either side of the road. He knew the make and model of each car.

We arrived at the courthouse, and the adults went inside, leaving Dwain and me in the car. It seemed a long time before they all came out. Aunt Elsie got in the front with my parents on the bench seat. Aunt Nora got into the back, between me and Dwain. No one said a word on the two-hour trip home.

Alcoholics live on the wrong side of a crashing wave. For some people, life is a continual battle with themselves as well as the rest of the world. Aunt Nora came to grips with her alcoholism when she was threatened with the loss of her job. She went to the Alcoholics Anonymous group in Upper Darby. She was one of the prime movers in setting up a special women's program there.

Years later, after Aunt Nora died, I helped Mother go through her things. We found a package of love letters tied up with a frayed blue ribbon. I, of course, was eager to open and read them. The letters were from her longtime boyfriend. They were very romantic and descriptive of their love-making. The last letter told her that he had met the girl he wanted to marry. I thought I detected a tear stain on the last page.

Love can be cruel.

I was excited when Aunt Nora invited me to go with her to the Shubert Theater to see *Showboat*. I could afford to go to a movie, but not to a play. Aunt Nora went to movies, concerts, and plays in the theater. Aunt Elsie went to the opera, and Aunt Bea went to Philadelphia Orchestra concerts with the Pitcairns. My parents, who said they "wouldn't understand" the Art Museum, took me to places like Valley Forge Park, the Zoo, the Museum of Natural History, and the Franklin Institute. They were happy to have me go to plays with Aunt Nora.

In those days, new plays would try out in Philadelphia to see how the audience responded. Then they would adjust things before opening in New York. One time when we went into the lobby for intermission, I saw Oscar Hammerstein walking back and forth, smoking a cigarette. He had a craggy face and a solemn look. Hammerstein wrote the lyrics for *Showboat*; Jerome Kern wrote the music. Many of Kern's songs are still familiar today.

I loved being transported to another world. And it wasn't just a screen—real people were singing to us. I loved living in a dream. In a dream, you can make things turn out the way you want them to. It's more comforting than living in reality.

After the play, we went to the restaurant in the Bellevue-Stratford, an upscale hotel a few blocks away. The restaurant was part of the hotel, but accessible from the street. We walked down some stairs to the restaurant in the basement. Aunt Nora ordered coffee for herself and ginger ale for me. She did not drink alcohol anymore. Then she ordered some clams on the half shell, and asked if I'd like to try some. I'd never seen them before. She said they were sweet tasting and you could chew them a little and they would go smoothly down your throat. They were a delicacy. Mother would never eat anything so exotic. But Mother would never have gone to the theater either. I said, yes, I would try them. When they came to the table, I looked at them suspiciously.

"Have they been cooked?"

"Oh, no, they're raw. They're still alive," said Aunt Nora.

"Oh dear," I said.

But I tried one. They tasted like the ocean, and reminded me of the seashore I loved so much. I've liked seafood ever since.

It was a thrilling day, and we had many more like it over the years. Once we went to a revue, which wasn't a whole play with a story, but a series of brief episodes that were usually funny. Aunt Nora expanded my world.

GLAMOR

The movie stars in the magazines looked
down from the lofty heights of sophistication.

The Mastbaum Theater was the most glamorous movie theater in the city of Philadelphia. The huge, opulent lobby had patterned rugs and glittering crystal chandeliers hanging from an ornately carved and painted ceiling. It was ready for a party like the ones in the movies. Women wore long evening dresses and smoked cigarettes. Handsome men looked suave and knowing in their black-tie dress suits. When I was about 12, I would go downtown on the subway to watch a movie and smoke a cigarette in the ladies' lounge.

Glamor was a word that had a lot of meaning to me. Movies transported me to another world where everyone was beautiful, poised, and well spoken. The movie stars saw the world through clinking wine glasses and cigarette smoke. Robert Taylor, for instance, might take a puff of a cigarette with a look of disgust followed by a pensive gaze into the distance. Then he might turn, look down, smash it into the ashtray, and run out of the room with determination.

Depths of feeling were expressed with all the small actions involved in drinking and smoking. Humphrey Bogart would sit at a bar looking thoughtfully down into his drink. We felt the tension in his soul each time he took a tortured drag from his cigarette.

Barbara Stanwyck might stare through a window at the far distant trees with a look of longing. A close-up camera shot would show her taking a long, thoughtful drag from her cigarette with a look of resignation. Then she would take another drag, firming up her lips and straightening her shoulders. She would walk away from the window with a new look of confidence, her eyes sparkling with a new idea.

Movie stars used cigarettes as props, I guess, often not knowing what to do with their hands. Holding a cigarette was the answer.

By the time I was eleven, I had become fascinated with "noir" movies as well as the musicals and comedies. I wanted to see films with psychological depth, showing the darker side of life. I liked *Mildred Pierce* (1945) with Joan Crawford, and *Double Indemnity* (1944) and *Sorry, Wrong Number* (1948) with Barbara Stanwyck, dark movies with psychological aspects. Barbara Stanwyck was one of my favorite actresses. She played in serious stories, and usually had a profound role with important things to say and do.

Movies filled me with unrealistic expectations, and fantasies filled the searching void in my mind. I lived in two worlds, and felt the sensibilities of both worlds. I tried to connect them. The differences between myself and my parents became wider and wider, and I felt estranged from them. Our attachment became uncomfortable, like a fraying string stretched to breaking. They seemed to stay in place while I moved in another direction, away from the core.

MOTHER AT THE MOVIES

I wanted to bring my parents out of their own "ruts" into the modern world of movies and current ideas. I thought they were old fashioned "Fuddy Duds." My own scope was broadening beyond my narrow world of friends and school. I read movie magazines, and

Daddy's *US News and World Report*. I wanted my parents to get out and experience current culture.

So I suggested that the three of us see a movie together. *The Lost Weekend*, starring Ray Milland, was the award-winning current hit movie in 1946, and depicted alcoholism.[61] For me, alcoholics had a certain mystique. I thought they had an impenetrable sorrow that even they themselves couldn't understand. They were falling like *Alice in Wonderland*—falling, falling, into a hole with slimy muddy sides they could not hold on to. I wanted to penetrate that inner sorrow.

I was anxious to see this movie, and I thought Mother would like it because of her professional experience with alcoholics. I'd always gone to the movies with Mary. But this time, I led the way down the aisle, chose a row, and chose seats in the center. I went in first, followed by Mother and then Daddy.

The feature progressed, and Milland's character began having problems. I watched eagerly, but Mother was becoming visibly uneasy. When the character went into delirium tremens, we saw through his eyes as a rat emerged from a hole in the wall and squirmed around. Mother started up from her seat to leave the theater.

"It's only a movie," I said. I remembered her saying that to me when I was four years old, and frightened by Shirley Temple's huge face.

Mother was upset and wanted to leave, but I wanted to see how it all turned out. So we stayed. Mother kept her head down, twisted her fingers, covered her ears and closed her eyes. I couldn't understand why she was so distressed, but I felt bad. I was sorry I hadn't suggested a musical comedy. It never occurred to me that Mother would be so upset by a movie.

My little mother was diminished in my eyes. I was as tall as her by this time, so physically we were eye to eye. But our viewpoints were not eye to eye. I don't think she ever went to a movie again. (My mother's full growth was 5 feet and half an inch. I would grow three inches taller.)

---

61 Made in 1945, *The Lost Weekend* got seven nominations and won in four categories at the 1946 Academy Awards in May

Sometimes I wondered what I would think of my parents if I were their contemporary instead of their progeny. I asked Aunt Elsie how she and my mother's friends perceived her. Elsie thought for a minute. I could tell she didn't want to hurt my feelings, and she thought it was a strange question.

"I would describe her as somewhat eccentric," she said.

I liked having eccentric parents, but I didn't know if I wanted to introduce them to my friends. I was shy. I always wanted to fit in and do what was expected. But I always admired outrageous people who strutted forward, revealing their inner compulsions.

GLORIA BASTIANI
The food was strange to me

Bea and Gloria

My friendship with Gloria Bastiani began in fourth or fifth

grade. She went to my school, but was always in the other section. She lived at the other end of our block in an all-brick, two story, semi-detached house with a front porch and an attic. Sometimes when Mother went downtown to a class, Gloria's older sister Hilda came and sat with me. I would tell Hilda great stories, some from movies I'd seen and others spun out of my own imagination. She listened with interest. I began going to movies with Gloria, and we became good friends in Junior High.

Gloria's parents were from Italy, and spoke English with an accent. I don't know how much education they had, but Gloria's mother had wisdom and everyday common sense. She made astute observations that would pinpoint a problem and find the answer. Gloria was the third of four daughters.

Mrs. Bastiani was short and plump with dark hair, a pleasant demeanor, and a practical outlook on life. She spoke broken English with an Italian accent, and I could converse with her. The Bastianis were more middle-class than the Gregorias, and more assimilated to American culture. The children went to public school, and the parents spoke English. But like the Gregorias, they had a boarder and made wine in the basement. The Bastianis' boarder was an elderly man, Uncle somebody or other, who lived in the back room upstairs and spoke no English.

The Bastiani family sat at the table on most Sunday afternoons, with friends and family speaking Italian and English. They were jolly and happy, laughing and drinking the wine from the basement kegs. They had a pasta course and a meat course. They always invited me to partake, but I always refused. I just sat and watched. The food was strange to me. Now I think with some regret of all the delicious meals I could have eaten.

When Gloria and I would laugh uproariously, I would feel a migraine headache coming on. It felt like shards of broken glass at the side of my head and around my eyes. I would get sick to my stomach and have to go home.

Mary Gregoria got an after-school job through St. Colman's

church with Dr. and Mrs. Bonner, who lived on the same street as the church. They were Catholics with five small children. Sitting in front of their house was a new Pontiac in the postwar style with fins.

Mary helped with the children and did the ironing. She sometimes invited me to go with her and sit and talk to her while she was ironing. I admired her for being able to do ironing and other household chores at her young age. She now had a certain independence and earned her own money.

I don't remember Mother ever teaching me to do household chores or to clean anything. Her idea was to get the chores done as quickly as possible so she could get on with sewing, making crafts, or reading. But I remember learning something on my own when I was very young. I had a set of child-sized teacups, teapot, plates, and spoons. Mary and I had served "tea" to our "guests," in our apartment, using milk and cookies. Our guests may have been Mary Joyce and Dolly. Afterwards, I put all the things back into the box without washing them. When I got them out again some time later, they were encrusted with stale milk and cookie crumbs. I noticed that they were harder to clean than if I'd washed them immediately. But I usually didn't notice this kind of thing because Mother did everything for me.

I realized that my family had different values from the families of my Italian friends. They bought large houses for their families, and focused on learning to speak English and making their way in America. We lived in an apartment and spent money on education and educational toys and books. They didn't care about such things.

JAX CONTEST

Gloria and I played Monopoly at her house after school. We didn't want the game to end, so we created more money and shoved the board with the green houses and red hotels on it under the couch. We would continue playing the same game the next day.

When the weather was good, we played jax outside. We played a lot, and we both got very good at it, but I considered myself better than Gloria. I was sure I would win the sixth-grade competition at the end of the year. Jax was considered a sport along with marbles for the boys.

As the end of the school year came near, girls played against each other, and winners played against other winners. Gloria and I easily beat the other girls, and it came down to a final round between Gloria and me. The winner would be the champion jax player. I was sure I would win.

It was a sunny day, and we decided to sit outside on the stone landing of the school steps. We played the required number of games. We were up to the last round, and we were both nervous. We got to the end where we had to pick up all the jax—I flubbed it—and Gloria won!

I was *chagrined*! Humbled, wounded, vexed, mortified—that is just the way I felt.

I knew I should be a good sport and congratulate her, which I did. But inside I was indeed chagrined. My defeat deflated me. My parents' accolades and my own hubris had led me to believe I was a superior person. I needed to be brought down a peg or two.

GRADUATION DRESS

Among the cast-off clothes from Glencairn that Aunt Bea had given Mother was a beautiful white cotton dress with wide lace inserts. Mother pulled it apart and remade it into a beautiful sixth grade graduation dress. I was looking forward to wearing it to the ceremony.

When I woke up the day of graduation I had a terrible migraine headache and was sick to my stomach. I couldn't possibly go to the graduation. I was deeply disappointed not being able to go to the ceremony and wear my beautiful dress.

The next day I was better and I decided to wear the dress anyway. One of the boys in the class said, "Hey, Beatrice, didn't you know graduation was yesterday?"

I was humiliated.

❦

Nature was coming into its full-fledged glory, with long June nights and the welcome last day of school. Janet Vollmer's parents put on a graduation party for our class in their large, elegant home. One of the boys asked her if we could have a "kissing game." A boy would pick out a girl and go behind the curtain to kiss her. Mrs. Vollmer seemed reluctant, but she said we could.

I was surprised. I thought we were too young for that. Nobody asked me to go behind the curtain to be kissed. I was just as glad because I didn't know how to do it anyway.

❦

John L. Lewis

I had thought that when the war was over we wouldn't have any more news on the radio. The news was all about the war, so what would there be left to tell us? I found out.

The name was John L. Lewis. I saw him in the newsreels in the movie theaters, and heard him on the radio. He was a large, burly man with a "massive leonine head, forest-like eyebrows, firmly set jaw, powerful voice and ever-present scowl [that] thrilled his supporters, angered his enemies, and delighted cartoonists."[62]

I asked Daddy who he was. Daddy said he was the union leader and president of the United Mine Workers. The coal miners would be going on strike. I asked Daddy what a strike was. He told me that the management of a company was content to pay as low a wage as they could to the workers. The unions were formed so workers could go on strike, all of them refusing to work until they had a contract for a higher wage. Strikes had been forbidden during the war, but now that it was over, the unions would be demanding higher wages.

As Daddy explained it, the company and the union president would sit down and negotiate, each side giving in a little until the two sides could come to an agreement that would benefit all. He told me

---

62 John L. Lewis - Wikipedia. https://en.wikipedia.org/wiki/John_L._ Lewis

that Henry Ford paid a high enough wage to his employees that they could afford to buy one of his cars. That spread prosperity around so that everyone could have a good life.

COMMUNISM AND THE RED SCARE

In school we'd been given a "Weekly Reader" about events going on in the world. But one day near the end of the year, our homeroom teacher, Miss Hartman, stood to the left of her desk and cleared her throat. I remember it to this day because she had such an air of importance about what she was about to tell us, it seemed she had learned her speech by rote.

There was a grand new experiment going on in the Soviet Union, she told us. All the people are equal. Everyone is assigned a job for which they are suited, and the government gives everyone the money they need. There are no rich people or poor people. This will lead to a prosperous country with happy people, she said. She painted a glorious picture for us sixth graders. If this great experiment worked out, all the countries in the world would be having it. She obviously approved of this new system.

I think this caused a stir when the parents heard about it. Possibly Janet's father, who was a leader in the community, voiced an objection. The Cold War was on now, and people were afraid that communists were influencing American culture and education.

I remember a snow scene in a Gregory Peck movie. Peck was telling his female companion, in heartfelt words, "There is something to this wonderful new experiment to raise all mankind from poverty." He was speaking of communism in the Soviet Union, where the slogan was: *From each according to his ability, to each according to his need.*

I liked Al Jolson. I flipped around the radio dial to find him singing in his raspy voice. Even in a thunderstorm, I kept the radio on to hear him through the static. I bought movie magazines and read everything about him that I could. He came from Russia and had a career on Broadway singing in musicals and doing comedy in blackface. In *The Jazz Singer* in 1927, he sang "Mammy" on bended knee, in blackface. I had no sense that there was anything wrong with this. Jolson was credited for bringing African-American culture to the white mainstream and sticking up for black people in the entertainment industry at that time.[63]

When I went to see *The Jolson Story* starring Larry Parks, I was still of the age when I could become "part of the movie" rather than just watching it. I read about Larry Parks and his wife, Betty Garrett, in my movie magazines. When the newspaper said that Larry Parks was coming to Philadelphia, I was so excited I jumped up and down, clapping my hands.

"*Pleeease* let's go downtown to see Larry Parks at the Art Museum," I pled with Mother.

Mother was reluctant, but she didn't say why. Finally she agreed to take me. We got off the train at 30th Street Station and walked to the Art Museum, a long walk on a very hot summer day. The crowd was huge. We edged our way in as best we could, and waited a long time. Larry Parks finally came out and stood on the steps in front of a microphone. We were too far away to hear him very well. Every so often there was a burst of applause. We couldn't see him very well either. Though I was too big for her, Mother tried to hold me up for a few seconds to get a glimpse of him. I was thrilled.

He went on and on speaking. But since we couldn't see him or hear him, we left before it was over. But I had seen Larry Parks, and it had been worth it.

What Mother hadn't told me was that "The Red Scare" was in full force, and Larry Parks and his wife were "leftists." They were "fel-

---

63 "Al Jolson–Misunderstood Hero or Villian?" By Eddie Deezen, October 9, 2014 www.todayifoundout.com/index.php/2014/10/al-jolson-hero-villian/

low travelers" with the Communist Party. Communists were being ferreted out of the government and the entertainment industry. Senator Joseph McCarthy and the House of Representatives' *Un-American Activities Committee* were looking into the presence of Communist spies and fellow travelers in our government.

I didn't understand all this until a few years later when I read *Witness* by Whittaker Chambers, a former Communist who had been a *Time Magazine* journalist. He was a friend of Alger Hiss, the Soviet spy. Chambers broke with the party and suffered for it. He renounced Communism and wrote a book about its horrors. It was thought that famous people like Larry Parks and Betty Garrett were being enlisted to lure Americans into the Communist ranks.

BRYN MAWR COLLEGE

Word was spread around the Autocar Company that there would be a summer camp for 11- and 12-year-old children of the workers on the campus of Bryn Mawr College. Daddy signed me up to go. It was fun. We played sports and learned crafts. The boys and girls were separated, and we had mostly young girls. The counselors were college students.

One girl camper, named Betty White, was so enthusiastic, she told the counselors she would like to go to Bryn Mawr College when she was older. I thought to myself that none of us would ever get to Bryn Mawr College.

One day we had a man come and talk about birds. We all went into the auditorium, girls on one side boys on the other. The man talked about birds and showed us slides. But soon some boys started to hiss and misbehave. The rest of us were very embarrassed. The speaker tried to calm them down and talk over them, but I think finally he had to stop.

I learned that not everybody is willing to take advantage of a good opportunity when it's offered. The boys had to show their toughness, bravado, and rudeness. Some were allergic to learning, and immature students often had a *cheeky* way of describing the idiosyncrasies of their teachers.

❧

Gloria and I played "house" in her attic, where the red and green peppers from last summer's garden hung from the rafters. We hung curtains to separate our sides of the attic. Then we became "Mrs. Smith" and "Mrs. Jones" and talked to each other about our "daily concerns."

That summer, Gloria's oldest sister had a friend who had just gotten married and returned from her honeymoon. She described her honeymoon experience in great detail to our eager ears.

❧

CERAMICS CLASS

After summer camp, Mother and I took a ceramics class. We went downtown to Chestnut Street near the place where we went to church when I was little. We entered a storefront with a big window. Our teacher was a beautiful young woman who wore a white peasant blouse and a flowered dirndl skirt with sandals. She had long, straight hair. This style became popular and was a precursor to the hippy style.

We took the course for about six weeks, and learned to make slip-molds. We came home with a sugar bowl, cream pitcher, and ashtray. Mother made a bowl. We carved the design into the partially-baked pieces with a stiletto and fired them. I still have them.

Chapter Seven: Junior High

The future opens up like a stage performance when the curtain is pulled back.
The past hovers overhead like a dense cloud.
—Beatrice Pitcairn

Gloria at the beach

All those years I'd watched through the window as the older girls waited on the corner for the big orange school bus. Now I was thrilled to be getting on the bus myself. It felt good to be growing up, entering the new life of Junior High.

Each of us had a locker with a combination lock where we kept our lunches, coats, and books. We went to a different classroom for each teacher and subject. When the bell rang and I hurried from one class to another, I felt very grown up. We had two semesters. One was September to February, and the second from February to June. The halves of the class switched subjects in February.

Gloria and I were in different sections, but we sat together at lunchtime. Mother always gave me celery stalks filled with cream cheese. Gloria liked those, and I traded them for her Italian cookies. Mother made hard-boiled eggs, and so did another girl's mother. She liked the yolks, and I preferred the whites. So we traded, each of us for our own preference.

As I became more aware of the world around me, my parents depended on me to navigate the mores of contemporary American life. My parents considered me more savvy and knowledgeable about the modern world than they were, and depended on me to know things they didn't. I wandered around the halls with a vague sense that I should know more than I did. Other students seemed so self-assured.

Mr. Abrams was my history teacher, the first male teacher I'd ever had. He was young and handsome. He might have just come back from the war. He was easygoing and pleasant. During breaks between classes, he talked to Miss Castle, the beautiful young teacher in the classroom next door. She wore her dark hair in braids wrapped around her head, which was fashionable then, and she always dressed in style. I always had an eye on people's clothes.

I had flickering of a crush on Mr. Abrams. During his lectures, I focused on him intensely. When he walked by me in the hall, even if he didn't look at me, my nervous system went into high gear.

Sometimes we got off the subject of history, and students talked about their home life. Mr. Abrams listened sympathetically. Two friends talked about their mothers drinking too much. The mothers played bridge all afternoon while their cooks made dinner.

"My mother is always drunk when I come home from school. She doesn't pay any attention to me," one girl said.

"What does your father do when he comes home?" Mr. Abrams asked.

"He sits down and starts drinking with her," she said.

Another girl nodded. It was the same in her home.

My "other" self was still inside my head—the one that was a famous movie star, or the one that was smart and could say the right things to the people I wanted to impress. Or maybe the one that could think of witty things to say to Mr. Abrams or to Al Jolson. Or the one who could sing like Betty Grable while Harry James played the trumpet in a beautiful hotel in the Rockies.

After school, Gloria and I sometimes took the bus together. Other times we walked home, talking about Mr. Abrams, school, and life in general. When we got to my apartment we still had lots to say, and I would walk along Spring Avenue with her until we got to her house. Sometimes we had so much to say that she would walk me back again, or we would separate in the middle and each walk home.

GROUPTHINK

One morning when Gloria and I were standing on the very crowded school bus, a boy in the back told his neighbors, "Gail is a Pill, pass it on."

The kids passed it on. Then the boy in the back said, "Gail is a Pill, Gail is a Pill. Come on, everybody say it—Gail is a Pill."

One by one we joined in until we were all shouting in unison, "Gail is a Pill, Gail is a Pill."

It went on for a while.

I didn't know who Gail was or why she was a Pill. But I learned how a charismatic leader could get a crowd going and the power of "groupthink."

... a metaphor for life - blisters come before calluses,
vulnerability before maturity.
—Supreme Court Justice Clarence Thomas,
My Grandfather's Son

The Biology classroom had block tables and stools for us to sit on. I walked in and saw Anna Mae, the friend I had abandoned years ago at the library to go with Mary instead. I averted my eyes, and Anna Mae ignored me. She stayed true to her promise to never

173

speak to me again. That's when I realized that actions taken quickly can have long-term consequences. Some bruises remain. In seventh grade, there was definitely an *in group* and an *out group*. I believe Anna Mae was part of the *in group*.

In the first semester, we were taught how to sew. Of course I already knew. We used a treadle sewing machine that gave our feet plenty of exercise. I thought of my grandmother in England sewing all her family's clothes and uniforms for the Army on a machine like that. We made an apron; the teachers saw our future. Our cooking class would be next semester.

On Friday afternoons in the auditorium, the cheerleaders led us in appropriate cheers for our football team. They were perky and cute in their pleated plaid skirts, bobby socks, and penny loafers. They had the air of nonchalance that comes with being comfortable in your own skin. They were the very popular girls. They spoke knowledgeably about the plays in football which I knew nothing about.

We had a girlfriend who was tall and thin. We would say "skinny" now. She hunched herself over to come down to our height. In today's world, she would be a perfect model. Back then she was called "a tall drink of water."

I went into a prolonged, furious, impotent, adolescent sulk.

—Christopher Buckley[64]

It often happens in life that just as an equilibrium is attained, something unexpected comes along to weigh down one side of the scale, and the carefully crafted balance goes awry. As I turned 12, adolescence was the juggernaut that put more weight on one side of the scale. Life was no longer up front and flat. It was gradually becoming layered and secret. It was time for my attitude to transform

---

64 Christopher Buckley, *Losing Mum and Pup*. New York. Hachette Book Group, 2009. Kindle edition, page 81

from bemusement to seriousness. My childhood energy was gone. The lethargy of adolescence arrived softly but surely.

At this age, I realized my parents were different from other parents. I was still the shining light for them. Their hopes could be fulfilled by me. I resented that. In lots of ways I had entered another world, a magical world that was true in many ways. But it also wasn't true in other ways that they could never understand.

Daddy said it was time for me to call him "Dad," and I did so from then on.

Gloria and I laughed a lot. We laughed at the silliness of established order and the foibles of adults. You became "yourself" through dissent, not conformity. Peel off the onion rings of protection and reveal your inner self. On the other hand, I remember Jean Paul Sartre saying that we are defined by other people. Both are correct.

We had flashes of feeling the absurdity of it all; of the rules, the conventional forms we had to follow, or the arbitrary expectations. A flash of insight: Why one way and not another? Gloria and I giggled at things that were funny only to us. We were too old to "play house" now. We began listening to Frank Sinatra records and trying to dance to them. We practiced the jitterbug with each other in her living room. Gloria liked Frank Sinatra. I liked Bing Crosby.

In sixth grade, I would bring a baseball bat and ball to school. After school, I played baseball with a group of boys and girls. I remember once an older boy came around wanting to talk to one of the girls. She had breasts and the rest of us girls didn't yet. We waited around to play baseball while this boy distracted our friend. By seventh grade, boys had become alien creatures. They were no longer baseball friends, but serious "others." I didn't have the easy repartee of some other girls who were used to intermingling with boys or had brothers. When I couldn't cope psychologically, my head would feel encased in a balloon. I wouldn't look outside, but turn inward and empty my mind of everything possible and say as little as I could.

We had dancing classes on the second floor of a building on Lancaster Pike. Girls would sit on one side of the room, boys on the other. When the music started, the boys would walk over and ask us to dance.

I was asked. I put a hand on the boy's shoulder and he put a hand on my waist. We put our other two hands together and looked down at our feet. The dulcet tones of a saxophone radiated from the Victrola. We tried to shuffle our feet in time to the music, and form the square as we had been taught. I think this dance was called *The Fox Trot* although I don't remember trotting. A joker I knew later called it "The Businessman's Shuffle."

After the music was turned off, the boy would escort the girl back to her seat. Or I could walk back to the security of my girlfriends and wait for another boy to come up and ask one of us to dance again. I longed to do the jitterbug, but when the time came to try it with boys, I was too self-conscious to step out on the dance floor.

I believe one of those dance classes was the last time I saw Richard Leach. He was in the other section of my class, and I didn't know him. Word came around the neighborhood that Richard had been killed in an automobile accident. Several days later, Mary and Gloria asked if I wanted to go with them to see him laid out. I had seen neighbors or acquaintances laid out on several occasions, but never someone my age. We approached the casket reverently, and looked at the lifeless, waxy figure all spruced up in the casket. We said a little prayer to ourselves and walked away.

CHRISTMAS AMBIANCE
Opulent or lowly, everyone was celebrating!

As Christmas approached, I went to Strawbridge & Clothier to buy *Heaven's Scent* perfume for Gloria. I bought her perfume for her birthday or Christmas. She would give me *Evening in Paris* perfume. The department stores with glittering lights in bright colors welcomed me in to browse, and I walked along gazing into cases made of dark walnut and glass, full of luxurious items I would never be able to afford. It gave me a good feeling that they were there.

I loved the ambiance of the season. The smell of Christmas:

balsam and fir. The twinkle of lights under the cloudy, ominous sky outside. Snow. The feeling of warmth and coziness inside. Sweets and cookies made with loving hands. All these things represented the Christmas season to me. Opulent or lowly, everyone was celebrating! The Christmas carols sung by choirs, the music playing on the Victrola, put me into a mood of excitement.

At home, Mother would be making Christmas gifts. One year we both made chenille corsages. We put a few in the store downstairs. I was thrilled when I sold one. The handmade gifts were mostly for women. To men we gave a carton of cigarettes if they smoked, or a bottle of shaving cream.

Mother made some lampshades out of parchment and poked holes in them to make designs. Marguerite liked them so much, she bought several and gave them to her family and friends.

❧

MY NEW CHURCH LIFE WAS SEPARATE
FROM MY OTHER LIFE

The older children in our church society were given red velvet Word covers and red satin bookmarks for Christmas, for their own copies of the Word. "The Word" was the books of the Bible that Swedenborg said contained an internal meaning. Mother would sew the velvet book covers, and embroider a seven-candlestick candelabra with gold thread on the red silk bookmarks.

The Reverend Morley Rich taught Bible Study classes for us older children. My mother would drive me to Bill Kingdon's house in Clifton Heights in her little blue coupe. Some of the students were: Bob Furry, Bill Kingdon, and Ann Carroll. We read Bible chapters and discussed them.

I kept waiting for someone to tell me why I should believe in this religion and not in any other. They never did, but they taught me the beliefs of our church. We didn't believe God was three persons, but that the Trinity represented three aspects of the Lord. We didn't say that Christ died for our sins, which I had heard in the summer camps I went to as a child. Mother was very anxious that I learn as much as I could.

Janet Abbey and Betsy Doster

Bea and Betsy Doster

Gloria and I were best friends, but we had a few other friends as well. Janet Abbey lived in a tall apartment house in Wynnewood. She had a little sister. Her mother was staying in bed to prevent a miscarriage with her third child, hopefully a boy. I don't remember how that turned out.

Another good friend was Betsy Doster. She lived with her parents and older brother in a large, old, high-ceilinged rented house in need of repair. It was on Linwood Avenue, which was on our way home from school if we walked. They had moved in from somewhere, and were going to move somewhere else eventually. Things were like that after the war. People were resettling. There was energy to get back to normal.

Betsy's mother was fairly tall with a medium build, except for her legs. They looked swollen with heavy thick ankles. (Mother would have said she had kidney trouble). She dyed her hair black. Betsy's brother, several years older, had just returned from a sanatorium out west, and was recovering from tuberculosis. Betsy said he was no longer contagious, but he was thin and gaunt. We sat on the couch, and he sat near the window in a tall, overstuffed armchair in the opposite corner, listless and silent. He wore a heavy sweater with a blanket around him. The room was sparsely furnished, with thin white curtains on the windows. Middle class people didn't decorate their homes so much in those days.

LATIN WAS MY NEMESIS

When I studied Latin for the first time, my brain didn't click in with understanding. My mind was going hazy, like there was gauze over my thinking. My quick insight was gone, and my learning was slow and plodding. I wasn't jumping from the question to the answer as quickly as before. In class, I dissolved into thoughts of other things, thoughts encapsulated in a balloon drifting over my head.

In elementary school, I had done well in spelling, arithmetic, and most of all, parsing sentences, which I loved. But now, I was completely befuddled as to how the Latin declensions worked and how to memorize them. I tried to work through each sentence, but it was all "Greek" to me. The words wouldn't set themselves in the correct order. The vocabulary had to be learned. The words had different places in the sentences than they did in English. The ending of each word had its own meaning.

Latin was my nemesis. At the end of the semester I got a D. I was humiliated.

MOTHER'S INTERESTS

One day back in about fifth grade, I had come home from school to find Mother lying on the bed, meditating. She had drawn a black circle in ink on a piece of paper and pinned it to the curtain on the opposite window over the trunk. She was concentrating on this circle, relaxing her muscles, and getting in touch with her inner consciousness.

She continued to study various things pertaining to spirituality and health, and she talked a lot about whatever she was learning at the time. She taught me how to set up an astrology chart, and how numerology worked. I read her astrology magazines and books. She set up different charts for people to learn what made them tick.

Wilma Baird was Mother's astrology teacher. Mother went once a week for astrology lessons and went another evening for numerology lessons. Wilma read my birth chart, and said I was an "old soul." She said I had Neptune conjoining my sun so I would be dreamy and impractical. She said I had Venus opposing Saturn so I would have difficulty having children, if I would have them at all. I told her I wanted to be a writer when I grew up. She said I would have artistic talent.

Mother was interested in Edgar Cayce, who was a well-documented psychic. I remember her reading *There is a River*, a book about his life published in 1942.[65] Cayce could detect ailments and recommend cures. He was well known, and many people sought his advice. He also predicted the future. He met a young man and had an insight that he would be killed in WWII.

Cayce has been called the father of holistic medicine, and his writings brought words like "holistic health," "soul mates," "spiritual growth," and "auras," into common use.[66] Mother belonged to groups that studied these things.

⤳

EXUBERANCE AND STUPIDITY

I don't remember why Gloria and I took the subway downtown that summer to a prestigious office building on Walnut or Chestnut Street. We may have been looking for summer jobs. We were going to an upper floor, so we headed through the sleek, modern lobby toward the elevators. I saw the doors opening, and said, "Come on Gloria, hurry up!"

---

65 Thomas Sugrue, *There is a River: The Story of Edgar Cayce*. New York. Holt, Rinehart and Winston, 1942, 1945.

66 Edgar Cayce's Association for Research and Enlightenment. www.edgarcayce.org

As we ran to catch the elevator, I collided head-on with a man coming out, carrying a file drawer full of papers. I fell down, the file drawer fell down, and the papers went sliding all over the polished marble floor. As an avid movie-goer, I thought the proper response was to laugh. But the man wasn't laughing.

"Are you all right?" he asked.

"Yes," I said, getting up quickly. "I'm sorry! I'm so sorry!" I apologized profusely. "Can I help you pick up the papers?"

He said no, and Gloria and I ran out of the building. I don't know what we were there for, but it couldn't have been very important. I don't think the BLACK SPOTS applied. This was a case of exuberance and stupidity rather than malice.

჎

LATER TRIP TO OHIO

The backwoodsman is a lonely man.
... he is self-willed; being one who less hearkens to what others may say about things, than looks for himself, to see what are things themselves.
If in straits, there are few to help;
he must depend upon himself;
he must continually look to himself.
—Herman Melville, *The Confidence Man*

In the summer of 1947, gasoline was again plentiful, so we went to Ohio for our summer vacation. We went to look at a piece of property that Dad's sister had told him was for sale. Dad discussed it with the men in the family that was selling it. I pictured a two-story house on the hill with a nice bedroom for me and a window on each side. I mentally decorated it with a pink-flowered chintz bedspread and ruffled curtains. I thought living in Ohio would be a new adventure. But Mother sat in the car, not saying a word.

We also took a trip across the Ohio River to Maysville, Kentucky. Rosemary Clooney lived there in the John Brett Richeson house built in 1832. She wasn't famous yet. We visited some historic houses two centuries old, one of them an abandoned stone house that was falling down. I walked through, imagining living there. The house was an empty wreck, but I imagined ladies in long skirts and men wearing big hats. I wondered what it must have been like to live at that time.

We went to see the schoolhouse where Dad had gone to school, but it had been torn down. On a whim, Dad thought he would see if his old school buddy Willie was still around. We drove up a steep hill on a rocky dirt road to the house where Willie had lived with his parents when he and Dad were in school. The unpainted shack was not more than 10 by 15 feet. Willie came to the door and looked warily at the mysterious black car intruding on his space. Dad got out of the car. Mother and I stayed inside.

Dad stood outside and Willie opened the door. He wore scruffy overalls. He looked startled when Dad told him who he was. His wife peered out from behind him, fleshy and careworn in a formless housedress. She had a large goiter in her neck.

Dad and Willie looked at each other. They would have been about eleven years old the last time they saw each other. Their past struggled to float to the surface through the long space of 35 years. The friendships, hurts, adventures, or whatever Dad and Willie had shared seemed locked in their respective memories, and stayed there.

"How are you doin'?" Dad asked.

Willie's pale brown eyes, the windows to his soul, were reticent. "It's been a tough year," he said.

"Do you have any children?" Dad asked.

"No," Willie mumbled.

It was the first time I had seen true poverty. It seemed as if his passions and worries were all wound up inside him like a spool of yarn. Words were there in his head, but were so seldom used that it was hard to retrieve them from his brain. Dad got back into the car. He didn't say a word as he drove us away. He held his lips tight together and seemed moved.

We are all part of the world, contributing each in our own way. Some mostly with our heads, some mostly with our hearts, and some mostly with our hands. Willie's brain wasn't cluttered with book learning. He was a man of the earth, sun, and rain. They were his friends and his enemies.

FLYING WITH DADDY

I shared Daddy's feeling of wonder, not so much for mechanical things, but for the world in general. We sometimes got to watch the Pitcairn Autogyro or the Pitcairn Mailwing when we went to Bryn Athyn or stopped at the Flying Field in Willow Grove. Sometimes we would drive down to the Philadelphia Airport, go to the rooftop of the terminal building, which was only about two stories high, and watch planes taking off and landing. It was hard to imagine actually flying in one. Neither of us, of course, had ever flown in an airplane.

That summer Daddy suggested that the two of us take an airplane to Washington, D.C. I was excited to do that and he got two tickets. It was a bright, sunny Saturday when we boarded the plane and settled into well upholstered seats. The stewardess came around in her trim uniform and high heels, and asked us if we wanted something to drink. I sat next to the window and traded with Daddy halfway through. We passed puffy white clouds and saw tiny houses below, and tiny cars driving on the streets. We saw farmland divided into squares. This was an exciting new experience. The half-hour trip was over and we landed, gliding along the runway. We got out and walked to the terminal and sat there until it was time to take the next plane back to Philadelphia. That was a memorable day.

I was skimming through the surface of a universe not
of my own making. I felt somehow disconnected.

I didn't go to Bryn Mawr camp that summer, a decision that I would regret. It was the last year that I could have gone. I would have gotten lots of exercise at camp. Instead I sat around a lot, reading movie magazines and gaining weight.

Mother and I took china painting lessons once a week for the summer. The teacher lived in Lansdowne in a large, pre-war stone house. It had a center hall with a staircase, the living room on the left and dining room on the right. She had turned the living room into a classroom with long tables and chairs. Most of the class was older or elderly ladies. I was the only young person. I painted six dinner plates with different flowers, and the teacher had them fired for me. I had fun doing things with Mother.

We also made hats. We bought felt and a balsa wood head frame. We coerced the felt onto the frame with steam from the kettle and a warm iron. When it was dry in a day or so, we decorated it with artificial flowers. Women wore hats to church, downtown, and to any dress-up occasion. We girls did too.

I took the trolley to another school every day for a few weeks to play violin in their orchestra. One day as I was coming home, I noticed a red spot on my dress. Gloria and Mary had told me about what they called "the curse." My mother tried to tell me about it, but I already knew. About this time, I moved out of the bedroom and began sleeping on the lounge in the living room.

⌖

Then I decided I wanted to be a ballet dancer. I was tired of lying around reading magazines, and thought I could lose some weight if I were a dancer. I'd taken dancing classes when I was seven, in the gymnasium of the Ardmore Avenue school next to the library. Mother and I had gone to Baum's Dancewear downtown to buy soft black felt dancing slippers. In the window there were lots of pretty dance costumes with sparkles and colorful trimmings. But we didn't buy any of those. Mother could make me a costume if I needed one. I had learned all five positions, and I went back the next year. But just about the time that I would need a pair of beautiful pink toe shoes, I quit. I don't remember why. Maybe I lost interest, or Mother thought it would be too expensive.

Now I wanted to be a dancer again. I found a dance teacher in Upper Darby, and Mother drove me there. The middle-aged teacher lived with her sister, who was also a dancer, in a semi-detached house, where she gave lessons on her bare living room floor.

I was the only pupil. I reached back into my past, remembering the five positions. The teacher turned on the ballet music, and I had visions of floating around gracefully on stage. But my childhood energy had vanished. My enthusiasm was fragile—in my head, but not in my body. I was overweight and desultory.

The teacher didn't have much vigor or enthusiasm either. I imagined the sisters as young beauties aspiring to Broadway, then gradually fading in spirit and body to where they were now. The fire had burned out and turned to ashes. After a few lessons, it all resonated with emptiness. I realized I was playing piano in an empty hall. I realized how much concentration and practice it would take to be a dancer. After a few classes, my mind came back into alignment with reality and I quit.

Later on, I read in the newspaper that the two sisters had committed suicide, putting their heads into the oven to asphyxiate themselves. The fervent energy of their hopes and aspirations, encapsulated in a balloon, had burst in a sorry wreckage.

Years later I read that Zelda Fitzgerald (F. Scott's wife) had a maniacal obsession with becoming a ballerina. She was in her 20s, and in order to catch up, she willed herself through sheer focus and frenzy to push her body as far as it would go. She practiced and practiced, but eventually she had a breakdown and had to be consigned to a mental institution.

Since I'd gotten fat, I needed new clothes for eighth grade. I designed what I wanted, and Dad and Mother got busy. They got out the scissors and tape measure. Dad said, "You won't be fat. Nobody in my family is fat, and nobody in Mother's family is fat."

That was no consolation for me when I looked at a photo of myself in shorts. I had a large appetite. Why hadn't I signed up for summer camp? Now I was going back to school fat.

The dreamy nightingale that hardly sings,
And all the lassitude of happy things
    —Sir Edmund William Gosse, "Lying in the Grass"

I would lie on the couch in dreamy discontent, reading books and magazines and waiting for some momentum. In relation to my school work, I had a general lassitude with intermittent spurts of concentration.

I argued with Mother all the time now, but I don't remember much of what we argued about. Sometimes I wanted to know why I couldn't go out with friends at night. She was a stone wall I couldn't penetrate. It was so unfair. Sometimes I argued for the sake of arguing. I knew I would probably be too shy or afraid to do some of the things I wanted to do. I knew Mother was right, but I didn't want her to know, so I just walked away in a snit.

Dad quit smoking, hoping it would prevent me from starting. It didn't work. Cigarette smoking was everywhere in those days. People smoked at home and in restaurants. We saw smoking in movies, and cigarettes were advertised on radio, in magazines, and on billboards. When I got to college, salesmen came in and handed out little packs of four cigarettes to the students, hoping we would like their brand.

I suggested to Gloria that we learn to smoke. We went sheepishly to a corner drugstore and bought the cigarettes, thinking that if we were questioned we could tell the proprietor that we were getting them for our parents. We were never questioned, but were always nervous about it. Then we went behind Gloria's bushes and tried to smoke. It didn't taste good and we didn't know how to inhale.

Our small apartment was no longer large enough for both my parents and me. My mind was expanding along with my body. Sleeping on a couch was not acceptable anymore. I made up the couch at night with sheets, blanket, and pillow. In the morning, I put them away. I had my vanity table and a small closet in the hall. That was all that was mine. I had nowhere to be alone, no place of my own to get away from my parents.

When Dad disapproved and spoke forcefully against something, I paid attention. I didn't argue with Dad. He was quiet, but had a more formidable presence for me. Besides, he was sensitive and I knew I could hurt him with my bluster. If he spoke against something I wanted, I would go sit at my vanity and sulk. But with Mother, I would argue and protest. We had a prickly relationship.

Mother said I was *headstrong* (not easily restrained; ungovernable; obstinate).

As I got taller, the apartment got smaller until I felt like I was in a vise. I felt like bursting out of the walls that were closing in around me. The wooden rocking chair was always welcoming. Sometimes I sat and rocked back and forth, seething with rage, silent and grim-faced.

I was advancing from the tantrums I'd had as a young girl to the studied performances of an adolescent. Most arguments were about me doing something Mother didn't want me to do. I thought I was most sensible and could overcome her protestations. Sometimes I did, and she gave in. If she didn't, I sulked and walked away. When I couldn't cope, I would revert back to my imagination where I was in control, and the Queen of all!

When I turned 13, Aunt Bea gave me a watch. I was thrilled. I'd never had a watch before. This one had a gold-rimmed face and two narrow black cords to fasten around my wrist. A week or so later, sitting in Aunt Bea's room at Glencairn, my mother was describing some infraction that I had committed. I don't remember what it was, but Aunt Bea suggested that Mother not let me wear my new watch until I straightened out. I thought that was ridiculous. I was a teenager now, and she wanted to treat me like a baby.

The idea seemed stupid to me. Not wearing the watch wouldn't erase my anger and frustration or deter me from any act they considered foolish. I wouldn't consider it foolish, but standing up for my independence.

My mother described me as *contrary* (given to opposition; perverse; captious; froward; wayward)

Everything depends—not on the mere fact of disappointment,
but—on the nature affected and the force that stirs it.
—George Eliot, Daniel Deronda

Gloria and I took the bus together for our first day of eighth grade. The class was divided into English Grammar in the fall semester and Creative Writing in the spring. I was looking forward to Creative Writing with Mr. Donald.

Creative writing! Where would our aspirations lead us? To awaken the slumbering muse, to pry open a new inspiration. A jumble of words barreling forth to the center, then elusively drifting away, becoming faint, then disappearing altogether. I was crestfallen when Gloria got into Mr. Donald's Creative Writing and I got English Grammar.

"Oh well!" I said to myself. "I will have it next semester."

I was envious that Gloria would have the wonders of writing opened up to her while I would be stuck with the mechanics. I liked the world of the imagination better. I wanted to wander in dense thickets searching for a theme, a word, making choices—not to learn clear-cut unambiguous answers as if I were doing arithmetic.

I walked down the hall past Mr. Abrams' classroom. He was standing outside his room. I said, "Hello, Mr. Abrams." He looked at me curiously before a glint of recognition crossed his face.

"Oh, it's Beatrice," he said with a lopsided smile, "You've gotten fat!"

Once again I wished I had gone to Bryn Mawr summer camp. My ego was flattened, but I carried on.

⁂

Gloria got an assignment from Mr. Donald to write a short story. She didn't know what to write. I wanted so much to write a story. I wanted to be a writer. I had the emotions for writing but no ideas to hang them on.

"I'll write a story *for* you!" I said excitedly.

Gloria acquiesced. I conjured up the muse. I think my story started with the usual "It was a dark and gloomy night." I think I wrote the story straight from my head onto the paper. I don't remember much about it except that my heroine was full of restlessness and anger. In a large house on top of a hill, she lived in "torment," far away from everything, in a psychological conflict with her mother.

I was as flowery and descriptive as my vocabulary would allow.

Being trapped, escaping, running away. The house was reminiscent of a Charles Addams cartoon.[67] The heroine struggled against adversity, but overcame and triumphed in the end. I poured my heart out. It was a gripping tale of suspense and intrigue!

Gloria turned this story in to Mr. Donald as her own. She got an A. Mr. Donald was suspicious and quizzed her, but she stuck to saying that she wrote it. I was thrilled that she got an A, and couldn't wait for the next semester when I would be in Mr. Donald's class myself. Gloria kept the story and I never saw it again. I guess Gloria would have gotten the BLACK SPOTS.

A sapling that is stepped on will not grow and thrive.
—Beatrice Pitcairn

My cousin Dwain's misbehavior had been getting more serious. As Dwain grew, his father had continued to encourage his misdeeds and a resentful attitude.

Roy Barnes died in August of 1946, when his son was thirteen. Dwain's transgressions now included appropriating street signs and hubcaps, which he proudly displayed in his room. He played tricks on neighbors with stink bombs. He shot out lights with a B.B. gun, and once shot an elderly woman in the eye. It was almost as if he was the designated "Bad Kid." He was always conjuring up trouble, and always had an "angle."

As I began eighth grade at Ardmore Junior High, Dwain was starting high school in Bryn Athyn. But the Reverend Karl Alden, the principal of the Boy's School, found him unmanageable. He suggested that Dwain go to The Hershey School for Boys in Hershey, about 90 miles away. Aunt Bea, for whom he was a source of embarrassment, agreed, and so did Mother and Dad. But Aunt Elsie resisted. He was her only child and she wanted him near. I believe he went to the local public high school, but didn't graduate. He may have gone to a tech-

---

67 Charles Addams: *New Yorker* cartoonist who created the Addams Family characters

nical school.

I remembered seven-year-old Dwain standing beside me at the Christmas service in the Advent Church, singing his heart out. He was torn between the values of his community and the surly, negative father who resented it.

❧

I felt like a fish caught on a hook thrashing around, frantically trying to break free. But I also knew I couldn't swim alone in the dark, vast sea.

—Beatrice Pitcairn

I simmered inside when Mother told me I wasn't allowed to do something. I considered myself a self-contained teenager now, perfectly capable of making my own decisions. I tried to beat her into submission with superior logic, and often Mother would acquiesce even though she wasn't convinced. Although I rebelled, deep inside I wanted to hear Mother's point of view. That's one of the reasons I kept on with the argument even after I tired her out. I wanted to prove logically that I was right. Even if I did what I wanted, I kept her admonition in the deep recesses of my brain in case she might have been right after all. Or when she finally said, "You can't go because I said so," I knew she had lost the argument. Then I went back into my shell, resentful and sullen.

Though I hadn't heard of it then, I would use the *Socratic Method* (a series of questionings the object of which is to elicit a clear and consistent expression of something supposed to be implicitly known by all rational beings).[68] Mother would tip-toe around the reality of the questions at times, tentative and uncertain. Other times she knew she was right and went full force. For instance, if I wanted to go with people I didn't know very well down to South Philadelphia for a party on a Saturday night.

When my parents were unreasonable or out of touch I would be belligerent. I would out-shout Mother and dig in my heels. I would

---

68 Webster's, 1934

fight for my right to do what I considered to be grown-up things. I was never sure my argument was reasonable, but I was sure hers was not.

I felt like one of the strings on my violin, strung too tightly, ready to snap. I threatened to run away to New York City. I sassed Mother, but I didn't sass Dad, who was too sensitive and easily hurt. I railed against their indecision. Life with Mother was a tug and pull.

I wasn't used to being respectful toward my parents. We were either an equal triumvirate or I was arguing against them. Mother talked a lot, and I did like hearing about her interests. But I thought the world should belong to me now, too. I believed I was ready for it. The constraints wound like ropes around our small apartment. Inside those confining walls, there was no escape from the stultifying atmosphere. It was full of Mother's narrow focus on her world of health, astrology, and philosophy, and her loquacious gossiping with fellow nurses on the phone. It was full of Dad in silent contemplation, reading *Popular Mechanics* and *U.S. News and World Report*, or working in his shop in the garage. Where was a budding adolescent to go? I walked to Gloria's house and we went for a walk and a smoke.

The frustration was overwhelming. This was before Cognitive Therapy or the Primal Scream, which became a popular way to vent rage at the narrow encapsulation of one's inner world and the confinement of one's outer world.

I noticed Mother reading books on *How to Raise a Teenager*.

> The remains of childhood cling like a vine
> wrapped around a pillar,
> hanging on with fierce intensity,
> becoming part of the whole,
> sometimes sprouting out in defiance.
>
> —Beatrice Pitcairn

One evening in a combative and petulant mood, I blurted out at Dad, "Why do we have to live in this crummy dump? I'm going to run away to New York. Why can't we get a house? How long do we have to live in this crummy apartment?"

I knew I had hurt him and I sulked in the rocking chair while Dad went to the window, put his hands on the windowsill and looked out for a long time. Mother tiptoed around. None of us said anything. All three of us closed into ourselves. I went back to sit at my vanity in the hall, feeling an intense need for a place of my own to withdraw to. I knew I'd hurt Dad, and I felt sorry, but I was raging inside. I knew he worked hard, and he was trying hard to make a better life for us. He had dreams which would never be fulfilled.

It's good to dream. It's what pulls civilization along to better things. Dad was always interested in new inventions, and did get a patent or two of his own. But then you have to sell them to somebody.

"SHE IS DEFIANT," MY MOTHER SAID.

I was the instigator with Gloria. We saw movies together, and I suggested that we go to New York City to see some movie stars. We began planning our trip. We talked about it on our walks, and got excited about it. We saved our money, Gloria from her babysitting and me from my allowance. I think the bus tickets were about $12.00. One bright Saturday morning in October we set out after telling our parents we were going to a movie and doing things together that day.

We walked to the P&W (Philadelphia & Western) Railway station. We took the train to 69th Street, and then the subway downtown. We walked to the bus terminal. (I must have looked it up in the phone book to find out where it was.) I hesitated a little bit, but the demon in my head said, *Go ahead, go ahead! You can see the Winter Garden Theater where Al Jolson sings, or you can see the Stork Club where all the movie stars go. You can walk along Broadway, THE Broadway, and see the theaters where the movie stars act in plays. Maybe even see a movie star walking down 42nd Street!*

I put my fears aside and went to the ticket window. Gloria stood behind me. I was excited and thrilled. *Go ahead!* the demon said boisterously. The angel in my head said quietly, *Make sure you buy round trip tickets.* Which I did.

The demon in my head empowered my excitement. The idea that the fantasies from the movies and the magazines would become a reality! To make things real when you are thirteen is an overwhelming prospect, one that presages adulthood.

The bus was so crowded we couldn't sit next to each other, but we found seats across the aisle from each other. The lady next to me was going home to Elizabeth, New Jersey. She asked me where I was going. I told her that my girlfriend and I were going to New York, and threw the conversation back to her. I didn't want to reveal too much. She told me she had seen a play in New York, *The Voice of the Turtle*. I have always wanted to see that play. She got off before our stop. We got off the bus at 38th Street, and walked outside. We walked up the street a little way and I stopped to ask a passerby where Broadway was. "You're standing on it," he said.

We walked a little further. I turned around occasionally to make sure I could still see the bus terminal. We walked through Times Square and admired its wonders. There were big flashing signs. We didn't see any movie stars. There were lots of people walking—many more than in Philadelphia, very fast and purposefully. They made Philadelphia look like a sleepy town in comparison.

Everyone was in a hurry. We heard lots of cars honking. We looked up at the news ticker, which went on continuously. We looked down some streets and saw the marquees of theaters. I turned around again to make sure I would know the way back to the bus terminal. In spite of my bravado, I really was apprehensive. We must have walked many blocks—eight or twelve. We saw a sign for the Winter Garden Theater. *Maybe Al Jolson had walked on this same pavement.* I could hardly contain my excitement. "Gloria, can you believe it? Here we are in New York City!" I said.

We stopped at a little place to get some lunch. "I guess we better go back now," I said, after lunch. I did have a little bit of common sense that kicked in when I needed it. Sometimes just in the nick of time. We walked back to the bus terminal and got on the next bus back to Philadelphia. It was a two-hour bus ride back. Then a walk back to the subway station and a ride to 69th street. Then we caught the P&W back to Ardmore. It was almost dark by then. We walked up the hill to Spring Avenue where we parted company.

My parents were in a state of panic.

"Where have you been?" Mother demanded. "I've been calling

Mrs. Bastiani. She didn't know where you were going. She thought it was to a movie."

I looked past Mother, then hung my head and told her we took a bus to New York. Mother was aghast. Dad's countenance was stern. I looked at the floor trying to summon up a line of defense. My emotions coiled around me like a snake. Why was this such a big deal? We'd gotten back all right, hadn't we? My parents stood there grim-faced, but I wouldn't be cowed. I stood my ground. The three of us stood apart from each other, like in a Eugene O'Neill play, each in his own space not saying a word to each other.

I didn't know whether to be contrite or aggressive. Finally, I decided contrite was the way to go. I'd had the experience. They couldn't take that away. So I held my head down.

Dad didn't get mad at me often, but when he did he spoke with a strong decisive voice. I resented it, but I didn't argue with him like I did with Mother. The BLACK SPOTS in this case were no laughing matter. I walked away sullenly.

My parents always expected good behavior from me, and were surprised when I misbehaved. But this rebellion truly alarmed them. They feared I would end up a reprobate like Dwain. Worse yet, I might marry a Catholic!

"She is *defiant*," said Mother. (Bold, insolent, willing to fight, disposed to resist, in contempt of opposition)

MY PARENTS DIDN'T WANT ME TO BE ANOTHER
EMBARRASSMENT FOR AUNT BEA

I was getting out of control and something had to be done. My parents talked it over with Morley Rich and Stella. They all decided that I would stay at Ardmore Junior High until after Christmas, and finish eighth grade at Bryn Athyn Elementary School. I would stay at the Riches' home in Rockledge during the week. The Riches were in their thirties and had five adopted children. Stella said later that she was flattered that my parents thought they could take on the responsibility of having me.

PART THREE:
LIFE IN BRYN ATHYN

Benade Hall, Bryn Athyn
Photo by Stephen Conroy, 2019

CHAPTER EIGHT:
AT THE RICHES

At Ardmore Junior High, my free-wheeling thoughts had been anonymous. At a religious school, I would have to learn the rules of thought and behavior.

The night before I was to leave for the Riches' house, it was hard to sleep. I was about to step into a new world that would change my life forever. The buck sheds his antlers and grows new ones. Dandelion seeds fly off into the wind. It is the way of nature. My regulated life at Ardmore Junior High, where I knew what to expect, was over.

My things were packed into a suitcase and a couple of bags. I had put my sheets, blanket, and pillow on the living room couch as usual. I laid my head back on the pillow. I was fearful, timid, and apprehensive, but also excited and ready for a new adventure. I didn't know what to expect in a New Church community. The rage I had carried around inside me dissipated.

I thought I would feel secure and comfortable with "Aunt Stella." She was optimistic and cheery. She was in good touch with the school, and knew its ways. She would guide me. I closed my eyes to fall asleep. I saw a Ferris wheel with indecipherable facets whirling around me. I would meet my new life with fear as well as enthusiasm. My only regret was that I couldn't take Mr. Donald's writing class.

Dad drove the three of us to 127 Elm Avenue in Rockledge. He carried my heavy suitcase up the steep steps and across the narrow porch into the house. Aunt Stella welcomed us, and showed me to my small bedroom on the first floor. The other bedrooms were on the second floor. I had my own room!

Aunt Stella was short and square. She had a buoyant spirit and a soft, determined voice. She had a smile on her face most of the time, and an air of good humor swirled around her. She was a perfect minister's wife, being all things to all people, peppy and cheerful, lending a helping hand or needed advice. "Uncle Morley" was more quiet and thoughtful. He was slim and of medium height.

They had five adopted children: Michael was the eldest at seven; Danny was five; Matthew three; Stephanie two; and a baby, Leila. A friend of theirs, a female physician in charge of a home for abandoned children in Western Pennsylvania, had facilitated the adoptions.

The next morning, the children had juice and oatmeal for breakfast, and Uncle Morley had an egg. I was surprised. I was used to having the best and my parents would be the ones to do without. After breakfast, Michael and I got into Uncle Morley's station wagon. We made the rounds to pick up children of various ages from Rockledge and Fox Chase who went to school in Bryn Athyn: Stella and Barbara Blickle, Joanne Walter, and the Renn children, who were younger and quieter. In those days you didn't have to wear a seatbelt, so the kids piled in and sat wherever they could.

We drove the five miles to Bryn Athyn and entered the grounds of the school buildings. The first building was deCharms Hall, a modern building with a flat roof, rebuilt after the original one was destroyed by a fire. That was our elementary school. The second was a larger building called Benade Hall, built in the late 19th century for the college and secondary schools. The third building was the library. Uncle Morley pulled up in front of the elementary school and we all got out. He went in with me and introduced me to the homeroom teacher, Miss Margaret Bostock. Then he went to his office in the Cathedral to study the Writings and prepare a sermon and doctrinal class.

There was one eighth grade class of about 25 students. I was given a desk in the left row halfway back. One of my classmates, Judith (Jid) Pendleton, spoke of her uncle, Rev. Willard Pendleton, the assistant bishop. Diene (Deana) Pitcairn, might say that her chauffeur was picking her up early because "Uncle Gene" was coming for lunch that day. "Uncle Gene" was Eugene Ormandy, conductor of the Philadelphia Orchestra. Deana would tell funny stories that she'd heard from her elders about his predecessor, Leopold Stokowski. Franklin Allen and Leo Synnestvedt were smart and funny. They sat behind me, making comments that made me laugh. Leo's uncle was Raymond Synnestvedt of the Synnestvedt & Lechner law firm. Beryl Cranch was the only person in my class whom I already knew, but only slightly.

Any bravado I had was chastened away very quickly. In Bryn Athyn, I changed my name from Beatrice to Bea. The unknown culture that I had entered was something bigger and finer. As I grew into it, I would become smaller and more defined.

I instinctively knew that I wouldn't be able to let my emotions flower into raucous stories like the one I wrote for Gloria. This frustrated me. But conforming to my new life gave me a new focus. My sensibilities were flattened—afraid of blurting out something unacceptable, I didn't say anything until I knew that what I said would be okay. Since I had such a different home life from most people and from the other kids my age, I held back and waited to find out the popular opinion or taste of others.

The atmosphere was more informal than in Junior High, and all subjects were taught in the same classroom. But the students stood up when a teacher or any adult came into the room, which I wasn't used to. Friendships were carried on after class with most of the girls gathering together when they could. I'm sure their mothers told them to be nice to the newcomer, and they were.

FRESH BREAD AND SENSIBLE SHOES

Stella was a good homemaker. On a minister's salary, she had to be frugal. She made her own bread once a week. The smell of fresh bread greeted us when we came home from school on Tuesdays. She served a roast or a chicken for Sunday dinner. She would save the bones to make a broth, adding vegetables and leftovers all week. We would have homemade soup and homemade bread every weekday for lunch. We ate oatmeal every morning for breakfast.

The Riches furnished their home with sturdy secondhand furniture, including a couch and chairs resilient enough to withstand the battering of five young children. Aunt Stella cut out colorful pictures from magazines and framed them as wall hangings. They had a bookcase full of books and knick-knacks and a worn rug on the floor. Cheerful and optimistic by nature, Stella did her best to make a cozy home. I was shocked when she told me she paid $18.00 for a pair of shoes. I always bought the cheapest shoes for about $4.00 or $5.00. Stella said it was important to have well-fitting shoes of good quality for your feet and for your posture. Hers had a high vamp and Cuban heels about 1½ to 2 inches.

I was a little afraid of Uncle Morley, but I felt very comfortable with Aunt Stella. I felt I could reveal my feelings and pour out my soul to her. I could tell she was amused at some of the things I said, and I asked a lot of questions. I had a lot to learn. We talked about my shyness. She said it was a very selfish thing to think only of yourself instead of thinking about other people and how to relate to them. I took that to heart.

Aunt Stella started a subtle makeover on me. I had long stringy straight hair, which I tried to curl in curlers with limited success. Aunt Stella told me I should wash my hair more than once every two weeks. She coaxed me in pronunciation. I was to say "man," "can," and "fan" with a long "a" instead of "mee-an," "kee-an," or "fee-an" with my Philadelphia accent.

It was unfamiliar at first, but I gradually copied my classmates. Aunt Stella taught me correct deportment. Later I learned from others about writing Thank You notes and other proprieties.

The Riches' household was lively with so many children. I couldn't relate well to small children, and realized I had never really experienced the give and take of a big family. I had seen it only as an onlooker. I had gone babysitting with Mary and Gloria, but never took on the responsibility myself.

I was happy to go into my room and read a book, but I felt uneasy doing that. I sensed that I was expected to play with the children while Aunt Stella was cooking dinner. Gradually I learned to play with them, but what I liked best was reading a book to them. I could read in a dramatic fashion that entertained the children.

By being a fly on the wall for my mother's adult conversations, I had learned something about human nature and some of its pitfalls. But I had learned no practical skills like doing laundry, cleaning a room thoroughly, or taking care of a child. I had little to offer in the way of cooking. But I settled into the rhythm of the house. Soon I was babysitting when the Riches went out, usually to give a doctrinal class.

One evening when I was babysitting, and all the children were asleep, I noticed a book of Shakespeare's plays on the bookshelf. I took it down, settled on the velvety couch, and read *Romeo and Juliet* all the way through. I was very proud of my accomplishment. Not to imply that I was a "bluestocking." At home, I would read *True Story, Modern Romances*, and movie magazines like *Photoplay* and *Modern Screen*.

Aunt Stella was amused when I thought she was the same age as my mother, who was 47. Stella was about 35. They were both just adults to me. One evening when Mother and Dad brought me back from a weekend at home, Mother began proselytizing in earnest to Aunt Stella and Uncle Morley about health food, telling them that white flour and white sugar were "vicious" foods. After she left, Stella and Morley treated this statement as an object of gentle humor. They thought Mother was acting as if a tiger would come out of the forest to threaten you if you ate candy, and they laughed about it. But in later years, the Riches bought into the health food idea, and followed it themselves.

‍

NUNC LICET

Now it is permitted to enter with understanding into
the mysteries of faith.
—Emanuel Swedenborg, *True Christian Religion*, #508

Ministers taught Religion class. One day the minister mentioned some "Old Church" religion that believed in "faith alone." The
whole class laughed derisively, as if to say, "How could they possibly believe that?" This shocked me. Of course, in public school you
wouldn't dismiss other religions.

We were taught that our religion was rational. There was a
solemnity and seriousness about religion there that was not like the
jovial Catholics I was used to. On the other hand, they were informal
and fun loving.

I felt unworthy, as if there were hidden explanations I wasn't
privy to. I felt self-conscious, shy, and bashful. I had grown up surrounded by children with religions different from mine. If the occasion arose to argue about it, I just stayed silent. I learned to be
tolerant. If someone asked me about Swedenborg, I couldn't explain
very well.

I had gone to the summer camps of various churches, and
played in Catholic homes. I even sat through "Three Hours' of Ag-
ony" in St. Colman's church with Mary on Good Friday. Now I sat
back and absorbed the ideas of my peers. I never revealed much
about myself. I asked a lot of questions of others, sometimes to the
point of rudeness, I'm sure.

Occasionally, when I was uneasy about what to say, I would
blurt out something inappropriate. Afterwards I would ask myself,
why did you say that? I did my best to deflect attention away from
myself. I was afraid I'd be asked for an opinion on something I knew
nothing about, and my ignorance would be revealed. I thought it was
*better to remain silent and be thought a fool than to speak and remove
all doubt,* as Maurice Switzer said.

I wanted to have a good education. My parents put great store in a good education, and I did too. But not so much that I was an excellent student. I was mostly lackadaisical with brief spurts of focused attention. At Wynnewood Road School, I had caught on fast and had a hard time repressing myself. But through the rest of my schooling I was a B to B+ student.

Labor to keep alive in your breast
that little spark of celestial fire, called conscience.
—George Washington, *Rules of Civility and Decent Behaviour in Company and Conversation*

It was decided that I would continue my violin lessons with Mr. Frank Bostock, our music teacher in Bryn Athyn. I went to a school room on a weekday afternoon for lessons. He said I could play in the Bryn Athyn Orchestra when I felt more confident. I thought I would be too scared to do that.

A few weeks after starting the lessons I somehow didn't practice for the whole week. I went to my lesson with trepidation. When I started to play, it was obvious I hadn't practiced. I realized it would have been much easier to practice my violin than it was to lie my way out of it. But it was too late now. I fumbled through the lesson, and felt ashamed. He asked me "Did you practice this week?"

I hung my head and said "Yes." The BLACK SPOTS swirled around me like furies. He knew I was lying. I knew he knew I was lying. I felt like a long-haired dog who is shorn of his hair, who hides under the couch in shame. I wished I could hide under a couch. I gave up trying to play the violin.

BACH OR BEETHOVEN?

I had a date with Leo Synnestvedt, who lived in Bryn Athyn. I think we walked from the dorm to his house. His parents were home, in another part of the house. Leo's father, George Synnestvedt, had a construction business. His mother was a musician who taught piano lessons, and Leo was well versed in music. He went to the record player to put something on.

"What kind of music do you like, Bach or Beethoven?" he asked.

I didn't know Bach from Beethoven, so I mumbled something and he chose.

MY TIME TO SHINE

Mother was thrilled when she got a new stand-up electric sewing machine with legs and a chair to sit in. She gave me the old Willcox and Gibbs table machine to take back to the Riches. I wanted to make a new summer dress. It was late spring, and the weather was getting warmer. I went to Strawbridge's fabric department in the store downtown. I bought a pattern, some pink cotton material, and matching pink buttons and thread. It would have short sleeves with white piqué cuffs.

I asked Aunt Stella if I could use her dining room table to cut out the material. I worked on it a little bit every day. I pinned the pieces together and basted it. Then, one night, when I was babysitting and the children were in bed, I sewed it up on the sewing machine. I hung it up on the door frame so Aunt Stella would see it. I went to bed and fell asleep.

The next morning Aunt Stella expressed amazement that I could make a whole dress so fast. She didn't know how to sew herself. I was proud that I could do something that she could not. The next day she pinned up the hem for me.

PARTIES AND CHAPERONES

My classmates took turns having class parties on Saturday nights throughout the year. If there was to be a party that Saturday, I would stay at the Riches' for the weekend or go home Friday and come back Saturday.

Uncle Morley would drive me to parties in Bryn Athyn. One

of the first parties I went to was at Leo's house. Aunt Stella told me to make sure I shook hands with his parents after the party, and thank them for the nice time. She reminded me again before I left. At the party, the boys and girls danced together in the living room to music played on the Victrola. The students had all had professional dance instruction in seventh grade. I'd had a little bit of instruction so I could follow pretty well. We had refreshments, then a little more dancing as I remember.

Then it was time to leave. I saw a young couple, one of them holding a small child. The class members were going up to say hello to them. I didn't know who they were so I held back. I was expecting the parents to come in so I could thank them for the nice time. Class members were getting their coats on and leaving. The young couple came over and said hello to me. I don't know what I said, but I didn't say, "thank you for the nice time."

The next day several of the parents called Aunt Stella and told her I didn't thank the chaperones. The young couple was Leo's sister Freya and her husband, Louis King, who was in theological school. They were there with their first baby. They were the ones I was to say "thank you" to.

I had embarrassed Aunt Stella.

HOME FOR THE WEEKEND

If there wasn't a class party on Saturday, I would go home for the whole weekend. School was over at 12:30 on Friday, and I would leave after lunch. I took the bus from Rockledge to Fox Chase, and a bus or trolley to the Frankford El (elevated train).

Even though I didn't want to be fat, if I had any extra money I would stop at a fudge shop across the steps beneath the girders and iron trusses of the elevated track. I would buy a little box of assorted fudge pieces, and then trudge up the iron steps onto the platform.

The elevated train would go snarling down the tracks, screech around a bend, and release a gasp of exasperation when it stopped at a station, which was frequent. I liked looking out the window as we passed blocks of brick row houses with porches. Sometimes I could see into the second story windows. Lights would be on inside the buildings and apartments, especially in the dark of winter. Shops below on street level were mostly dull brick with painted white window sills. Otherwise I would either read a book or observe my fellow passengers while eating my fudge.

When the train got near Center City, it suddenly swooped down under ground into the darkness. I heard it glide on the tracks, and sigh when it stopped to let out and take on more passengers. It was called the subway at this point. It emerged from the ground again in West Philadelphia, and I rode to where it ended at 69th street. If I hadn't finished my fudge (too much would make me sick), I threw the rest in a public trash container at 69th street so Mother wouldn't know. Then I would walk to the P&W station and take the train to Ardmore. The whole trip took me 1½ to 2 hours.

Back home in our apartment, I dumped out my dirty clothes and called Gloria as soon as I could. My Bryn Athyn self was like the stalk of an exotic flower being grafted onto an ordinary plant. At home, I reverted to the ordinary plant, but full of new ideas and experiences.

Gloria looked forward to me coming home. She was eager to hear about my new life, and she saved up things to tell me about the people I knew and happenings in the neighborhood. We would buy some cigarettes and go behind her bushes to smoke and talk. We didn't smoke often, and we still choked when we tried to inhale. With more practice, I would learn.

Gloria would tell me what the Italian men were talking about at their club. Many immigrant groups had clubs for people from the same district in the "Old Country." The Italians were talking about Anna Moffo, a rising star in the Italian immigrant community, who was a couple of years older than us. She was a beautiful girl with a beautiful soprano voice, born in Wayne, Pennsylvania. She'd made her singing debut at the age of seven. Though she was offered an audition in Hollywood, she had chosen to study music in Philadelphia. In the 50s, she became a famous opera star. People called her "La Bellissima."

Italians were also proud that pizza pie was becoming a popular American food. Poor Italians had been making pizza for centuries, but American GI's returning from Italy had brought home a taste for pizza. Now pizzerias were popping up all over the United States.

Gloria was the only friend I would see on weekends. She wanted to know all about my new life, and asked a lot of questions. I answered them. But I couldn't explain to her the profound transformation and transition that was happening to me. I was distracted. I was still her best friend, but she was no longer my best friend, and I was sad about that.

A Man in a Trance

Some of my mother's friends studied the occult. They believed in reincarnation, and believed that by going into a trance, you could conjure up lives that you lived centuries ago.

On one of my weekends home, a man and wife came to our apartment with a couple of other people. The man lay down on our couch for a long time trying to go into a trance and summon up his past lives. Mother and the others were transfixed. Dad and I looked on with a bemused intensity. We were both interested in new ideas, but we didn't know what to think of this. Nothing happened. The man wasn't able to make a connection.

A few years later, these friends got excited about the Bridey Murphy story. An American housewife was believed to be the reincarnation of Bridey Murphy, an Irish woman from the 19th century. Under hypnosis, the woman spoke with an Irish brogue and described details of her life in Ireland.

Needless to say, I never told any of my Bryn Athyn friends about this. But I was eager to embrace the world and learn as much about it as I could. I was divided between two worlds, a different person in each. I told my parents about my new life as best as I could. The apple was falling farther from the tree. In fact, it was rolling downhill and picking up speed. As I integrated myself into Bryn Athyn and my friends there, I felt more and more distant from my parents. But then I spouted forth my parents' ideas to Aunt Stella, as 13-year-old children will, even when they don't get along with their parents.

❧

TELEVISION

Several new houses had been built on Wynnewood Road around the corner from Gloria. A young couple had moved into one and asked Gloria to babysit their young children. I was too shy and too insecure about my abilities to babysit on my own. I'd never had any training, and wouldn't know what to do. But Gloria babysat, and her mother was just around the corner if she needed help.

I went with her. It was a perfect small house; a compact traditional Cape Cod style with a sloped roof. Inside they had modern furniture and a TV set. The television faced the couch, and on each side of the TV was an armless, chartreuse upholstered chair in the modern style. Neither of us had TV in our own homes yet. This new invention was exciting, and I was mesmerized. I asked Dad when we would get a television, and he said he didn't know.

Dad had put our names in for a two-bedroom apartment in a new development called Drexelbrook in Drexel Hill. Ninety buildings were planned, and our apartment wouldn't be ready for a year or so.

❧

All happy families are alike;
each unhappy family is unhappy in its own way.
—Leo Tolstoy, *Anna Karenina*

One of my new classmates was Miriam Yvonne Lyman. As we were getting to know each other better, we went to a movie at the opulent Mastbaum Theater in Philadelphia. It was a Friday, and I was on my way back to Ardmore. After the movie we went down to the ladies' lounge, where we talked for a couple of hours and I smoked cigarettes. Then we went our separate ways, north and west.

Miriam and I clicked into each other's thinking. We were a good fit in our ideas and outlook, as well as our backgrounds and aspirations. Miriam wasn't a conformist and she didn't expect anyone else to be either. We both made our own clothes. We liked all forms of art and reading. Miriam loved books, and read more than I did. She read classics like *Ivanhoe*. We thought we could go on talking forever. We developed a lifelong friendship, much like two musical instruments playing in harmony.

Miriam was fun. She saw the humor in things, which led me to see it as well. We both saw the whimsical and capricious side of life so we played off each other and had a good time.

Miriam's family came from Allentown, Pennsylvania, but was originally from Germany where they'd had a pretzel factory. She was the youngest of three daughters. They were a happy family that laughed a lot. Her father, Mr. Addison Lyman, was born in North Carolina and had a slight southern accent. He had a throaty laugh that stood out in a household of women. He could see humor in many places.

Before moving to Willow Grove, Miriam's family had lived on Huntingdon Pike with her maiden aunt, Ora. Aunt Ora kept her house on the Pike until after the war, when she sold it for $9000 and built a house in Bryn Athyn.

The Lymans' house in Willow Grove was a narrow single house with morning glories adorning a trellis behind the front porch swing. It must have been about fifty years old by then. The small living room had a brick-sided fireplace, and a stairwell of beautifully varnished wood.

Miriam and I rode on her tandem bicycle around the neighborhood and played badminton on the empty lot next door. Old trolley tracks ran near the house. After the war, trolley cars and tracks were gradually being dismantled, making way for a national road system with everyone driving a car. When Charles Wilson, formerly president of General Motors, became Secretary of Defense, he was reported to have said, "If it's good for General Motors, it's good for the country." That's not exactly what he said, but both Wilson and President Eisenhower wanted a national road system. With trolley systems gone, everyone would have to buy a car—hopefully from General Motors, and if not GM, then Ford or Chrysler.

Mr. Lyman had studied to be a minister. He was well educated and could read Latin and Greek. But he didn't get a place in the ministry. During the Depression, he went to work for the Asplundh Tree Expert Company, and stayed with them all his working life. Miriam said he was offended at the crude language of his fellow workers and kept mainly to himself.

Miriam's mother, Rhoda, had trained to be a teacher. She taught music and piano lessons at home, and thrived as a homemaker. Her house was neat and clean, and she cooked delicious food. She adored her rose garden. We walked around and she showed me the large pink Helen Traubel rose and the yellow Pearl Buck rose, both in full flower. God's gifts to beautify the earth.

In those days, most women did not work outside the home. They worked at making comfortable homes for their families. The sisters Rhoda and Ora sometimes worked in the kitchen together. They would make pies or can vegetables from their backyard garden to store in the cellar for the winter. They made jams and pickles. They talked effusively, sometimes both at the same time. Since they were sisters, I think they could divine each other's thoughts. They appreciated the small joys of life—a delicious piece of pie or a beautiful flower.

I think musical families who sing together are happy families. The Lymans all had good voices and they sang a lot. In the winter they had friends over to eat dinner. Then they would all sit by the fire playing cards.

Since Mother was a nurse and often worked on holidays, the Lymans sometimes invited me for holidays or Sunday dinner after church. Their holiday dinners were festive, with flowers or decorations, and sometimes a little wine.

Once when I was visiting, Miriam's mother got after her to clean her room. Her closet was a mess and books were everywhere. I said, "If you clean your room, it will just get dirty and have to be cleaned all over again next week. But if you read a book, you will learn something that will stay with me forever."

Miriam and I laughed about this. There was no doubt in our minds that we were intellectually superior to Mrs. Lyman.

❧

Charlotte Austin

My classmate Charlotte Austin was a dynamic person, lively and eager. She had read lots of books I had never heard of. She was the eldest of three children, and her mother was a widow. Charlotte had become good friends with Miriam when the Lymans lived down the street from her on Huntingdon Pike. It was Miriam who told me that Charlotte's father was Bertrand Austin, a cello player with the Philadelphia Orchestra. Her mother had taken cello lessons from him when she was a young girl, and he was quite a bit older than her. Charlotte's mother became an accomplished cellist as well.

Miriam remembered Charlotte's father dying of cancer when the girls were about ten. He stayed in bed in the front room upstairs. They would be playing outside and he would yell out the window for them to be quiet. When Charlotte's father died, no one consoled her; she had to grieve alone. People didn't indulge in grief in those days, or talk to children about it. You had to keep a stiff upper lip. Later on, Charlotte said she was upset that no one talked about it. Miriam moved to Willow Grove after that.

Charlotte's mother supported the family with a novelty store in the front room of her house downstairs. She was a lovely, soft-spoken lady, who gave her daughter free rein, trusting her to take care of herself.

Charlotte was tall—about 5'8". (I was 5'4".) She had wavy brown hair and a strong face with regular features. She looked like Maureen O'Hara. She was also one of the smartest girls in my class. She exuded confidence, and I felt comfortable and protected with her. Once when I took her to Aunt Stella's house, we talked to a neighbor over the back fence. Later the woman told Aunt Stella that Charlotte was the most beautiful girl she had ever seen.

Charlotte understood things in a way I didn't, and I looked up to her. She expressed strong opinions and I adopted them. She had a forceful personality. She was progressive and liked to live outside the box. Once she suggested we go to a movie. I was all for it. It required taking a bus to Fox Chase and a trolley car to the Lawndale Theater. I don't remember what the movie was, but I remember getting a good talking to for going without telling the adults. I don't remember how Charlotte's mother reacted, but Aunt Stella was furious. She blamed Charlotte for leading me astray. I was humiliated.

I felt like a dandelion wandering in a field of voluptuous lilies.

I went for walks with the girls in my class on the unused railroad tracks or nearby paths. The girls commented on the beauty of the flowers we passed along the way. They knew the names of most of them. I didn't. They would sing church hymns in harmony as we walked along. They knew the words to the hymns and the alto and soprano parts. I just walked along and listened. They talked about the books they were reading.

I remember them discussing *The Scarlet Pimpernel.* The hero was a dashing detective who lived through the French Revolution. I had never heard of him; they were all enamored with him. Charlotte sighed with a dreamy look on her face, describing his exploits to me in great detail. She also knew opera, and some of the girls would listen to opera on Saturday afternoon on the radio. I kept quiet so as not to betray my ignorance.

The girls in my class were naturally interested in where I came from. They had all grown up together in the Bryn Athyn community, and many were cousins. They asked me questions, and I gave the briefest answers I could.

TEA TIME

After our walks, Rhona Synnestvedt, Claire Campbell, and sometimes Beryl Cranch would invite us to their houses for tea. There were about twelve girls in the class. Not everyone came to tea, but everyone was respected and invited. In my class in Bryn Athyn, we did not have *in groups* and *out groups.*

Rhona would serve us tea with cookies that she'd made herself.

It was a warm, homey atmosphere. Sometimes the girls, wanting to include me, asked my opinion on something. I tried to keep quiet, or agreed with what they said. But while preparing for luncheon at Claire's, she might ask something like, "Bea, do you think we need an extra salad fork?"

At my Italian friends' houses, everyone used their own forks to serve themselves from a large bowl of spaghetti in the middle of the table. At my own house and Aunt Stella's, we used the basic knife, fork, and spoon. How could I have an opinion about salad forks?

After the tea, I would take the bus back to Rockledge. One day I missed the bus, and started on the five-mile walk home from Bryn Athyn. I got about halfway, to the top of the hill where Holy Redeemer Hospital is now. A car pulled up next to me. A grown man was driving, and a boy my age in the passenger seat rolled down his window and asked me if I wanted a ride. I didn't know who they were, so I said no. They kept rolling beside me.

"Hey, don't you recognize me?" the boy asked, several times. "I'm in your class. I'm Jerry Odhner," he said. Finally I recognized him, and realized that they were who they said they were. The driver was Charlie Cole, a teacher at our school. Then I happily got into the car and they drove me the rest of the way home.

One night Charlotte invited Miriam and me to stay overnight at her house. The three of us slept in a big double bed. Charlotte passed around a cigar for us to smoke. I fell asleep, and woke up with a headache. I think the other girls stayed up all night.

Sometimes Charlotte or Miriam would regale me with a detailed restatement of a book they had read or a movie they had seen. Later on, I sometimes couldn't remember if I'd actually seen the movie or just remembered it from their vivid description.

Miriam Yvonne was called Miriam in her younger years. Miriam connotes a steadfast, conservative homemaker. As an adult, she changed to her middle name, Yvonne, which connotes the free spirited, creative person she had become.

> She didn't say a word the whole time.
>
> —Deana Pitcairn

In the spring, Deana Pitcairn invited me to her home for lunch. The chauffeur picked us up at school and drove about a mile before turning between stone pillars at the entrance to the estate. We proceeded down a long driveway flanked by blooming apple trees. The flowers were white with a hint of pink in the centers.

Deana's father, the Reverend Theodore Pitcairn, was a New Church minister. A small chapel on his property served a congregation of The Lord's New Church which is Nova Hierosolyma, an offshoot of the General Church founded in 1937 with a different interpretation of Swedenborg's Writings.

On the left was a French barn built of stone. I didn't know then that the barn complex was influenced by French Norman architecture and designed by the famous architect Howe. On one side of a cobblestone courtyard, there were stalls for horses, and a garage. The barn later became a meeting room for their church group. We went up a gentle hill, and to the left I saw the church, a small stone construction in the manner of a French country church, big enough for about 100 people. Then we arrived at the main house.

Deana's family lived in France during the Depression, and had cousins in France. They moved back to Bryn Athyn just before the war broke out in Europe. Her father originally planned to complete the estate by adding a French chateau to house his family of nine children. He had enlarged the farmhouse that came with the property, adding a large living room with a fireplace and a big window looking out over the greensward. The living room was furnished with French antiques and a grand piano, with Oriental rugs on the floor. A large medieval Gobelin tapestry hung on the wall, and also *La Terrasse à Sainte-Adresse* by Monet. There were many large paintings by well-known artists, purchased in Paris. I remember a painting of a fat woman on a train with a basket of potatoes, which I thought was a van Gogh.[69] In the small living room and entrance hall from the original house, I saw *John the Baptist* by El Greco hanging over the fireplace.

Portraits of Reverend Pitcairn's family members, his wife Marÿke, and their children, were painted by Philippe Smit, the second husband of Marÿke's mother, Berendina Urban. They called Marÿke's mother "Omassie" (grandmother) and she was a formidable person. I saw her on some other visits.

Smit had lived in Paris, where he'd met Monet and Picasso. Marÿke's mother and her first husband befriended him and supported his work. Theodore Pitcairn bought Smit's portrait of Marÿke before he met and married her, and he then became Smit's most important patron. Smit came to Bryn Athyn and painted portraits of the General Church bishops as well as the Pitcairn family. He married Berendina Urban in 1940.[70]

Awed by all that I saw, I followed Deana into the dining room, where ornately carved high-backed chairs stood around the table. There seemed to me to be a solemn stillness in the hushed environment. An invitation to speak was an invitation to speak softly.

Theodore Pitcairn sat at the head of the table, with his shy wife Marÿke to his right. He was a dignified man, tall and thin with a gray goatee, who sometimes had a mischievous twinkle in his eye. Marÿke was a solidly built Dutch woman. At dinner, Deana's family continued the customs of her mother's European background. They held their fork in their left hand and the knife in their right to cut meat. They held the fork upside down and used the knife to gently coax the food onto the fork prongs. Dutch and English were both spoken at the dining room table. The butler asked "red or white?" as he served wine for lunch. It was even offered to us kids, but we declined. The house man who waited on us was married to the cook—their names were Henry and Lucille.

Johanna sat across from me next to Marÿke. She was a nice

---

69 Deana's father owned four van Goghs: The Sowers, Mademoiselle Ravoux (Blue Girl), van Gogh's Mother, and Sorrow. – Siri Hurst

70 See biography at www.philippesmit.com

Beryl Cranch

Rhona Synnestvedt and
Charlotte Austin

Joanne Cranch

Miriam Yvonne Lyman

Diene (Deana) Pitcairn

lady from Holland who became the children's nanny when she was 20, and they were living in France. The children were mostly adolescents now. Jo (pronounced "Yo") asked me about myself to include me and put me at ease. Of course this did the opposite for me. When the spotlight was on me, I shriveled up inside and hoped I wouldn't

Emmy Lou Soderberg and
Claire Campbell

Leo Synnestvedt

blurt out something wrong.

Deana's mother didn't say much, and I gathered it was more comfortable for her to speak Dutch with Johanna than English with us. I don't remember any conversation, only that I didn't participate in any. I wanted to be as small and insignificant as I could be, and looked down at my plate most of the time.

After our lunch, Deana asked me what I would like to do. I guess I said, "I don't know." She asked, "Would you like to see the barn?" I must have said yes. Later when Deana described my first visit to her home, she said, "And she didn't say a word the whole time she was there."

Miriam Yvonne told me about her own lunches at Deana's when she was a younger child. She said the arms of her large chair hit the table and she had a hard time getting the spoon from the soup bowl across and up to her lips without spilling it. After the main course, a maid brought around a cut glass bowl of water with slices of lemon in it. Miriam was puzzled, and thought, *this can't be dessert*. She found out you were supposed to squeeze the lemon pieces into the water and dip your fingers into the water so you wouldn't get your napkin dirty. If you were a member of the family, you put your napkin back into a silver napkin ring engraved with your initials.

In my later visits to Deana's, when I didn't know what to say,

I asked questions so I wouldn't have to talk. Years later in the same vein, the Reverend Theodore was talking about the voices of opera singers. I thought that as a guest, I should say something. Someone had told me that female Chinese singers had the sweetest sounding voices in the world. I interjected that sentiment.

"They can be shrill, thin, and screechy," said the Reverend Theodore.

I had nothing more after that.

BABY HOLLY

I was more at ease playing with the Riches' children now, and babysitting them when the parents went to a doctrinal class. Aunt Stella was on the list with a Children's Aid Society as a caregiver for babies who needed temporary homes. Holly was one of the babies who came to our house. Her mother was diagnosed as mentally ill, and Aunt Stella volunteered to care for Holly until she could find a permanent home. Holly's mother came for an interview with Aunt Stella and talked continuously, for hours, about her struggles and how she came to be left with a baby she couldn't take care of. I was fascinated and hung on every word. I loved listening to adults' tales of woe. However, this woman went on for so long, even I began to get restless.

After she left, I told Aunt Stella that I had a hard time believing she was mentally ill. She seemed perfectly coherent to me, and her story was riveting.

"Oh yes," Aunt Stella said, "She lives in a fantasy world. She has to be institutionalized."

I was horrified that someone who seemed so sane would have that happen.

One night Stella and Morley went to a class and left me to babysit Holly. I was apprehensive; I had never cared for a newborn before. A bottle of formula was ready. When Holly woke up and started to cry, I held the tiny being in my arms and carefully tried to put the nipple in her mouth. She resisted it, and kept on crying. I was as gentle as I could be. I held the nipple near her mouth, but she wouldn't take hold and suck it. I didn't know what to do. Holly kept on crying and finally went to sleep.

When Aunt Stella came home, she saw that Holly hadn't drunk enough and showed me how to force the nipple into her mouth instead of waiting for her to grab onto it. Poor Holly finally got fed. I had failed my first attempt to take care of a baby.

Holly didn't stay with us very long; she went to stay somewhere else. Sometime later I learned that she had some kind of congenital defect and had not been expected to live. In the tug and pull of life forces she had succumbed.

On the whole, I was uncomfortable with responsibility. But after I had lived with the Riches for a while, I settled into babysitting.

A Party and a Play

In the Spring, when it was my turn to give a party, Aunt Stella invited the class. The weather was good, and we had the party in the backyard. I wasn't at all ashamed of my surroundings. If you were a minister with a wife and five children, it was acceptable to live in genteel shabbiness. Stella had a buoyant spirit and a smile on her face most of the time.

The eighth grade was getting ready to put on a play, and our graduation was near as well. We discussed the play in class. We were doing a play called *Toad of Toad Hall* by A.A. Milne, adapted from the book *Wind in the Willows* by Kenneth Grahame. I had never heard of it. My classmates all knew it by heart. The clever students had the main parts.

There were two performances with a different cast for each performance, so we could all have a part. Some were in the background cast and did not have speaking parts. We all wore animal

Toad of Toad Hall

Zanna, Miriam, and Leo

Rhona

costumes.

Our eighth-grade graduation ceremony took place in the Assembly Hall. The following year we would be freshmen in high school, the boys in the Boys' School and the girls in the Girls' School.

Life is always a rich and steady time
when you are waiting for something to happen.
—E.B. White, *Charlotte's Web*

Bea in New York City with Dad

In the summer after eighth grade, waiting to go into high school and live in the dormitory, I was ready to reinvent myself.

I was invited to a week-long day camp at Sweetwater Farm. This was a nearby farm that belonged to a member of the community. The owners' daughter was a year younger than the girls in my class, but she drove us around in a truck on the property. We practiced archery, went on imaginary "snipe" hunts, and swam in the pond. The girls called me "Honey Bea."

After the camp, I wanted to earn some money, and decided to use the china painting skills I had learned the summer before. I bought glasses and paint in the 5&10, and painted a different spring flower on each glass. Then I put them up for sale at the Philadelphia New Church picnic. Arlene Archer, one of the parishioners, loved children and liked interacting with us. She had one glass eye due to an accident when she was younger. She was a sweet person. She praised me up and down for my work and artistic ability. She said she would like to buy the glasses, which puffed me up.

Sweetwater Farm Summer Camp

But I think, after a few washings, the paint wore off the glass.

Dad took me to see New York City. Since I'd threatened numerous times to run away there, and had actually done so once, I guess he thought it would be good to take me there. We took the train to the city, and went on a bus tour. We went to the top of the Empire State Building. We had lunch at the Stork Club, where movie stars went in the 30s and 40s. We got the first room near the window, and I brought home a black ceramic ashtray with "The Stork Club" in white lettering. We took the bus south to see Chinatown.

Chapter Nine:
Glenn Hall

You can't go home again.

—Thomas Wolfe

The Deka sorority in 1950

New Church people from smaller communities often sent their children to Bryn Athyn for the upper grades of high school or for college. Glenn Hall and Stuart Hall housed the high school and college students from away. Freshmen and sophomores were sometimes allowed as special cases. Five of us from the Philadelphia society went into the dorms before we were juniors, but only Emmy Lou and I were freshmen. All of us were only children except Emmy Lou, who had an older brother. Emmy Lou's family was dysfunctional due to her father's alcoholism, and her mother thought she would be better off in Bryn Athyn.

I was excited about living in the dormitory. Emmy Lou would be my roommate, and we could plan things together. I was just turning 14, the same age as Mother had been when she began her new life in America.

Dad and Mother got busy making me a new winter coat. I picked out the patterns and fabrics. Dad measured and cut—Mother sewed it up on her sewing machine. Except for those I made myself, Mother made all my clothes until I got married and left home for good.

We packed my things into the car and drove to Bryn Athyn. Dad parked close to Glenn Hall, and the three of us made several trips from the car to my room with all my things. In the room I would be sharing with Emmy Lou, we were each provided with a bed, a desk, and a closet. We brought our own curtains, bedspreads, towels, and a small rug to cover the bare wooden floors. Below the window between our beds was an old-fashioned radiator. It was a comfortable room.

When we were finished moving me in, we went outside. My parents stood side by side, and I faced them. Mother looked wistful, and Dad's hands were folded across his stomach. We exchanged a few words about when I would be coming home for a weekend. I gave them each a hug and walked back to the dorm. Mother and Dad walked back to their car. We all knew I was starting a new life and things would never be the same.

The room I shared with Emmy Lou was the one closest to the dorm mothers' office, as we were the youngest girls in the dorm. All the other girls were sophomores, juniors, and seniors, and at least 15 years old.

One of our housemothers was Mrs. Carswell, who had a calm demeanor and spoke slowly. Another was Mrs. King, who was a genteel lady. They both had a "presence" in my eyes.

Our classrooms were in an old stone building called Benade Hall that emanated a feeling of lush private-school class. We ascended wide, creaky wooden stairs to the high school classrooms on the second floor. The boys were on one side of the second floor, and the girls on the other.

◠⟍⟍◡

Latin, again

We had Miss Margaret Wilde for first year Latin. I had an advantage over my nemesis now. Having already struggled with Latin, I was able to pass it with a mediocre grade. I would have remembered if it were a D. I've always been glad that I learned some Latin, which is helpful for learning new words. Other than Latin, we had the usual subjects like English, algebra, science, music, and art.

◠⟍⟍◡

Typing at last

I was delighted to take typing. As a child I had used the "hunt and peck" system, and longed to learn how to move my fingers at a rapid speed as I saw grownups do. Some of the girls chose typing instead of Latin, or as an elective. Typing would give us a job skill for when we graduated.

Our teacher was Miss Florence Rhoener. She was a middle-aged woman who stood up very straight herself and encouraged us to have good posture as well. She also articulated her words very precisely. She had a lovable French Poodle dog called "Pierro." She would tell us about Pierro in her well-modulated voice.

Miss Florence brooked no nonsense. There were about ten students, and the typewriters were set up on tables for each of us. We typed to music. At first, the music was slow. Miss Florence would turn on the record player, and we would start typing *asa asa asa* or *fgt fgt fgt fgt* over and over until our brains were in sync with the letters. It was like learning to play the piano—once your fingers know the letters, you never forget. After we had learned the fingering, we moved to typing words and sentences, all in time to the music. With each record, the rhythm would be faster. We would do 30 words a minute, then 40, then 50. One song we used was *Anchors Away*. I loved that class and found it fun after all the intellectual stimulation of the morning.

Miss Florence was also in charge of the student work program. Most of us did some work for the school to reduce our tuition payments, a certain number of hours in different jobs. Freshmen usually got Dining Hall jobs. We would carry food from the kitchen to the tables, and clear the dishes. One of the boys ran the dishwasher. On Saturday mornings, we would do things like polishing silver. The sobriquet for the Dining Hall was "Bean Hall."

When we were sophomores, we would clean classrooms and dust the furniture. Upper class girls would be allowed to work in the library. It was a good way for us to be integrated with other students outside our own little group.

⚬〰⚬

AN ARMATURE FOR OUR LIVES

Reason's essential delight is to envision from love the effect in thought, not at the time of the effect, but prior to it, or not at the present time, but in a time to come.
—Emanuel Swedenborg, *Divine Providence* #178

We had Reverend Karl Alden for Religion. He was a confident, breezy man who obviously loved his subject. He told us about the Trinity in real life, illustrating the concept with a chair. There was the idea of a chair in your mind, then a physical chair, and the use to which it was put. That was a Trinity.

I liked Religion class and the symbolism of the Trinity. I was excited to learn these new ideas. I began to see why this religion made sense. The things I'd learned in my Bible study classes were now filled in with a new understanding. We were entering the world of "becoming," taking the knowledge we were given and expanding ourselves. We were building a solid armature of beliefs on which to craft our lives.

Rev. Alden told us about influx from the "Other World." Our minds were vessels, being prepared with learning and knowledge. Our prepared vessels would be receptive to influx from the Lord according to our Wisdom for intellectual things, and the Love in our hearts.

Glenview girls

Sally Smith, Sylvia Gladish, and the Brickman twins were all good friends from Glenview, a New Church community near Chicago. They all helped me conform to my new situation. Sally Smith and the Brickman twins taught Emmy Lou and me how to play bridge. You need four to a table to play, and we would have to race back to the dorm right after dinner to get a place at one of the tables. If eight girls wanted to play, we were fine. But usually there would be six, and only the first four got to play.

The Brickman twins, Doris and Audrey, became good friends of mine. They were smart, and could see a problem with razor sharpness. They were used to bickering and bantering back and forth with each other. They were direct in their assessment of life, and they were fun.

In the evening, we had a worship service led by the housemother, and then study hours from 8:00 to 10:00 p.m. In the middle of the study period we had a break, and boys would bring ice cream for some of the girls from the snack bar we called the "J.D."

The snack bar originated in deCharms Hall, and was officially called the "Dutch Kitchen." But "some enterprising student renamed it the Jive Dive or Juvenile Delinquents (J.D. for short), and that was the name that stuck."[71] The J.D. shared the first floor of a large building on Alden Road with Soneson's, a small grocery store. Astrid Odhner ran the J.D. The Bryn Athyn Civic and Social Club (C&S Club) had the second floor.

First formal dance

The first formal dance of the school year happened in October; it was part of the celebration of the Academy's Charter Day. I

---

71 *Reflections on the First 100 Years: Girls School Centennial Album 1884-1984.* Academy of the New Church, 1985. Page 78

loved designing dresses and dressing up, but going to my first dance was another thing. I was awkward; it was my first real date. I felt shy with boys, and didn't know what to talk about with them.

The boys were required to take a girl to the dance, and not all the students were enthusiastic. After I was married, I had a nephew who chose to do three hours of "Coal Pile" rather than take a girl to a dance. I thought that was funny. In my day, the buildings were heated with coal, and boys who got detention had to shovel coal. By the time my nephew was there, they had changed to oil heat.[72] But detention work was called "Coal Pile" for a long time after the change, like "ice box" for refrigerator.

POISON IVY

I got a terrible case of poison ivy that fall. It was my second case of poison ivy. The first happened when I was seven or eight, after I climbed Driscoll's tree, which was covered with it. I got large blisters all over me, that oozed all over the bed sheets. I was in bed for a week or more.

I didn't get it again until I was in high school. People were burning leaves in the backyard of Glenn Hall, and I went out to watch the leaves burn. Poison ivy was mixed in with the leaves, and I breathed in the oil with the smoke. This is the worst way to get poison ivy, and I came down with the worst case ever. I was swollen all over, and my face swelled up so I couldn't eat. My throat was so swollen, I couldn't chew. All I could do was drink liquids through a straw.

My friend Claire Campbell brought me ginger ale. I was the center of attention for all the girls who walked past my room and saw my grotesque appearance. Someone brought flowers, which were placed in a vase on my bedside table. I stared at them all day. I couldn't do anything else. I learned to appreciate the beauty and intricacies of flowers.

---

72 The change to oil heating probably happened in the summer of 1954. The graduating class of 1958 was the first class that never actually shoveled coal. –Sam Yardumian

❧

Dewey wins!

In November, we had the first presidential election since the war ended. Everyone expected the Republican Thomas Dewey to win. It was time for a change after sixteen years of Democrats. Harry Truman was a plainspoken man who had ended the war by ordering the dropping of atomic bombs on Japan. The Japanese were forced to surrender, and fewer soldiers were killed than if our troops had invaded Japan. Truman had gone on a train trip around the country, stopping in small farm towns and waving to people from the caboose. But he was not expected to win.

The *Chicago Tribune* went to press early with the headline: "Dewey Defeats Truman," and H.V. Kaltenborn, a famous newsman, announced "Dewey wins" on the radio. But the next morning, after all the votes were counted—surprise, surprise!—it turned out Truman, the Democrat, had won.

I saw the newspaper photo of Truman with a big smile on his face, holding up a copy of the *Tribune* with its erroneous headline. Truman the populist, the man of the people, from a small town in Missouri, had defeated Dewey, the city slicker lawyer. Dewey had dark hair and a clipped moustache, and his public image had been damaged when he was described as the "little man on the wedding cake."[73]

❧

Flames and BLACK SPOTS

About a week later, on a balmy November evening, we had just finished our worship service in the downstairs room of Glenn Hall. The school nurse was giving us a "female talk." The fire alarm went off with a prolonged blast. The nurse was getting frustrated, trying to

---

[73] The remark was published by *The Washington Post* and attributed to Theodore Roosevelt's daughter, Alice Roosevelt Longworth. *https://en.wikipedia.org/wiki/Alice_Roosevelt_Longworth*

talk over the alarm, which wasn't stopping. Other sirens joined in the cacophony. One of the girls got up and went to the window. "Benade Hall is on fire!" she shouted. We rushed to the windows and watched as flames leaped high into the evening sky. An arsonist had set our school ablaze!

Mrs. Carswell told us to stay inside Glenn Hall. But Glenn Hall was a wooden building, and Emmy Lou feared the fire would spread. She went to our room and gathered her things into a blanket. She planned to throw the bundle out of the window and jump onto it if the fire spread to our building.

Miss Morna Hyatt had noticed smoke when she went back to work in her office that evening.

> As the siren sounded, wailing from the top of the Library, the flames burst through the roof of Benade Hall. Many fire companies were called, but could do little more than keep the combustion from spreading to the Library and De Charms Hall. As the fire burned on out of control, it drew crowds of onlookers and the press. Rumors as to how the fire started were flying and the word "arson" was in the air. Next day one of the Philadelphia papers erroneously reported that Bishop Benade had burned down Evan Hall.[74]

The next day Benade Hall was a shell. Mrs. Carswell gathered us together and told us emphatically not to go into the burned-out building. But I was, once again, a bad kid. A couple of friends asked if I wanted to sneak over just to see it, and I said, "Sure." We tiptoed carefully around the burnt debris, and thought we would just peek inside. Somehow we found ourselves in the chemistry lab, where paraphernalia was scattered around. I backed into a table, and felt a wetness on my seat. It was almost time for lunch at the Dining Hall, so we thought we had better leave.

As I sat down at the table to eat, I was feeling a burn on my backside. After lunch it was getting worse, so I had to tell Mrs. Car-

---

74 *Reflections,* 67

swell that I had been in the chemistry lab and backed up against something. I didn't know what. Mrs. Carswell took me across the street to see Dr. Cronlund, who bandaged it with a salve. Neither of us said a word. I was chagrined.

I was encapsulated in BLACK SPOTS. I was required to write a paper confessing my disobedience. After Mrs. Carswell gave me a serious talk on disobedience, my emotions cascaded in my head like falling bricks, the solidity of bricks replacing the ephemeral balloons that were my usual companions. I wrote a long essay of apology and atonement for bad behavior. Mrs. Carswell said it was a very good essay.

Months later, a fireman from another town confessed to setting a number of recent fires, including one at Theodore Pitcairn's barn five days before the one at Benade Hall.

Miss Wilde teaching freshman girls in the "Ivory Tower."
Bea in the middle of the front row

Our school building had burned, but our classes did not stop. The girls were assigned to rooms in the Cathedral. Freshman girls climbed a circular staircase to the stone room over the porte-co-chère, which we called "The Ivory Tower." It had been Morley Rich's office, and he was moved into the crypt! Teachers came to the assigned rooms to teach. Classes were taught in the Women's Vestry, the Choir Hall, the Undercroft, and the Council Chamber. Long ago, Benade Hall had served as the community's church building. Now the Cathedral was serving as its secondary school. The typing room was moved to the basement of Glenn Hall.

More BLACK SPOTS!

We had an assignment to write a report on a book about World War II by Ernie Pyle, who was a war correspondent. A couple of the girls hadn't had time to read the book, so I wrote some extra book reports. I wrote in styles different from my own and told the girls to put it in their own words. I was quite proud of my ability to create different writing styles. I think I deserved a BLACK SPOT or two for that. But then again, so did the other girls.

Christmas

Christmas was upon us before we knew it. Girls from nearby and far away packed to go home for the holidays. The Christmas break was about two weeks, and most of us could go home. Some who lived in other countries or couldn't afford the fare to go home stayed with relatives or friends in Bryn Athyn.

One girl in the dorm was going home to the Midwest on the train. She had an extra-large suitcase packed full of clothes and gifts. She called two of us into her room to sit on her suitcase so she could get it closed. We both sat on it and jumped up and down a few times until she got it fastened. I hoped *Samsonite* made good sturdy fasteners.

That year Mother was making some little princesses by gluing together shells and beads. After living away from home, I found that my parents did not annoy me as they had before. But Gloria and I no longer shared the same world. She didn't know mine and I couldn't relate to hers. After the Benade Hall fire, she kept teasing me about "Burnt Athyn." My mind would wander. I felt sad and uncomfortable that she missed me so much while I was too involved with new friends and experiences to miss her at all.

The Gregorias had a television now. Mrs. Gregoria would sit and watch it, laughing and smiling. I had never seen her so animated except when wielding a butcher knife or kitchen spoon. Otherwise she was laconic. I could see that she had a crush on the Italian singer Perry Como. When he came on the screen and sang, she sat transfixed with a beatific smile.

Though Mary was mature for her years in some ways, in other ways she was totally "ignorant." In her house, "ignorant" was a pejorative word that meant you didn't know how to behave socially. Mary and her sisters were always calling each other that.

Gloria and Mary became close friends after I moved out of the neighborhood, and Gloria told me about a double date they went on together.

Mary had insisted on opening the door and holding it open for her date.

He said, "No, I'll open it for you." They had a go-around. Her date was perturbed. "The man is supposed to open the door for the lady," he said.

The boy never asked Mary for a date again, and Gloria had to tell Mary how to behave with a boy.

Mary never married. She got an office job, and continued to live with her parents and help them when they needed someone to speak English for them. They changed their name to Gregory.

We're Moving!

My parents told me that we would have to move out of 248 Spring Avenue before our new apartment at Drexelbrook was finished. The apartment house had new owners who wanted our place for their relatives, and my parents' lease would not be renewed. My parents would have to find somewhere else for us to live while we waited for our apartment.

So that was my last Christmas at the apartment where I grew up. My parents would move us from there to a furnished room across the street at Mrs. Finnerty's next door to the Dougherty's. Then they found an apartment in a converted house on our road, at the bottom of the hill near the P&W station. In that apartment, we would have our sleeping areas separated with a curtain.

❦

The summer after my freshman year, Aunt Nora gave me a part-time job working for her in the dietary department of Delaware County Hospital. Her office was a little glassed-in cubicle at the corner of the kitchen when you walked in. It had a desk and a couple of filing cabinets. I organized receipts and wrote down numbers.

Aunt Nora ordered the food. Salesmen would come in from time to time. At noon, I would eat my lunch with Aunt Nora in the hospital dining room. After work, I walked to the corner and took the bus home.

There was no air conditioning in those days, and I remember that the kitchen was sweltering. But I was thrilled to have my first job and earn my own money. Aunt Nora paid me out of her own pocket, and as a special treat, she invited me to visit her in Maine for two weeks in August.

❦

MONHEGAN ISLAND

Life is a comedy for those who think
and a tragedy for those who feel.

—Horace Walpole

Aunt Nora rented a cottage on the island of Monhegan in Maine for a month every summer. The owner was a professor from Bryn Mawr College. I spent the last two weeks there with her. I went up on the train with a doctor's wife, a friend of Aunt Nora's. I got off

Bea on Monhegan Island

at Rockport. Aunt Nora was there to meet me.

We took a ferry boat to Monhegan Island, about ten miles out from the mainland. A large island loomed up in the distance. Formidable rocks cropped up out of the water all around it. We got off at the dock. There was a small island across the water, with a little shack on it. Aunt Nora pointed it out as the home of a hermit who lived there alone.

We climbed the steep hill to her cottage. There was a wood burning stove for heat and cooking, and kerosene lanterns for light. The screen door was wobbly and had to be slammed shut. There was a wooden bookcase full of paperback books. It was definitely a place to relax away from the cares of the world. In the morning, I would help with chores and make my bed. Then we would lie outside sunning ourselves on a big, flat rock and read a paperback mystery story. I took photographs. In the afternoons, we went for a walk. Without street lights at night, we could see a myriad of stars in the sky. It was miraculous. We fell asleep to the roaring sound of the ocean, and I slept like a log.

If you go to Maine, you must have lobster. It was one of the foods Aunt Nora introduced me to. I had never even seen a lobster except in a picture. One day Aunt Nora took a large bucket and we went down the hill and filled it with salt water. Then we went to the dock. A fisherman came in and sold us two lobsters. We climbed back up the hill with our lobsters in the bucket, and Aunt Nora lit the wood burning stove. When it was hot enough, she put the bucket on the stove and cooked the lobsters. Then she chopped them into parts. We sat on a rock in our shorts and T shirts, and she showed me how to get the delicious meat out. I liked lobster right away.

The next day we walked around the island. There were a few paths among the weeds. The sky was clear, and the ocean sparkled in the sun. Our nostrils breathed in the sea air. The ever-undulating water lapped against the rocks, splashing up with little droplets, forming a mist. Sea gulls were squawking overhead.

We saw other cottages placed up high for a good view of the great beyond. Some belonged to college professors, and one to the playwright Clifford Odets. A well-known psychologist who taught at Harvard had a cottage near ours. He and his wife invited us for a drink one night. We both had ginger ale.

One evening we went up to the local school house. People, young and old, were milling around, and some were dancing. A young man about my age with bright red hair came over and talked to me and asked me to dance. We danced, but I was too shy to say much. He didn't say much either.

As we walked home in the dark with a flashlight, Aunt Nora teased me. "I think he took a shine to you," she said.

One day we were both lying on flat rocks in our bathing suits, soaking up the sun and listening to the waves splashing up on the rocks one after another. We started talking about Dwain.

"I can't understand why Dwain behaves the way he does," Nora said.

"I understand it," I said.

"Can you explain it, then?" she asked.

"I can understand it, but I can't explain it," I said. She looked at me, perplexed. I raged against the world, too, and I couldn't explain it, except that I was on the edge of adulthood and wanted freedom. I didn't want my life to be programmed by someone else.

There was very little sand or beach. I tried going into the water, but it was freezing cold.

My cousin Dwain came to a bad end as might be expected. Aunt Elsie remarried in 1955, and hoped her new husband would be a good influence on her son, but it was too late for him to make a difference. Dwain married at age 23 and had three boys and a girl, but later he left his family and went to Texas. Aunt Elsie moved into their house in Rockledge to help support the family. Dwain ended up in prison in Galveston, and I believe he was killed by another prisoner there.

I saw the Monhegan experience as a happy interlude before my life would really begin. When my two weeks were up, Aunt Nora and I took the train back to Philadelphia. My world was enlarged by that wonderful experience, and I was grateful to her for taking me.

When Aunt Nora was dying in the summer of 1954, I was living in Cape Cod with Miriam Yvonne and Deana. We were working on a boat that went to Nantucket. We drew profile sketches for the passengers. The terrain in Cape Cod was similar to that of Maine, so I gathered some of the grasses and interesting weeds that I had seen on Monhegan Island. I put them in a large envelope and sent them to Aunt Nora with a note saying I hoped they would bring back good memories for her. She died the next year in Delaware County Hospital of lung cancer and breast cancer.

BACK IN GLENN HALL
GOSSIPING IN ROOMS

Often several of us dorm girls would get together in someone's room, sit on the beds and talk. We'd talk about our family situations. We vied with each other about who was the poorest and whose family suffered the most during the Depression. Many of them revered President Roosevelt. It turned out that all of us had enough to eat, a comfortable place to live, and a loving family. So we weren't really deprived.

Once we were discussing one of the girls from the Midwest who was beautiful and popular and had a lot of nice clothes.

"Her father is a minister," one of the girls said. "How can she afford all those nice clothes?"

"I think she and her mother make most of her clothes," said a girl who knew her.

"I know, but still—it doesn't look good," the first one said.

INDEPENDENT, CAN-DO GIRLS

As a pampered child, I admired girls with an independent spirit and a "can-do" attitude, accomplished in the mundane aspects of life.

Jane Wilson came to the dorm as a sophomore. She was from Florida, where she lived with her mother and two brothers. Her father wasn't in the picture. She had lived in Maryland for the summer as a mother's helper for a family with five small children. She helped with the children and housework, and earned her own spending money. She was mature and independent; I was coddled and dependent. I would have liked to be like her but I really had no skills of that kind and not much interest in learning them. Aunt Stella had taught me a little about housework. But I was happy to be in my own reverie, except that I would have liked to earn money.

Jane took responsibility like my friend Mary. She was good at making her own way. She did scholarship work like all the rest of us, to help pay for her tuition, but also cleaned houses for people in Bryn Athyn to earn spending money.

Barbie Barnitz showed me how to use a washing machine with a wringer. Doris Brickman wanted to be a nurse and worked toward that goal. Any time any of the girls was sick she would rush into her room to help. I admired how she knew what she wanted, while I dreamed wistfully about my future. My ideas of what I wanted to do weren't fully formulated. They floated from my grasp like helium balloons. I did enjoy learning to type. That was fun and would be useful.

I knew I had to have a good education as a starting point. It was a thrill for my parents to see me getting the education that they could not. None of Dad's brothers or sisters went to college, but many of their children did, and I would go as well. We were lucky to live in the United States of America where those things were possible.

The house was full of cactus plants

Aunt Bea got me a job with her good friend Olive Wells. I cleaned the house, sometimes cut up carrots for dinner, and ironed her husband Arthur's shirts. I told Mrs. Wells I wasn't sure I knew how to iron a shirt properly. She said I had to iron only the collar and front of the shirt since he never took off his jacket in the office. I thought this was funny.

Arthur Wells walked to the Bryn Athyn train station every day and took the train downtown to work at the University of Pennsylvania. There were cactus plants all over their house. He was a well know cactus expert.

What are you doing, you fool?

One day some girls were together in one of their rooms, and one told us that we could get "high" by taking too many aspirin. Some girls were going to try it, so I went back to my room to try it, too. I was about to swallow the third or fourth aspirin when the angel in my head said, "What do you think you're doing, you fool?" I spit out the aspirin and threw the bottle in the trash.

Rationality and aspirations don't always coincide in the mind of a teenage girl.

An aspect of maturity is to not wish away reality.
—Dennis Prager, radio host (heard on radio)

One afternoon two slender girls came into my room and asked me how I got my eyebrows to arch. I looked at them, perplexed. I didn't do a thing to my eyebrows. I didn't *think* about my eyebrows. They also asked me how I got my breasts to grow. They thought of themselves as flat-chested. I was dumbfounded!

My whole focus was on not being fat. I had heard that a grapefruit diet was good for losing weight. I went to the store and bought three grapefruit. I didn't go to the Dining Hall for a whole day and ate grapefruit. The next day I still ate only grapefruit. I even ate the skin. Finally by the evening meal, I succumbed and went to the Dining Hall. My roommate, Emmy Lou, was tall and slender. She could eat anything she wanted and not gain weight, and she was too sensible to indulge in such foolishness. Her mother, Emily Soderberg, sometimes brought us homemade fudge.

⌒ ⌒

WEDDING RECEPTIONS AND WINE

Nancy was a pretty girl from New Orleans. She had nice clothes and a good figure to show them off. The first time she saw snow, she was thrilled, and gushed over it. She had a charming southern accent and was everyone's favorite.

The whole society was invited to weddings, and receptions were held in the Assembly Hall. Wine was served, and we dorm girls would drink it. One night after we'd gone to an event, the heel had come off one of Nancy's high-heeled shoes. She went into Mrs. Carswell's office to tell her about it. I admired Nancy for doing that. You could tell by her voice she'd had a little too much wine. She kept repeating, "What can I do with my shoe?" in her soft Southern accent. I'd had some wine also, but I tip-toed unobtrusively to my room.

Sometimes I felt the happy verve of adolescence. But when I was in a very uncomfortable situation not knowing what to say or do, I would suspend reflection and sensation and concentrate like an automaton on the matters at hand. Housemothers described me as phlegmatic.

⤳

I was ashamed of my parents,
but I was standing on their shoulders.
They would gradually crumple up underneath me
and I would stand alone.
I was ashamed of being ashamed.

Before the Christmas break of my sophomore year, the bishop's wife, making nice conversation, asked me if my family had any special traditions at Christmas time. I quickly said no, and deflected the conversation back to her. She told me about her family traditions. I couldn't very well tell her that I'd be sleeping on a mattress on the floor at Mrs. Finnerty's house. I also couldn't tell her that the highlight of the season would be Christmas dinner at Horn and Hardart's restaurant.

I loved living in the dorm and having girlfriends, playing bridge, and even cleaning homes to earn my own money. But I wanted to grow up. I wanted freedom. I drew little calendars on my school papers and crossed out the days until I would graduate.

The summer after our sophomore year, Emmy Lou and I took a train to Glenview, Illinois, where some of our friends lived. Emmy Lou's father worked for the Pennsylvania Railroad, so she got a free ticket. I paid my own, or my parents did. We each stayed in one of our friends' homes. I stayed one week with Sally Smith, and the next with the Brickman twins. She stayed with Franny Barry. They allowed us to smoke and drink cocktails. *This is the way to live*, I thought.

Emmy Lou and I got summer jobs at the John Wanamaker Department Store. I put addressograph plates back in their proper places. Emmy Lou had a job that was one step up from that.

৹৵৩

DREXELBROOK

I was away at school when my parents moved into our brand new, two-bedroom apartment at Drexelbrook. I was excited to have my own room at last. We were moving up in the world. Most of the residents were upwardly mobile college graduates. There were new-lywed couples with husbands starting out in the corporate world, working for firms like Burroughs, G.E., Westinghouse, and Philco. They would have to move where the company sent them, perhaps to another city, to move up the ladder. Some young families had chil-dren. They would eventually buy a house and move. There were also some older people who were downsizing.

This was postwar suburbia. Drexelbrook was one of many suburban apartment complexes constructed after World War II. It consisted of about 90 long, two-story red brick buildings with ga-rages underneath in the back. The apartments were all alike, each having a living room, kitchen, and two bedrooms. Ours was on the second floor. There was a "Club House" with a swimming pool, a restaurant, and a common hall that could be rented for events.

I liked my old neighborhood where the dwellings were indi-vidualized. To my mind, each dwelling reflected the character of the people living in it. There was a stiffness in Drexelbrook that I didn't feel in my old neighborhood where I knew who everybody was. I felt isolated; there was nobody my age.

Dad wanted to look like he belonged among the people there. This was not a working-class neighborhood, and he didn't want to come and go looking like a "workman." He now had to drive a few miles to the Autocar. He would leave home in the morning wearing a coat and tie, taking his work clothes with him, and change into them at work. Then he'd change into casual clothes before coming back home. He found a garage in Ardmore from an ad in the paper and rented it for his workshop, working on his inventions and fixing cars for friends.

We got new "modern furniture," a proper couch with three pillows across the back, and two chairs. The old rocking chair that Dewey had built, in which I had rocked away so much frustration, disappeared. Mother and Dad wanted everything new and modern, and all the old things had to go. The beautiful marionettes that Aunt Bea gave me disappeared also.

My parents made curtains to my design. I chose a heavy beige cotton, and appliqued leaf-shaped chartreuse cutouts down the sides and across the bottom. Chartreuse was a trendy color. The living room windows looked out onto the street below and the opposite row of apartments across the street.

Dad took me down to a store near the waterfront in Philadelphia to pick out a new kitchen table. We chose one with chrome legs and a chrome band around the gray formica top. The old wooden table with its peeling paint and oilcloth table cover was gone. After the war, people were getting rid of their old wooden furniture. They loved the easy care of formica. We got stainless steel chairs with dark green vinyl seat covers.

For oft, when on my couch I lie
In vacant, or in pensive mood,
They flash upon that inward eye
Which is the bliss of solitude;
And then my heart with pleasure fills,
And dances with the daffodils.

—William Wordsworth,
"I Wandered Lonely as a Cloud"

I would put my feet up on the back of our new couch and read my magazines—*True Story, Modern Romances, Modern Screen*, etc. We got a television. I don't remember Mother ever watching TV, but Dad and I watched the news while Mother was cooking dinner in the kitchen. I was never "dying" to learn to cook. I wasn't domestically inclined. I did like to sew, and I did help Mother make carrot and celery juice, pushing the vegetables through the electric juicer.

Mother made friends with the close neighbors. An attractive single woman in her thirties lived downstairs. I don't remember what her work was, but she held an executive position somewhere. She was a prototype for the liberated feminist of today. I was interested in her work, and she invited me down to tell me about it. I believe she'd gone to an Ivy League college, and she was working her way up the corporate ladder. I was very impressed, and asked her a lot of questions. She had strong opinions. She thought the corporate world was stacked against women. She would be a "feminist" when that idea and designation came into being. I remember that she didn't eat vegetables. She said she was a "meat and potatoes girl."

After a while, the career woman moved, and was replaced by a couple with a young son. The wife was pregnant. She drank a lot of coffee, and invited me down a few times for coffee. "Always keep the pot going," she said.

Neighbors noticed Mother going out in the morning in her nurse's uniform. A woman one street up from us struck up a conversation with her. She told Mother she had been trying to get pregnant for several years to no avail. Mother suggested chiropractic adjustments. At that time, she was giving treatments in our apartment on her black folding Naugahyde table. She gave this lady a few treatments. She did get pregnant, and she was ecstatic and grateful. Unfortunately, three months later she had a miscarriage.

We heard later that she never did have children. But she loved gardening. After she and her husband got a house and moved away, we heard that she was happy working outside, putting plants and flowers in front of her place.

BABYSITTING

I had the audacity to put my name in the Drexelbrook news sheet advertising for babysitting jobs. No one was ever more unprepared for babysitting than me. My only experience of babysitting was with friends, or at the Riches, where I knew the children. I didn't know how to relate to children. I didn't know any games to play. I mostly read books to children in a dramatic way that was fun for them. But I wanted to earn more money.

One New Year's Eve I babysat some newborn twins. The parents had called all around for a babysitter, and they were desperate.

I don't know how they got my name, but they did confirm that my mother was a nurse. They paid about 50¢ an hour. The father picked me up, and we drove some distance to the Main Line. Their house was new and modern—one story with a flat roof and large plate-glass windows. The babies were asleep in their room, and I hoped they would stay asleep because I didn't know how to change diapers. The parents went out with their parents and a few other people.

After a while, I thought I should go check on the babies, but I was afraid I'd wake them up. I opened the door a crack, and listened. I didn't hear a sound, so I closed it again.

The group stayed out quite late. I didn't have a number to call, and I had no idea where I was. I sat there and smoked. Finally they came back, all quite tipsy. After the parents paid me, the parents of the parents put a roll of cash in my hand. So I did pretty well that night.

At another babysitting job, there were dirty dishes in the sink. The mother hadn't asked me to do them, so I didn't. But when she came home and realized I hadn't done them I knew she wasn't happy. She never asked me to babysit again.

Sometimes I invited Bryn Athyn friends home for the weekend, and Aunt Nora took us to some plays. We saw *Guys and Dolls*, *Carousel*, and some other plays.

❧

Benade Hall: New and Improved

The schools moved back into Benade Hall in 1950. Our English teacher, Miss Lyris Hyatt, wrote a poem expressing appreciation for the new building and a bit of nostalgia for the old one that was loved by so many.

"Momentary Sentimentality"
The halls are tiled and straight and bright;
The windows let in lots of light;
Everything is fixed up right.
Remember the squeaky floors?

The firetraps are all demolished;
Useless corners are abolished;
Everything is waxed and polished.
   We used to hide in the closets.

The rooms are painted lovely hues—
Pale greens and yellows, pinks and blues.
The corkboards carry all the news.
   The Egyptian tapestries burned.

The furniture is modern steel
And has a good substantial feel.
This modern stuff has real appeal.
   We sat on the chapel stairs.

The chapel now has room to spare.
It's wonderful to have fresh air.
It's nice to have the whole school there.
   I liked going *up* to chapel.

—Lyris Hyatt

Our Good Angels Were With Us

At Glenn Hall, only seniors were officially allowed to smoke, and only with their parents' permission. The smoking room was in the basement where we had evening worship. Smokers who did not have permission would go up into the attic during the break in the middle of the study hours. There was a small window at the end of the attic with the glass partially missing. We would blow the smoke outside through the hole in the glass. The problem was that during the fall season, dry leaves would blow through that hole into the wooden building. Our good angels were with us, for sure.

One of the girls I smoked with was Carolyn Hicks, who was a class ahead of me. She went to the doctor because she was having stomach pains and swelling. She was diagnosed with ovarian cancer, and died in her senior year shortly before graduation. Her diploma was given to her at the hospital. It was a sad time for us all.

Dates and Railroad Tracks

Bryn Athyn Post Office
Photo by Stephen Conroy, 2019

On weekends, we might have a date. We liked to walk along the old, unused railroad track that had brought New Church people to Alnwick Grove Park long ago. The old train station was now the Bryn Athyn Post Office. Couples were not allowed to go for walks alone. We had to go with another couple and be together at all times. Then we went to the J.D. for refreshments, and we might smoke there also. We were allowed only two dates, on the weekend, and only if our school work was good. This was a hardship for couples who were going steady.

On Fridays, there was "Friday Supper" in the Assembly Hall, put on by the ladies in the community and followed by a doctrinal class. Mildred Pitcairn paid for all the dorm students to attend Friday Supper. For steady couples, Friday Supper was a chance to sneak a third date into the week. Emmy Lou and Charles Echols, who were going steady in the upper grades, took advantage of this loophole.

YOUTH CONCERTS

The Philadelphia Orchestra had a program of Youth Concerts to expose young people to classical music. They were given downtown at the Academy of Music on Broad Street, once a month during the school year in the evening. This was a thrill for me. I had never been to a concert at the Academy of Music before. We girls would take the train to Reading Terminal.

Some of us asked to go downtown ahead of time a few times. We might go to the Ladies' Lounge in the Bellevue-Stratford to smoke cigarettes. The Bellevue was a block or two from the Academy of Music, and the lounge was large and comfortable. Or we might go to the nearby Harvey House Restaurant, which served mountains of ice cream. A couple of times when I was with some of the more daring girls, we went to a bar restaurant for a whiskey sour. We always allowed plenty of time to get to the concert which started about 8:00 p.m.

In spite of all that, we were treated to some beautiful music played by the Philadelphia Orchestra, which many of us might not otherwise have had.

INSECURE OPINIONS

The girls in my class were all bright, with opinions that they expressed with vigor but without animosity. I, on the other hand, was the two-handed person who thought, "on the one hand, or on the other hand," and waited to see which way the wind would blow before committing. I had a tolerance for differences, and could see both sides. I was what you would call "wishy washy." Years later, when I did a self-portrait for an art class, I painted a chameleon with my head sticking out of its mouth.

I was too insecure to state any opinion of my own. I didn't think my opinions had any value. My modus operandi was to ask questions and learn from others how to form opinions and what to think. A friend of mine told me I asked too many questions. But I learned that we receive self-awareness from other people. So I always asked a lot of questions. I wanted to see how the pieces of the puzzle fit together. I came to realize later that the puzzlement of life would always be there.

❧

FORMAL DANCES

After the Charter Day dance in October, we had a number of other formal dances throughout the school year. Some dances were put on by the student sororities and fraternities, which had existed since the early days of the Academy. The *Deka* was the dorm girls' sorority. They would put on a dance jointly with the settlement boys' fraternity, *Sigma Delta Pi*. The settlement girls' sorority *Alpha Kappa Mu* (AKM) would put on a dance with the dorm boys' fraternity, the *Phi Alpha*. There was also a Senior Dance which the Juniors put on for the Seniors, and the Glencairn dance, hosted by Raymond and Mildred Pitcairn.

Barbara Merrell was in charge of decorations for one of the Sigma-Deka dances, and chose a Fairyland theme. I loved working on the scenery for that dance. We used a Fairyland book for reference, and created wonderful scenes. I remember pixies. We hung huge sheets of paper on the wall in the basement of Glenn Hall.

Mother would make my long, formal dance dresses. I looked at fashion ads in the newspaper and magazines for the latest styles. I thumbed through Butterick and Simplicity pattern books. Sometimes I'd design a dress with a skirt from one pattern with the top from another. I remember a bright red tulle I had in one of the upper grades. It was strapless, so I had to have a stole. We weren't allowed to wear strapless without a stole.

Mother was pretty good at improvising, and Dad liked to figure things out, too. I would go to Beck Shoes on 69th Street. It was half way up the hill on the right-hand side. They usually cost about $4.95 or $5.95.

ONE SHIP DRIVES EAST

One ship drives east and another drives west
With the selfsame winds that blow.
Tis the set of the sails
And not the gales
Which tells us the way to go.
Like the winds of the seas are the ways of fate,
As we voyage along through the life:
Tis the set of a soul
That decides its goal,
And not the calm or the strife.

—Ella Wheeler Wilcox

ANC Girls School Class of 1952

Charles Echols, who was dating Emmy Lou, had access to a car for one of our dances. He suggested sneaking out of the dance and driving down to the Rockledge Tavern to have a drink. Charles' best friend, Jerry Odhner, was my date. Jerry asked me if I wanted to go. I said, "Sure."

So the four of us got into the car and drove down to Rockledge. Jerry held the door open for us. The tavern was dark inside. I thought that was good. The waiter wouldn't see how young we were. We got a table for four. But demons were hiding in secret places.

None of us was anywhere near age 21. The boys got Seagram's 7 and soda, and us girls got whiskey sours. I felt uncomfortable. Surely we would be called down by the manager. We stayed long enough to have one drink and then drove back and snuck into the dance in progress at the Assembly Hall without being observed (that we knew of). But as I was getting quickly out of the car, the door slammed before my thumb was out of the way, and smashed it hard. The unreal became real.

In my senior year, my vast accumulation of imaginary BLACK SPOTS transmogrified into a very real black thumbnail. It took months to grow out, and would have taken some mental acrobatics to explain, so I kept it hidden. For a couple of months, it kept reminding me of my spiritual BLACK SPOTS.

A New Sunrise

The next Sunday, our high heels clicked on the stone walkway as we approached the door into church. We wore long coats over our calf length dresses, and the required hats and gloves. We were confident and happy, joyful to be growing up. We had a spring in our steps, but we became hushed and solemn as we closed the heavy wooden door with its ornate metal handles behind us. As we reverently entered the hushed environment, we tried to keep our heels from clicking on the stone floor. We sat together in a middle row with a good view of the chancel.

We gazed in wonder at the tall stone pillars holding up the vaulted ceiling. I saw the grisaille glass windows with red and blue accents that I had studied as a child. It all now had a new importance. We watched the chancel girls come out in their long white robes and light each candle with a long taper. We gazed at the beautiful flower arrangements made by women in the community.

The window over the sanctuary faces East, which represents where the Lord is. Over it is a circular rose window with a representation of the Lord in stained glass. The large window is segmented into twelve sections, each with a reproduction of one of the apostles. The symbolism of the sanctuary is taken from the Book of Revelation.[75]

When I was a small child, I would look around the spacious cathedral in wonder. I would gaze up at the tall pillars and the inaccessible stained glass windows way up high. I felt the holy sphere then. Now I was here worshipping with my friends on the brink of adulthood. We were singing the psalms we learned in school. Sometimes, listening to the sermon, my mind would wander, but I knew I was in the right place, building a solid armature on which to craft my life.

Bright sunlight glistened through brilliant reds, greens and yellows in a background of French ultramarine blue in the tall window. The jewel colors sparkled with the promise of a new sunrise for all of us deeply flawed human beings.

THE END

75 See the photo on the back cover of the chancel window at the Bryn Athyn Cathedral. Photo by Stephen Conroy, 2019.

EPILOGUE

Emmy Lou and Charles were given permission to become engaged in high school because Charles had joined the Navy reserves, and had been called up to go to Korea. They married in 1953, and I was their maid of honor.

I got my Bachelor's degree at Bryn Athyn College, and studied for a year at Museum School of Art in Philadelphia. While in Bryn Athyn, I met Robert Pitcairn at the C&S Club. His father was John Pitcairn's third son, Harold. We married in 1957 in the Bryn Athyn Cathedral, and our reception took place at Cairncrest, their family home built in the style of an English country manor.

My soon-to-be mother-in-law took me to Bonwit Teller, a posh, upscale women's clothing store, to get a beautiful wedding dress. That was my debut for wearing store-bought clothes.

❦

Dad retired in the early 60s, but he never stopped tinkering. He moved with Mother to a mobile home park in Jensen Beach, Florida, where he continued to fix whatever needed fixing. Mother played Edie Arnold records and wrote stories for her "little friends," my husband's nieces and nephews in Fort Lauderdale.

After Mother died at age 72 from an unusual form of leukemia, Dad married a widow named Alice Northrop. They drove to Ohio together every year to visit Dad's family, and always spent some time visiting my cousin Elbert Matheny. Elbert lived on a farm all his life, flew his own airplane, and worked on the construction of a large highway going east from Cincinnati.

Dad stopped driving when he was 90, but he never stopped gardening. He was carrying a watermelon into the house when he collapsed and died at age 93.

Bea and Robert

Charles and Emmy Lou

Bea with Mother and Dad in Florida

Bea's children

Acknowledgments:

Over the years, many people have helped me pull together my voluminous writings and notes to make this book, and made many helpful suggestions. I will mention everyone I can remember, and I apologize to those I leave out.

My cousin Carolyn Jodrey Snyder provided some Sharp/Tamme family history; Janna King, Peter Bostock, and Clayton Walsh transferred my typed pages into computer files and did some editing; especially Tessa Rose who carried me through to the end and edited further, researched many things, and made sure nothing I wanted was left out; Greg Baker read through and made some helpful suggestions; Emmy Lou Echols and other old friends jogged my memory and provided details of their own; Michelle Chapin and Caroline Kline designed a beautiful cover; and Stephen Conroy and Larken Rose shot and edited photos.

—Beatrice Pitcairn

SOURCES CITED:

Butler, Nicholas. *The Story of Wivenhoe*. Wivenhoe: Quentin Press, 1989

Furnas, J.C. *The Americans: A Social History of the United States 1587-1914*. New York: Putnam, 1969

Glenn, E. Bruce. *Bryn Athyn Cathedral: The Building of a Church*. Charlotte, NC. Bryn Athyn Church, 2011.

Kasson, John F. *The Little Girl who Fought the Great Depression: Shirley Temple and 1930s America*. New York: Norton, 2014

Nicholson, George. *Dictionary of Correspondences: The Key to Biblical Interpretation*. West Chester, PA. Swedenborg Foundation, 2010

Okrent, Daniel. *Last Call: The Rise and Fall of Prohibition*. New York: Scribner, 2010

Reflections on the First 100 Years: Girls School Centennial Album 1884-1984. Academy of the New Church, 1985

Shlaes, Amity. *The Forgotten Man: A New History of the Great Depression*. New York: Harper Perennial, 2008

The History of Brown County, Ohio. Chicago. Beers, 1883